"America's leading source of s̶   information." ★★★★

—YAHOO!

LEGAL INFO
ONLINE A
24 hour

www.nolo.com

AT THE NOLO.COM SELF-HELP LAW CENTER, YOU'LL FIND

- **Nolo's comprehensive Legal Encyclopedia** filled with plain-En͏͏ ͏information on a variety of legal topics
- **Nolo's Law Dictionary**—legal terms <u>without</u> the legalese
- **Auntie Nolo**—if you've got questions, Auntie's got answers
- **The Law Store**—over 250 self-help legal products including: **Downloadable Software, Books, Form Kits and eGuides**
- **Legal and product updates**
- **Frequently Asked Questions**
- **NoloBriefs, our free monthly email newsletter**
- **Legal Research Center,** for access to state and federal statutes
- **Our ever-popular lawyer jokes**

Quality LAW BOOKS & SOFTWARE FOR EVERYONE

Nolo's user-friendly products are consistently first-rate. Here's why:

- A dozen in-house legal editors, working with highly skilled authors, ensure that our products are accurate, up-to-date and easy to use
- We continually update every book and software program to keep up with changes in the law
- Our commitment to a more democratic legal system informs all of our work
- We appreciate & listen to your feedback. Please fill out and return the card at the back of this book.

OUR "NO-HASSLE" GUARANTEE

Return anything you buy directly from Nolo for any reason and we'll cheerfully refund your purchase price. No ifs, ands or buts.

Read This First

The information in this book is as up to date and accurate as we can make it. But it's important to realize that the law changes frequently, as do fees, forms, and procedures. If you handle your own legal matters, it's up to you to be sure that all information you use—including the information in this book—is accurate. Here are some suggestions to help you:

First, make sure you've got the most recent edition of this book. To learn whether a later edition is available, check the edition number on the book's spine and then go to Nolo's online Law Store at www.nolo.com or call Nolo's Customer Service Department at 800-728-3555.

Next, even if you have a current edition, you need to be sure it's fully up to date. The law can change overnight. At *www.nolo.com*, we post notices of major legal and practical changes that affect the latest edition of a book. To check for updates, find your book in the Law Store on Nolo's website (you can use the "A to Z Product List" and click the book's title). If you see an "Updates" link on the left side of the page, click it. If you don't see a link, that means we haven't posted any updates. (But check back regularly.)

Finally, we believe accurate and current legal information should help you solve many of your own legal problems on a cost-efficient basis. But this text is not a substitute for personalized advice from a knowledgeable lawyer. If you want the help of a trained professional, consult an attorney licensed to practice in your state.

Mediate, Don't Litigate

by Peter Lovenheim
& Lisa Guerin

FIRST EDITION	April 2004
EDITOR	Emily Doskow
PRODUCTION	Susan Putney
COVER	Susan Putney
PROOFREADER	Robert Wells
INDEX	Victoria Baker
PRINTER	Delta Printing Solutions, Inc.

Lovenheim, Peter.
    Mediate, don't litigate / Peter Lovenheim & Lisa Guerin.-- 1st ed.
        p. cm.
      ISBN 1-4133-0030-8 (alk. paper)
    1. Dispute resolution (Law)--United States--Popular works. 2. Mediation--United
States--Popular works. I. Guerin, Lisa, 1964- II. Title.

KF9084.Z9L683 2004
347.73'9--dc22   2003070161

Quantity sales: For information on bulk purchases or corporate premium sales, please contact the
Special Sales department. For academic sales or textbook adoptions, ask for Academic Sales,
800-955-4775. Nolo, 950 Parker St., Berkeley, CA 94710.

Acknowledgments

I thank the staff at Nolo for their support and assistance, especially Jake Warner, Marcia Stewart, Emily Doskow, and co-author Lisa Guerin.

I'd also like to thank Andrew Thomas, executive director of the Center for Dispute Settlement in Rochester, New York. More than 20 years ago, Andrew was the first person I heard utter the phrase, "Mediate, don't litigate."

—Peter Lovenheim

Dedication

(from Peter Lovenheim)

To Irina

Table of Contents

7 Write an Agreement That Works

8 If You Don't Reach an Agreement

9 If Your Mediation Agreement Doesn't Work

10 Divorce Mediation

Introduction

You and your spouse are getting a divorce, and cannot reach an agreement on how to divide your property and share custody of your children.

Your neighbors' dog has destroyed your prize rose garden, and they refuse to compensate you.

You receive a stiff letter from a business claiming you are infringing its trademark and demanding $50,000 in damages.

Any of these situations—or a thousand others—are likely to send your blood pressure sky high. Why? Because the first word that is likely to come into your mind, of course, is court. And most likely, the second is lawyer. The litigation fever in this country—the often unthinking dash to lawyers and to court—is only one symptom of a society grown increasingly adversarial and violent, where ordinary people have lost the belief that they can sit down together and reason out a solution to their own problems.

But every year, the countless Americans who enter the legal system discover that the delays, costs, and stresses of litigation often leave them poorer and more frustrated—and less empowered—than when they began. Many would agree with Judge Learned Hand, who said in an address to the New York Bar Association in 1926: "As a litigant, I should dread a lawsuit beyond almost anything else short of sickness and death."

Fortunately, there is a much better way to resolve most disputes, an alternative that is often quicker, less expensive, more private, easier to navigate, and more likely to result in a solution that everyone can abide with in the long run. It is called mediation.

A. Understanding Mediation

Mediation is a process in which two or more people involved in a dispute come together to try to find a fair and workable solution to their problem. They do so with the help of a mediator, a neutral third person who is trained in cooperative conflict resolution techniques. Mediation can be used to resolve most types of civil (noncriminal) disputes that traditionally would end up in court, such as those involving personal injuries, contracts, leases, employment, and divorce. Mediators are also skilled at resolving interpersonal disputes between neighbors, roommates, business partners, coworkers, and friends.

Certainly, the most efficient way to resolve any dispute is simply to sit down with the other person involved and talk it out. But if that's not possible, mediation will usually be the best alternative.

Use of mediation as a means of resolving disputes has grown rapidly in the United States in recent years. Wherever you live, you should be able to find a mediator or mediation service to help with your dispute. And in most cases, you will not need a lawyer to go to mediation. The rules of mediation are usually simple and straightforward. The preparation may take some time and thought, but won't overwhelm you with complicated technicalities. The mediation itself will follow a simple procedure and will be conducted in plain English.

B. Using This Book

This book explains every step of the mediation process, from deciding whether to mediate your dispute and choosing a mediator to writing and enforcing an agreement reached in mediation. Chapters 1 through 9 describe the mediation process in detail, from start to finish—the information in these chapters will help you mediate virtually any kind of dispute. Chapters 10, 11, and 12 provide an in-depth look at some special issues that often arise in three types of disputes: divorce mediation (Chapter 10), mediation of business disputes (Chapter 11), and employment disputes (Chapter 12).

What this book does not cover. The book does not cover mediation of disputes between labor unions and management. This aspect of mediation is governed by federal and state laws, and by the terms of union contracts. Special rules apply that are not generally applicable to other types of mediation. Nor does the book cover multiparty environmental disputes or disputes arising in other specialized areas of public policy.

As a mediator and an advocate in mediation, we have seen the magic of mediation work time after time. We have seen people with seemingly insoluble problems come together with a skilled mediator and, after a remarkably short time, emerge with their problem settled. Mediation doesn't always succeed, of course, but most of the time it does. And when it does, it gives those who participate the valuable gifts of a fair and workable solution, an end to uncertainty and hostility, and the ability to put a problem behind them so they can get on with their lives.

That's the magic of mediation as we know it. We hope this book will help you know it, too, and that mediation will offer you meaningful and lasting benefits.

Icons Used in This Book

 This icon lets you know where you can read more about the particular issue or topic discussed in the text.

 This is a caution to slow down and consider potential problems.

 This icon means that you may be able to skip some material that doesn't apply to your situation.

 This icon alerts you to a practical tip or good idea.

This icon directs you to other books or sources of information that might be helpful. ■

CHAPTER 1

Mediation Basics

Chances are good that you picked up this book because you're in the midst of a dispute with someone, and you'd like to resolve it outside of court. Maybe you and your soon-to-be ex-spouse can't agree on how to divide your marital property. Perhaps you and your business partner don't see eye to eye about the future direction of your company. Or, you may be in the middle of a lawsuit that you'd like to settle before trial.

In these situations—and for countless other types of disagreements, large and small—mediation may be your best option. Mediation is cheaper, quicker, and much less complicated than going to court. And because mediating parties work together to find a solution to their problem, mediation can often help rebuild strained relationships and lay the groundwork for more positive interactions in the future. This can be especially important in situations that require ongoing communication between the parties, as might be the case when parents share custody of their children, partners own a business together, or neighbors use a common driveway.

This chapter will introduce you to mediation as a tool for resolving disputes. Here, we explain what mediation is, how it works, and what you can expect when you mediate a dispute. We also explain how mediation differs from other methods of resolving disputes. Armed with this basic information, you can then move on to the details of deciding whether to mediate, choosing a mediator, and preparing for the mediation, covered in subsequent chapters.

This overview chapter is designed for the reader who is relatively new to mediation. Because most of the topics mentioned here are discussed in greater depth later in the book, readers who are already familiar with mediation may wish to skip or skim this material.

A. What Is Mediation?

Mediation is a process in which two or more people involved in a dispute come together to try to work out a solution to their problem with the help of a neutral third person, called the "mediator." The mediator is usually trained in conflict resolution, although the extent of this training can vary greatly. Unlike a judge or an arbitrator, the mediator does not make decisions about the dispute. The mediator's job is to help the participants evaluate their goals and options in order to find their *own* solution.

Mediation is not coercive—that is, the mediator doesn't have the power to force the parties to do anything. Nothing will be decided unless both you and the other party agree to it. However, if you do arrive at a mutual agreement, you can make it legally binding by writing the agreement in the form of an enforceable contract. (For more on how to write a mediation agreement, see Chapter 7.)

Agreeing to mediate does not mean that you give up any other legal rights. If you can't reach an agreement in mediation, you are free to pursue other remedies, such as binding arbitration or litigation. (See Section D, below.)

1. The Goals of Mediation

The primary goal of mediation is for the parties to work out a solution they can all live with. In this sense, mediation looks to the future, not to the past. The goal is not to figure out where the truth lies or to determine whether any laws have been broken, but to solve a problem. This is a far different approach than is followed in a court trial, where the judge or jury looks back to determine who was right, who was wrong, and what should be done about it.

Mediation also has some important secondary goals. Even if you cannot resolve all of your differences with the other party, you can reap these other benefits:

- improved communication with the other party

- a better understanding of the other party's point of view

- the opportunity to meet face-to-face with the other party, speak your mind, and be heard

- increased awareness of the strengths and weaknesses of your position

- an understanding of any hidden issues or underlying problems (such as past grievances or personality clashes) that may be involved in your dispute, and

- exposure to creative ideas for settlement suggested by the mediator.

WHY NOT WORK THINGS OUT ON YOUR OWN?

Many disputes that come to mediation settle in just a few hours. In these situations, you might wonder why the parties didn't just resolve the problem on their own, rather than bringing in a mediator. Unfortunately, there are often barriers that prevent people from reaching their own compromises, including an inability or unwillingness to communicate directly, a lack of trust in the other party, or simply not having a private, neutral place to talk things over. People who are caught up in a dispute often need help to take a step back, evaluate the arguments on both sides, and identify creative solutions to the problem.

Mediation serves an important psychological role as well. Often, before people are willing to compromise and settle, they need the chance to tell the other person (ideally, in front of a third party, who can keep the exchange civil) how hurt they are and how wronged they feel. Once these feelings are expressed (and heard by the other party), people are much more willing and able to work things out. This opportunity for what psychologists call "catharsis" explains why mediation is sometimes necessary before a dispute can settle—and why mediation is so often effective.

2. The Role of the Mediator

"To mediate" means "to go between" or "to be in the middle." This, literally, is what mediators do: They go between you and the other party to help you find a solution to your dispute. The mediator's role is not to be a judge, deciding who is right and who is wrong. Neither is it to give legal advice (even if the mediator happens to be a lawyer); nor to be a counselor or therapist. The mediator's sole function is to bring the parties together to help them find a solution of their own making.

Exactly how the mediator does this may puzzle those who are not familiar with the process. Although each of us is, at times, a mediator—for example, department heads mediate between workers, parents mediate between children, friends mediate between friends—we probably would not attempt to sit in a room with total strangers and try to help them find a solution to a problem that has vexed them for months or years.

Our reservations about trying to do this would be well-founded. Although formal mediation involves a good deal of applied common sense, it also involves a lot more than just "getting folks together to talk about their problem." Done well, it features a mediator trained in successful conflict-resolution techniques who efficiently uses a multistage process to produce positive results. Employing these skills through the different stages of mediation (see Section C, below), the mediator attempts to unfreeze the parties from their fixed positions, open them to the possibilities of creative solutions, and finally guide them to a mutually agreed-upon result.

In most disputes, the mediator has only the power to listen, persuade, and inspire. These may not sound like strong tools, but a good mediator can use them creatively to help the parties improve communication, look at the situation from a different perspective, and eventually arrive at their own mutually satisfactory agreement.

The mediator does this by helping the parties:

- discover any hidden issues involved in their case (people often obscure—or don't even understand—the real problems underlying a dispute)

- understand the difference between what they want and what they need (people make certain demands in a dispute—the payment of money, cutting down a tree, or visiting children only on Tuesday—but these "wants" are not always the same as their broader needs for emotional and economic security, respect, or preservation of important relationships; once identified, needs are often easier to satisfy than wants)

- understand the wants and needs of the other side (parties may discover that some of their wants and needs overlap, which can open the door to a mutually satisfying compromise)

- realistically consider a variety of ways to settle their dispute (mediators often generate creative resolutions, and can help the parties weigh the pros and cons of proposed terms of agreement).

B. How Do Cases Get to Mediation?

Disputes come to mediation in several different ways. Most disputes are mediated voluntarily, after both sides agree to give it a try. However, some disputes *must* be mediated, regardless of what the parties want. If you are required to mediate by order of a judge, by state law, or by the terms of a contract, you won't have any say in the matter.

1. Voluntary Mediation

Most cases come to mediation when the people involved in a dispute or a lawsuit agree to bring in a mediator to help them resolve it. Usually, one party decides mediation might be a good idea and suggests it to the other or contacts a mediation service, which in turn contacts the other side to propose mediation. Or, an employer, trade group, or other organization might establish a voluntary mediation program that it promotes to employees or members.

2. Mandatory Mediation

In mandatory mediation, the parties are required—by contract, court order, or law—to attend at least one mediation session. However, only the process is mandatory, not the resolution. Although the parties have to attend the session, they don't have to agree to anything.

There are a couple of different types of mandatory, or required, mediation. In an effort to cut the flood of lawsuits and show people the benefits of mediation, many states have passed laws that require you to try mediation before you can move your lawsuit forward. Courts in some states routinely order small claims actions or regular civil claims for relatively small amounts of money to mediation. In California and other states, courts may order divorcing parents to mediate issues of child custody and visitation.

Contracts are another source of mandatory mediation. With increasing frequency, mandatory mediation clauses are contained in contracts people sign with their employers, banks, colleges, and even gyms. If you have signed one of these contracts, you will have to at least try to mediate any dispute you have with the other party before taking it to court or arbitration. Some of these contractual provisions require the parties to use a particular mediation service; more commonly, the parties are free to choose a mediator if and when a dispute arises.

⚠ You may be contractually obligated to mediate—even if you never signed a contract. Some companies impose mediation (usually followed by arbitration) on their customers as a condition of doing business, just as employers sometimes require mediation of their workers as a condition of employment. In these situations, the customer or employee may never sign a contract that explicitly requires mediation. Instead, the requirement appears in the fine print enclosed with a credit application, in an employee handbook, or on the company's website. These provisions often state that doing business with or agreeing to work for the company constitutes an agreement to resolve disputes through mediation and/or arbitration rather than the court system.

3. Mediators and Mediation Services

There are lots of different mediators and mediation services out there. Which one ultimately mediates your dispute will depend on how your case gets to mediation and what you and the other party are seeking in a mediator.

Here is some information on the most common types of mediators and mediation services (for more information on choosing a mediator, see Chapter 3):

- **Community mediation centers:** These nonprofit groups offer free or low-cost mediation services to members of their local communities. They offer a very efficient and cost-effective means of resolving relatively minor disputes (such as neighborhood disagreements and consumer claims). Some cases are referred to community mediation centers by local courts; others are brought directly by the parties.

- **Private dispute resolution companies:** These firms mediate all kinds of civil disputes, from contract and business issues to wrongful termination and personal injury claims. They provide not only mediation services but also help with paperwork, scheduling the mediation, and getting the other party to agree to mediate. Because they offer these additional services, their fees tend to be fairly high (see "Mediation Costs," below).

- **Independent mediators in private practice:** These solo practitioners mediate a wide variety of disputes, depending on the mediator's field of expertise. For example, you should be able to find an independent mediator who specializes in employment disputes or divorce mediation.

- **Court-connected mediation programs:** If a court requires you to give mediation a try, a mediator may be assigned to you or the court may give you a list of mediators to choose from. As long as you use one of the court-approved mediators, the court will pick up the tab for at least a couple of hours of mediation. Some courts give you the option of selecting your own mediator, but you will probably have to pay the mediator's fee.

MEDIATION COSTS

The cost of mediating varies greatly depending on the type of case and the mediator. In nearly all cases, however, mediating is far less expensive than going to court. Here is a quick overview of what you can expect to pay:

- **Nonprofit community mediation centers:** These groups offer mediation services free or for a nominal charge. For a one-day mediation of a neighborhood dispute, for example, you might expect to pay a $20 administrative fee (which the center might waive if you can't afford it).

- **Private dispute resolution companies:** These firms usually charge a set administrative fee plus an hourly rate for the mediator's time. Fees vary somewhat with location: companies in New York, Los Angeles, and other major cities may charge a $500 administrative fee per party plus $200 per hour per party. In medium-sized cities and small towns, expect fees to be reduced by about half. For a half-day mediation of a personal injury dispute, for example, you might have to pay $600 in total fees. For a complicated, three-day mediation between two large businesses, the parties might have to pony up $8,000 each.

- **Private mediators:** Most private mediators charge by the hour (there's no administrative fee). Divorce and family mediators, who specialize in divorce cases and other family-related problems (such as disputes between parents and children, siblings, and extended family members), might charge anywhere from $60 up to $300 per hour, with a rate of $100 being typical. The higher rates apply in the larger cities. For a couple that owns substantial property and has minor children, the mediation might consist of six two-hour sessions over the course of a couple of months, for a total fee of $1,200. (The mediator would charge an additional fee to write up the agreement.) Other private mediators might charge significantly more, depending on their area of expertise. For example, a mediator who works solely on disputes between employees and employers might charge up to $400 or more per hour, particularly in large metropolitan areas.

C. Anatomy of a Mediation

No two disputes are exactly alike, and the same is true for mediations. The personality and skill of the mediator, the temperaments of the parties, the volatility of the underlying issues, and countless other factors all affect how a particular mediation plays out. Nonetheless, most mediations follow similar patterns and similar rules. This section describes what you can expect at your mediation—starting with where the mediation will take place.

1. Where Are Mediations Held?

Not surprisingly, mediation is usually conducted in a conference room. Typically, the mediator sits at the head of a longish table and the disputants sit on either side, facing each other. Where the mediation conference room is located and what it looks like will vary greatly, depending on what type of mediator or mediation service you are using:

- Community mediation centers often mediate at the center's offices, typically in a downtown office building or in space provided by a government agency. It will probably be a bare-bones conference room, featuring pale green or yellow walls and a wobbly, wood-veneer table with folding chairs.

- Private dispute resolution companies generally hold mediations in fancier surroundings—often a suite of offices in an upscale office building or in the mediator-lawyer's law firm. If the law firm or dispute resolution company is prestigious, you may find yourself seated in a high-backed, leather-upholstered chair facing the other party across a 12-foot mahogany table.

- Local and state courts sometimes conduct mediations in conference rooms at the courthouse.

- Private divorce mediators may work in downtown office buildings, suburban office parks, or even in their own homes. Their meeting rooms are designed to give couples a private and secure feeling. Rather than being "squared off" across a conference table as would be typical in a business mediation, a couple typically will be seated on a sofa, or in armchairs arranged around a coffee table.

When parties live a great distance apart and cannot travel to the same location, mediation sometimes can be conducted by telephone, through videoconferencing, or on the Internet. Online mediation has become an increasingly popular way to resolve small consumer disputes—particularly disputes over products or services purchased over the Internet—and to continue mediations that began in person.

2. Mediation Rules

Though mediation is much less formal than litigation and arbitration, there are a few rules. Your mediator or mediation service should give you written rules well in advance of your first session. Read these carefully ahead of time, because you'll have to sign an agreement at the mediation, pledging to abide by them. If you have any questions, contact the mediator or mediation service, or review them with a lawyer or law coach.

Typically, mediation rules are a couple of pages long and cover these topics:

- **Matters of procedure,** including what forms you have to fill out to begin the mediation process and how the mediator will conduct the mediation

- **Confidentiality,** stating that everyone involved in the mediation agrees to keep whatever is said confidential, and that the mediator will not disclose what is said during mediation in any later court or arbitration proceeding

- **Fees,** including how much each party will pay and the deadlines for payment, and

- **Liability,** usually stating that the mediator or mediation service is not legally responsible for problems arising out of the mediation.

  Mediation rules are discussed further in Chapter 5, Section A.

HOW LONG DOES MEDIATION TAKE?

Depending on the type of mediation, mediators will often keep a mediation going as long as they and the parties believe progress is being made. If a mediation that begins at 9:00 a.m. produces quick results, the session might be over by 11:00 a.m. If the parties take longer to reach an agreement, the session may continue (after a lunch break) through the afternoon or longer. However, some mediation programs—particularly those run by court systems and community mediation services—do impose time limits. A two-hour limit, with the option to continue another day if the mediation appears to be productive, is typical.

Many cases that go to mediation, such as consumer claims, small business disputes, and auto accident claims, are resolved after a half day or, at most, a full day of mediation. Multiparty cases last longer: add at least an hour of mediation time for each additional party. Major business disputes—such as complex contract and construction cases that involve many issues, parties, and witnesses—may last several days or more.

Private divorce mediation generally takes quite a bit longer—both because the couples usually have a number of issues to resolve and because their ability (and desire) to communicate and compromise is likely to be at a low ebb. Some court-sponsored divorce mediation programs address only child custody issues and are limited to one or two sessions. However, divorcing couples who choose private mediation often aim for a comprehensive settlement, including division of marital property and spousal maintenance, as well as child custody, visitation, and support. Resolving all these issues generally requires half a dozen or more sessions spread over several weeks or months. (See Chapter 10 for more information on divorce mediation.)

Given the uncertainty over how long your mediation will last, try to clear your calendar for the whole day so you will be able to stay as long as you need to. Put another way, you should park in a lot, not at a meter.

3. The Six Stages of Mediation

Mediation does not consist simply of sitting around a table, talking to the mediator and the other party. Instead, mediators structure the process to give the disputants time to speak and be listened to, meet privately with the mediator, and work together toward a settlement. Although mediators agree that mediations progress through distinct phases, they don't always agree on how many phases there are (some say five, others six, and still others seven). We will split the difference and assume that your mediation will occur in six stages, as follows:

STAGE 1: Mediator's Opening Statement. After everyone is seated at the conference table, the mediator will make introductions, review the goals and rules of the mediation, and encourage each side to work cooperatively toward a settlement.

STAGE 2: Disputants' Opening Statements. Both parties will be invited to tell, in their own words, what the dispute is about, how it has affected them, and how they would like to see it resolved. While one person is speaking, the other will not be allowed to interrupt.

STAGE 3: Joint Discussion. At this point, the mediator may try to get the parties talking directly about what was said in the opening statements. This is a time to identify the issues that need to be addressed in the mediation.

STAGE 4: Private Caucuses. Often considered "the guts" of mediation, the private caucus gives both parties a chance to meet privately with the mediator to discuss the strengths and weaknesses of their positions and come up with new ideas for settlement. Typically, the mediator will ask one party to remain in the conference room while the other party waits in a nearby room or in the reception area. The mediator may caucus with each side just once, or several times back and forth, as needed.

Caucusing is not used in every mediation. It is commonly omitted in divorce mediation because divorcing spouses often experience a breakdown in trust, and the mediator doesn't want to exacerbate the problem by separating the spouses and creating anxiety about what either might tell the mediator in private. For the same reason, some community mediation centers do not use caucusing in cases involving interpersonal conflicts. And some mediator rarely caucus in any type of dispute, believing that the process is more effective when everyone involved is present at all times.

STAGE 5: Joint Negotiation. After caucuses, the mediator may bring the parties back together to negotiate directly.

STAGE 6: Closure. This is the end of the mediation. If an agreement has been reached, the mediator may draft its main provisions as the parties listen. The mediator may ask each side to sign a written summary of their agreement or suggest they take it to their lawyers for review. If no agreement was reached, the mediator will review whatever progress has been made and advise the parties of their options, such as meeting again at a later date, going to arbitration, or going to court.

 Chapter 6 explains each mediation stage in detail.

THE ROLE OF LAWYERS IN MEDIATION

If your dispute has not yet blossomed into a lawsuit and you haven't already retained a lawyer, there's no need to hire one just for the mediation. In most cases, you won't need to bring a lawyer to the mediation. This is because you are trying to work out a solution to your problem with the other party, not trying to convince a judge or arbitrator of your point of view. Usually you will understand the problem and your own needs better than anyone else, including a lawyer. Because mediation doesn't have a lot of rules (and the rules that do apply are straightforward), and the entire proceeding is conducted in plain English, you don't need special training to figure out how to do it.

Lawyers can be helpful, however, as consultants before and after the mediation. If your case involves substantial property or legal rights, you may want to meet with a lawyer before the mediation to discuss the legal consequences of possible settlement terms. You may also want to condition your agreement to a settlement proposal on a lawyer's review afterwards, to be sure it does not affect your legal rights in any way you did not intend.

If you're already working with a lawyer—because you're mediating a lawsuit or a dispute that may shortly turn into one—then your lawyer will probably attend the mediation. In this situation, your lawyer can also handle or help you with some of the work, including making the opening statement and writing a mediation brief, if necessary. Even if you have a lawyer, however, you should still plan to be an active participant in the mediation. After all, it's your dispute—and only you can decide whether to settle and on what terms. For more on lawyers and mediation, see Chapter 13.

D. Mediation vs. Other Forms of Dispute Resolution

Mediation is just one of a variety of ways to resolve a dispute. The legal system lumps together every method of resolving a dispute outside a courtroom—that is, all alternatives to litigation—under the heading "alternative dispute resolution," or ADR.

Arbitration (see Section D1, below) and mediation are the two best-known types of ADR available. However, the growing popularity of mediation and arbitration has spawned variations of each that can be attractive options for certain types of cases. In addition, there are several other methods of dispute resolution, including negotiation, fact-finding, conciliation, mini-trials, and private judging.

1. What Is Arbitration?

People sometimes use the word "mediation" interchangeably with "arbitration," another popular method of resolving disputes outside of a courtroom. However, these two procedures are very different.

Arbitration is an out-of-court procedure for resolving disputes in which one or more neutral third parties, called an arbitrator or arbitration panel, hears evidence and arguments from both sides, then reaches

Mediation, Arbitration and Litigation Compared

PROCESS	MEDIATION	ARBITRATION	LITIGATION
Who decides?	Parties	Arbitrator	Judge
Who controls?	Parties	Arbitrators/attorneys	Court/attorneys
Procedure	Informal—a few rules are designed to protect confidentiality and allow everyone to speak and be heard	Agreed rules of procedure are followed	Formal and complicated rules abound
Time to schedule hearing	A few weeks	A few months	Two years or more
Cost to party	Nominal or low (business disputes can cost more)	Moderate	Substantial
Rules of evidence	None	Established but relatively informal	Complex
Publicity	Private	Usually private	Public
Relations of parties	Cooperative effort may develop	Antagonistic	Antagonistic
Focus	Future	Past	Past
Method of negotiation	Compromise	Hard bargaining	Hard bargaining
Communication	Often improved	Blocked	Blocked
Result	If successful, Win/Win	Win/Lose	Win/Lose
Compliance	Generally honored or appealed	Often resisted or appealed	Often resisted

Source: "Mediation and Prepaid Legal Plans," by Kenneth Cloke and Angus Strachan, *Mediation Quarterly*, No. 18, 1987, p. 94. (The chart above is adapted from the referenced table and includes material that doesn't appear in the original.)

a decision. An arbitrator's job is to conduct a contested hearing—much like a court hearing—where each party will present witnesses, evidence, and arguments. Then, acting as a judge, the arbitrator makes a decision.

Arbitration has long been used to resolve commercial and labor disputes, but its popularity is growing as a means of resolving problems of all kinds. The arbitrator (sometimes called an "arbiter") is often an expert in the topic of the dispute, such as construction defects, labor-management relations, or securities fraud.

Arbitration can be binding or nonbinding. In binding arbitration, the arbitrator or panel issues a decision that both parties are legally obligated to follow, just like a court order. In nonbinding arbitration, either party is free to reject the arbitrator's decision and take the dispute to court, as if the arbitration had never taken place. Binding arbitration is far more common.

2. Variations on Arbitration and Mediation

There are some hybrid forms of arbitration and mediation. A few that you might consider or hear about include:

- **Mediation With a Recommendation:** If mediation ends without a settlement but the parties respect and trust the mediator, they can ask the mediator to make a written recommendation as to how the dispute should be resolved. Assuming the mediator agrees to do this, the parties are then free to accept the recommendation or use it to further their own negotiations.

- **Mediator's Proposal:** Some mediators offer their recommendation in the form of a mediator's proposal. In these situations, the mediator writes down a proposed settlement of the dispute—often simply a dollar figure. The mediator shows this proposal to both parties, who then have a certain amount of time to let the mediator know whether they accept or reject the proposal. If both parties accept the proposal, the mediator informs the parties and the dispute settles on those terms. If one or both parties reject the proposal, there's no settlement. A party who rejects the settlement is not told whether the other party would have agreed to it.

- **Med/Arb (pronounced "meed-arb"):** The disputants consent to mediation. However, they also agree that if mediation does not produce a settlement, the mediator (or another neutral party) can act as an arbitrator and make a binding decision. Med/arb gives assurance that, one way or the other, the dispute will be resolved: The parties will either reach their own agreement or one will be imposed on them.

- **High-Low Arbitration:** Like most types of arbitration, high-low arbitration is binding on both parties. However, to reduce the risk of an unacceptable award, the parties agree in advance to high and low limits on the arbitrator's authority. For example, they might agree that the arbitrator can award no less than $300,000 and no more than $500,000 to the winning party.

- **Baseball Arbitration:** Along with evidence and arguments, each party gives the arbitrator a figure for which he or she would be willing to settle the case. The arbitrator must then choose one party's figure or the other—no other award can be made.

- **Night Baseball Arbitration:** As in baseball arbitration, each side chooses a value for the case and exchanges it with the other side. However, these figures are not revealed to the arbitrator (the arbitrator is kept in the dark, which is why it's called *night* baseball). The arbitrator makes a decision about the value of the case, then the parties must accept whichever of their own figures is closer to the arbitrator's award.

OTHER TYPES OF ALTERNATE DISPUTE RESOLUTION

Here are a few other methods of ADR:

- **Negotiation:** In negotiation, the disputing parties talk directly to each other to try to reach an agreement. When it is successful, negotiation is the most efficient way of resolving a dispute because there is no cost or delay associated with the intervention of a third party. But if parties have trouble dealing with one another, negotiation may not work unless they hire agents, lawyers, or other representatives to negotiate for them.

- **Conciliation:** The conciliator's aim is not so much to resolve the dispute as to reduce tensions and get the parties talking. Parents often play the role of conciliator when their children are fighting. "I'm sure you two can work this out. How about something to eat while you sit and talk it over?" Conciliation is used fairly frequently in family and other interpersonal disputes, when a family member, friend, or a member of the clergy is asked to try to help the parties solve a dispute.

- **Fact-Finding:** When negotiations between the parties have reached an impasse, the parties may invite an independent "fact-finder"— often an expert in the field of the dispute—to analyze the issues (or sometimes just a single issue) and present findings of fact and recommendations for a solution. Fact-finding is most often used in labor disputes, although the process can easily be adapted to more general types of disputes. For example, if a construction dispute concerns a collapsed roof, the parties might agree to hire a physical engineer to examine the roof and report on what caused the collapse. The parties would then use the report to further their own negotiations.

- **Mini-Trial:** This method is most often used in disputes between large businesses. Typically, lawyers for each side are given the chance, within strict time limits (often half a day), to present their best case before top executives from both companies and a neutral advisor. The neutral advisor gives an advisory opinion to the executives, who then meet privately to negotiate a settlement based on what they've heard. For more on mini-trials, see Chapter 11.

OTHER TYPES OF ALTERNATE DISPUTE RESOLUTION, continued

- **Private Judging:** In about half the states, the law allows parties in non-criminal cases to try their case before a judge whom they choose and pay for jointly. To use this "rent-a-judge" procedure, the parties generally pick a retired judge or private attorney to decide their case. In other states, a real judge appoints the private judge (sometimes called a "referee"). Either way, the private judge usually has authority to decide the case as a real judge would. Most private dispute resolution companies that provide arbitration can also arrange for private judging. ■

CHAPTER 2

Deciding Whether to Mediate

A Chinese proverb says: "A lawsuit breeds ten years of hatred." In our experience, this may be optimistic.

All too frequently, lawsuits pit former partners, colleagues, spouses, neighbors, or friends against each other in a winner-take-all fight to the finish. The adversarial structure of our legal system encourages litigants to beat up on each other and win at all costs, rather than figuring out how to actually solve their problem once and for all. And when the lawsuit is over, the parties are too often left feeling even more agitated than when they began. Although money may change hands, the parties never get the chance to tell their side of the story—and to know that they have been heard. Feelings of anger, sadness, and dissatisfaction are common—sometimes for years after a lawsuit ends.

Mediation offers a way out of this trap. For much less money, time, and aggravation than you'd spend in a lawsuit, you can use mediation to come up with a solution that everyone can live with. And mediation can be effective in nearly all kinds of disputes. It can be used to decide who will own the Sinai Peninsula or who will park on weekends in the driveway you share with your next-door neighbor. It can be used to determine how one computer company will compensate another for infringing operating system software or how your dry cleaner will compensate you for damaging your favorite sweater. It can be used to determine if a shelter for the homeless can be operated by a church in a residential neighborhood in Atlanta or where children should live after spouses divorce in Peoria.

However, even though mediation works well for many kinds of disputes, it is not the best option in every situation. To decide whether to mediate your dispute, you'll have to consider your circumstances, your goals, and your relationship to the other party. This chapter will help you make the right choice.

A. What Types of Disputes Can Be Mediated?

You can mediate most kinds of civil (noncriminal) disputes that would otherwise go to court or arbitration. Disagreements over contracts, leases, small business ownership, employment, and divorce are all good candidates for mediation. Unmarried partners who are separating and need to divide their house and property, two small businesses squabbling over customer lists, or neighbors fighting over who will maintain a common fence are just a few examples of people who could use mediation to resolve their problems. Other types of disputes often settled through mediation include:

- consumer vs. merchant

- landlord vs. tenant

- neighbor vs. neighbor

- spouse vs. spouse

- employee vs. employer

- homeowner vs. contractor, and

- business partner vs. business partner.

Mediation is not just for problems that could otherwise be brought to court. Many kinds of interpersonal disputes can be mediated, even if neither party has legal grounds to sue the other. For example, siblings who can't come to an agreement on who should care for an aging parent, roommates arguing over who is responsible for household maintenance, or coworkers who just can't seem to get along with each other could all use mediation to work things out, even if they have no legal claims.

You can even mediate some nonviolent criminal matters, such as verbal harassment or destruction of property.

B. Advantages and Disadvantages of Mediation

We'll admit it freely—we strongly believe that mediation is one of the best ways to settle most disagreements. But, like any other dispute resolution process, mediation has some benefits and some potential drawbacks. You'll have to weigh how important these factors are to you when you're considering whether to mediate your dispute.

1. Advantages

Especially when compared to litigation as a way to resolve disputes, mediation offers these advantages:

- **Speed:** Once you and the other party agree to mediate, you can probably get a mediation scheduled within a few weeks. Most mediation sessions last from a couple of hours to a whole day, depending on your dispute. In contrast, lawsuits often take many months or, more typically, years to resolve. In some large cities, it can take two years or longer just to get a court date.

- **Confidentiality:** Most courtroom proceedings and paperwork are open to the public, but mediation is confidential. Mediation sessions are private—there is no "public record," as in court—so no one even needs to know that you have a dispute in the first place. What is said during mediation cannot be brought up later in court, and mediation rules often prohibit the mediator or the parties from revealing statements made during a mediation session. (For more on confidentiality in mediation, see Chapter 5, Section A.)

- **Low cost:** In many parts of the country, nonprofit community mediation centers handle relatively minor consumer, neighborhood, workplace, and similar disputes either free or for a nominal charge. Private dispute resolution companies, which typically mediate personal injury claims, business, contract, and employment disputes, and other cases involving large amounts of money are more expensive (some charge hundreds of dollars an hour), but still far less costly than bringing a lawsuit. Couples who pay divorce mediators $100 or more an hour often find that they end up spending many thousands (and sometimes tens of thousands) of dollars less than they would have shelled out for a litigated divorce.

- **Fairness:** In mediation, you tailor your own solution to the dispute according to your needs; legal precedents or the whim of a judge or jury will not dictate the outcome of your case. Best of all, if you don't think a proposed settlement is fair, you don't have to agree to it.

- **Flexibility:** In mediation, you can raise any dispute-related issues that are important to you. For example, in divorce mediation, a couple may go beyond the strictly legal issues of property division and custody arrangements and reach an agreement on matters that ordinarily wouldn't find their way into a judge's order, such as how each spouse will participate in their children's extracurricular activities or where the family dog will live. Many disputes harbor undiscovered or undisclosed issues, and mediation offers a forum where these matters can surface, be discussed, and become part of the overall resolution.

- **Reduced stress:** For many people, going to court is scary. You face complicated procedures, a winner-take-all scenario, and the frustration of being dependent on a system whose practitioners speak a foreign language full of terms like *motion in limine*, *order to show cause,* and *res ipsa loquitur*. Mediation, by contrast, is informal, conducted in plain English, and driven in large part by the parties themselves.

- **Success:** Independent mediators and mediation services report that in more than four out of five cases, the parties are able to settle all disputed issues to their mutual satisfaction. As compared to court, where the losing party is almost always angry, this is success, indeed.

2. Disadvantages

In some situations, mediation has disadvantages that might outweigh these potential benefits:

- **No imposed solution:** The mediator does not have the authority to decide on a resolution for the parties. Although this can be an advantage in many cases, it might also be a problem. If you are seeking vindication of your rights, nobody will tell the other party that he or she has done wrong. And mediation doesn't always result in a solution—if your case is one of the relatively few that don't settle, you will have spent some time, money, and energy without resolving your problem.

SOME COURT-ORDERED MEDIATIONS MAY BE COERCIVE

In some court-sponsored mediation programs, particularly for divorcing couples who have children together, judges have the power to order the parties to mediation and, if the case doesn't settle, to ask the mediator to recommend how the case should be decided. This type of mediation presents very different choices for the parties—we discuss them in Chapter 10. The remainder of the book assumes that the mediator follows the traditional role and doesn't have any decision-making power.

- **Power imbalance:** If the other party has far more power than you—whether financial, intellectual, emotional, or otherwise—you may be at a significant disadvantage in mediation, unless the mediator is willing and able to help you articulate your point of view and carefully evaluate any proposed settlement to be sure it's fair. For example, a person dissatisfied with the purchase of a home computer may find himself seated across the table from the computer store's district manager, who not only knows more about computers but is also trained in negotiating techniques. Similarly, a shy college student who works part time and has been sexually harassed by her manager may be at a serious disadvantage mediating with the owner of the company. Power imbalance can also be an important consideration in divorce mediation, if one spouse has a history of abuse or intimidation.

DEALING WITH POWER IMBALANCE

Power imbalance occurs when one party in a dispute has a significant advantage over the other in knowledge (financial, legal, or technical, for example), negotiating skills, or emotional strength. Power imbalance is also likely if there has been violence or abuse in the relationship between the parties—domestic violence or severe workplace bullying, for example.

Most mediators are concerned about the issue of power imbalance, but there are different approaches to handling it. Some quickly advise not to attempt mediation with a too-powerful person on the theory that it is like taking a lamb to slaughter (with you as the lamb). Others are a bit more relaxed, saying that fears about lambs being slaughtered are exaggerated and that the presence of an experienced mediator normally offers ample protection for the weaker party. They point out, too, that the alternatives to mediation (doing nothing, direct negotiations, litigation) may create worse problems, for a variety of reasons.

We cautiously favor the latter view and believe that under the right circumstances, you can mediate effectively with just about anyone. You should not agree to mediate if you fear for your safety and the mediator or mediation service cannot adequately address your concerns. However, many mediators will take an active, interventionist approach and do their best to ensure safety and fairness in the process and in the outcome. This is especially common in divorce mediation, discussed in Chapter 10.

Here are some constructive steps you can take to help prevent being overwhelmed by a powerful opponent:

- Prepare in advance by carefully identifying your goals, preparing your presentation strategy, and gathering evidence, as discussed in Chapter 5.
- Bring someone along—a friend, adviser, or lawyer—who can provide moral, practical, or legal support during the course of the session.
- Plan to leave the mediation if you don't like the way it's shaping up. In most cases, mediation is completely voluntary. If you don't like the direction it's taking, you are under no obligation to stay. (However, if you are going to mediation because a state law, court rule, or contract provision requires it, you may need to stay for at least one complete session—probably a couple of hours.)
- Don't sign anything until you've run it by your lawyer or other adviser. (See Chapter 7, Section E, for information on how to set this up in advance.)

- **Slippery slope:** Some people, including those who are extremely anxious or eager to please, may be a bit too willing to buy into the "compromise" goal of mediation and end up accepting an inappropriate agreement in order to appear cooperative. These folks might benefit from a more structured dispute resolution mechanism.
- **Showing your hand:** To mediate effectively, you generally need to reveal enough about the strengths of your position to persuade the other side to compromise. You also have to be open to seeing the other person's point of view, which may involve admitting your responsibility for some aspects of the problem. This is all well and good—unless the case doesn't settle. If you end up in court, the information you revealed in mediation might help the other side plan a more effective defense.

C. When Mediation Makes Sense

If one or more of the following statements are true, you might be well served by taking your case to mediation. (Some of these factors—and those listed in Section D, below—are adapted from *A Student's Guide to Mediation and the Law,* by Nancy H. Rogers and Richard A. Salem (Matthew Bender, 1987).)

1. The Law Cannot Provide the Remedy You Want

Although there are hundreds of thousands of laws on the books, many types of common disputes simply do not involve a legal claim that you can take to court. Disputes between family members or neighbors often fall into this category. In these situations, no law says who's right and who's wrong—the parties have a disagreement, but it isn't one that the law is equipped to handle.

Fortunately, mediation is available to you even when courts are not. For example, two sisters who owned and ran a jewelry store disagreed about who should control different aspects of the business. If they could not come to terms, the business might fail. Yet neither sister thought the other had violated her legal rights or broken the law—it was just a dispute between partners, which mediation could very likely help settle. Similarly, when a suburban homeowner found that lights around his neighbor's driveway shone in his window at night, the law offered no solution, because no local ordinance regulated residential lighting. However, the situation could still be hashed out in mediation.

Even if you could bring a lawsuit, you may not want to because of other factors. In the example above, for instance, the homeowner bothered by driveway lights might be able to sue his neighbor for creating a nuisance. But the costs of doing so, in terms of legal fees, delay, publicity, and damage to his relationship with the neighbor, would almost certainly be out of proportion to the underlying problem. In mediation, however, the neighbors could probably work out an agreement—quickly, cheaply, and privately.

Learn your rights before you make a decision. It's often wise to research your legal rights and responsibilities before you decide to mediate. That way, you can make an informed decision about how your case might play out in court if you decide not to mediate or the mediation isn't successful. If you do not know whether the law might provide a remedy for your dispute, you should do some research or consult a lawyer (see Chapter 13).

2. You Want to End a Problem, Not a Relationship

Does your dispute involve another person with whom—either by choice or circumstance—you need to remain on good terms? This may include family members, coworkers, your landlord, neighbors, or others with whom you have a continuing personal or business relationship. As compared to going to court, one of the advantages of mediation is that it can resolve a dispute without destroying a relationship. In fact, discussing the problem face to face and coming up with a mutually acceptable solution might even strengthen your relationship—or at least lay the groundwork for better communication in the future.

Let's face it—filing a lawsuit is almost always a hostile act. The common expressions "to be slapped with a lawsuit" or "hit with a lawsuit" accurately convey the level of combat and aggression inherent in going to court. If you are the one doing the suing, you can be sure that whatever relationship you had with your adversary before papers were served will be worse afterwards. In part, this is because your attorney, motivated by the legal necessity to prove that the other side is wrong, will use every means possible to show the other party's guilt or liability. From the lawyer's point of view, to do anything less could be malpractice. Even if you and the other party want to stay on speaking terms during a trial, your lawyers will likely forbid it, lest you reveal something to the other party that could jeopardize your case. The legal system is designed to be adversarial; even if you weren't on hostile terms with the other party when the lawsuit began, you are almost certain to be enemies by the time it's all over.

By contrast, mediation isn't about one side beating the other, but about all parties reaching an agreed solution to a dispute. For example, in the written mediation agreement, there is no place for stating who was right and who was wrong; the agreement speaks only of who will do what by when in order to remedy the problem. It is this absence of fault-finding, plus the experience of working cooperatively toward settlement, that helps parties in mediation preserve or restore their relationship.

3. Your Dispute Is No One Else's Business — and You Want to Keep It That Way

As noted earlier, one of the drawbacks of having your dispute settled in court is that, by and large, everything said or submitted in connection with a lawsuit becomes publicly available. Only by a special order of a judge can information be "sealed" from public exposure. So whether your desire is to protect trade secrets or just to avoid airing your dirty laundry in public, you will be more likely to succeed if you handle your dispute through mediation rather than a lawsuit.

For example, if you sued your employer for sexual harassment, much of the background information both sides collect to try to harm the reputation of the other would probably be available to the public. This would include not only what was said in court, but also what was revealed before trial in "discovery" proceedings, during which you may have had to answer very personal questions about your wages, work performance, associates, and personal habits on and off the job. And your employer would likely have had to answer questions about every-thing from the company's structure, ownership, profitability, and employee relations to whether lewd posters were hung on the men's room walls or dirty jokes were told at board meetings.

Also, lawsuits are sometimes publicized. Newspaper and television reporters who cover the courts know where to find the information that will make an otherwise boring legal story come alive with interesting (usually embarrassing) personal details. Don't take this threat to your privacy lightly; every day the media—including trade journals and other specialist publications with a narrow focus—report on thousands of legal actions. For example, even if a sexual harassment claim against a trucking company wasn't reported in the daily newspapers or on the TV news, it might be the subject of a big story in a magazine that covers the industry.

Mediation, by contrast, is a strictly private affair; there will be no stenographer or tape recorder. Mediators take an oath to protect the confidences entrusted to them. Many will even throw away their notes after the mediation session. And in some states, the confidentiality of mediation proceedings is additionally protected by so-called "privilege laws" that prevent a mediator from testifying in court (or arbitration) about what was said in mediation. (For more on confidentiality in mediation, see Chapter 5, Section A.)

Abuse won't be kept confidential. If evidence of spousal or child abuse or other criminal behavior is disclosed in a mediation session, the mediator may be required by state law or by the rules of the particular mediation service to stop the session and forward the evidence to authorities. This is one of the few exceptions to the general rule that everything said in mediation is confidential.

4. You Want to Minimize Costs

A Chinese proverb says, "Going to the law [court] is losing a cow for the sake of a cat." While this may sometimes be an exaggeration, parties all too often lose more than they gain in a lawsuit. And certainly, when going to court is likely to cost more than the dispute is worth, it makes sense to consider other approaches.

Over 90% of your costs in bringing a civil lawsuit will likely be your lawyer's fees, which can range from $150 to $300 per hour and up. Many contested court cases eat up literally hundreds of hours of lawyer time for both sides. For example, a basic trademark dispute often costs each party more than $100,000 in legal fees, and it's all too common for spouses involved in contested divorce or child custody disputes to spend all the money they have, and then some.

By contrast, mediation fees start at zero for nonprofit community mediation centers (their operations are supported by tax dollars and donations), and $500 or so at private dispute resolution companies that handle consumer and business cases.

Mediation can really save you money if you would otherwise hire a lawyer for a contingency fee—a percentage (usually between 25% and 40%) of any amount you are awarded. Suppose, for example, you are hit by a telephone company's service truck and suffer several serious injuries. If you sue the company and a jury awards you $100,000, your lawyer would take at least $30,000, leaving you $70,000. In addition to paying your medical bills (or reimbursing your medical provider), you would need to subtract from that amount many more thousands of dollars for court fees, as well as the costs of investigating and bringing physicians and other experts into court to testify. By contrast, if you can mediate the case without a lawyer, you could settle for a little less—say $80,000—and still end up with more than you would have taken home in a lawsuit. You won't have to pay attorney fees, court costs, or expert witness fees (although you will have to chip in for your share of the mediation fee).

5. You Want to Settle Your Dispute Promptly

"Our civil courts can be described as parking lots for civil litigation," Robert Coulson, former president of the American Arbitration Association, has correctly noted. It's not uncommon for a lawsuit to be pending for two, three, four, or five years before trial. Although more than 90 percent of litigated disputes settle before trial, settlement discussions often do not get serious until a trial date is near. This aspect of the law has not changed much since 1759, when the British statesman Edmund Burke observed, "The contending parties find themselves more effectively ruined by the delay than they could have been by the injustice of any decision."

Large business, consumer, and public policy disputes that might take years to resolve in court can often be processed and settled within a few months in mediation. Even small consumer disputes that might take three months or so to resolve in small claims court can be disposed of far more quickly in mediation.

6. You Want to Avoid Establishing a Legal Precedent

You may want to avoid a court ruling that would set an unfavorable precedent, particularly if the chances for a victory in court are slim and the consequences of an unfavorable decision are substantial. Suppose, for example, that you and a group of neighbors want to stop a local manufacturing company from building a new factory on several acres of undeveloped woodlands near your homes. If you sue to block the company's plans, you have only a small chance of winning under a state law designed to protect environmentally sensitive areas. However, if you lose in court, the judge's decision might set a legal precedent that would encourage other companies to build on other environmentally sensitive areas. So, rather than risk the bad precedent, you decide to mediate with the manufacturing company in an effort to get them to abandon or modify their plans, in order to protect your woodlands without putting other areas at risk.

7. You Are Having Difficulty Initiating Negotiations, or Lack Negotiating Skills

Even though you want to negotiate a fair settlement to your dispute, you may not be able to get the process rolling. Maybe the other party is a large company or government agency that has a policy of not negotiating with individuals. In this situation, your formal offer to mediate—especially if it is made through a respected mediation service—may be enough to get their attention, especially if it carries the implied threat of a lawsuit if you are turned down.

Similarly, if you have poor negotiating skills or are intimidated by the other party, you might want to mediate. The mediator's presence will allow you to negotiate in a safe environment and help you get your points across clearly to the other side. In this sense, the structure of mediation can often help parties who have trouble dealing with each other directly, thus reducing or eliminating the need for hired representatives. In addition, the mediator will make sure that neither party is threatened, browbeaten, or intimidated.

D. Factors Opposing Mediation

If any of the following statements are true, mediation may not be the best choice for resolving your dispute.

1. You Want to Vindicate Your Rights or Set a Legal Precedent

If you are part of an advocacy group—one that promotes environmental, women's, or immigrants' causes, for example—it may be important to your group to set a legal precedent by winning an important court case that interprets or defines the law in a particular way. You can't do this through mediation. Mediation agreements do not establish who is "right" or "wrong," but only what steps each party will take to resolve the dispute. And because a mediated settlement is binding only on the parties to that dispute, it does not establish a precedent—what the parties agree to in mediation does not affect the parties to any other dispute.

If there is a bad law that you want overturned, or if you want to prove the truth of something publicly—for example, if you have been unfairly maligned in the local newspaper and want to clear your name—you may sensibly choose to do this through the courts rather than in mediation.

2. You Want to Go for the Jackpot

If you believe you can win a million-dollar verdict against a big company (or even a small company with a big bank account or plenty of insurance), you might want to opt for a jury trial rather than mediation. In mediation, chances are good you would achieve a settlement more quickly and therefore get your money sooner than you would by filing a lawsuit. However, because mediation usually results in compromise, you would be less likely to get big money. This is especially true if there's a good chance that a jury might award you punitive damages (see "What Are Punitive Damages?" below) or a significant amount of money for pain and suffering. Of course, it's also true that you could lose in court and recover nothing. A lawyer can advise you in advance about your chances in court.

WHAT ARE PUNITIVE DAMAGES?

Sometimes, a judge or jury awards "punitive damages." This is payment over and above the value of the person's actual losses or injuries, and even beyond compensation for "pain and suffering," "emotional distress," and other types of trauma that are difficult to measure. The purpose of punitive damages is to punish the defendant and to deter him and others from committing similar acts in the future. Punitive damages may be awarded when the defendant acted maliciously, recklessly, or deliberately, or intentionally disregarded the rights of others. In most states, punitive damages can be awarded in cases involving personal injuries, damage to property, false arrest or imprisonment, fraud and deceit, interference with employment or business relations, libel and slander, nuisances, and interference with rights guaranteed by the Constitution. Punitive damages are generally not awarded in divorces or cases involving breach of a contract.

3. One Party Refuses to Mediate, or Is Absent or Incompetent

What is the sound of one party mediating? Nothing, of course, which pretty much sums up what happens when only one party agrees to try mediation. For any one of several reasons, the other side may:

- prefer litigation because he thinks he has a good chance to win in court

- not perceive enough of an advantage in mediation to consider trying it

- enjoy the dispute—or the prospect of beating you in court—so much that he's in no hurry to end it, or

- dislike or fear you so much that he doesn't want to be in the same room with you.

A significant percentage of cases referred to mediation never reach the table because one party declines to participate. You'll find some strategies to overcome a party's reluctance to mediate in Chapter 4. Often, a mediation service will actively work to bring the reluctant party into mediation. But if the other side keeps refusing to participate, there is little you can do about it. Perhaps at a later stage of the dispute (when legal fees are skyrocketing, a court decision goes the wrong way, or it becomes important to end the dispute quickly, for example), you can try to raise the topic of mediation again—it may look more attractive to the other party at that point.

Similarly, if one or more parties is physically unable to attend, then mediation may not work. For example, if a party is in jail for an extended period, then you cannot mediate. However, physical proximity isn't always required for successful mediation. Even parties who live in different cities or states can mediate a dispute through teleconferencing or the Internet.

Mediation requires both parties to be rational and able to participate in reasoned discussion and negotiation. If one party is mentally impaired or affected by alcohol or drug abuse, mediation won't work. A physical impairment such as a speech problem or an inability to speak English should normally be no bar to mediation—you can arrange for an interpreter or spokesperson to bridge the communication gap.

4. The Dispute Involves a Serious Crime

Cases involving spousal or child abuse or other serious criminal behavior, including murder, rape, and armed robbery, do not belong in mediation. By law, crimes must be prosecuted by the authorities. But even beyond that, mediation requires that both parties be able to engage in rational and effective negotiation; if one party has been the victim of serious criminal behavior, that party may be too intimidated or fearful of reprisals to participate freely.

On the other hand, minor criminal cases—for example, assault with no injury, personal harassment as might occur among neighbors or coworkers, and minor property damage—are often good candidates for mediation. The process allows parties to get at underlying attitudes and behaviors with the idea of heading off repeat problems. In many areas, these types of cases—which are often referred to mediation by prosecutors or judges—make up a significant part of the caseload at community mediation centers.

5. You Need a Court Order to Prevent Immediate Harm

Your dispute won't be a good candidate for mediation if, by taking the time to mediate, you might suffer immediate personal or business harm. For example, if another company in the same field as your small manufacturing firm has copied your trademark and is advertising their competing product widely, you need to stop them pronto, before your customers become confused. The best way to accomplish this (expense aside) is by getting a court to issue a restraining order. Similarly, if town officials announce their intention to cut down all the maple trees lining your street by next Thursday, you obviously need to get a judge to issue a court order preventing (enjoining) them from wielding the ax until the case can be heard. Once you get the court order stopping the tree choppers, you may want to ask the judge to put the case on hold while you try to resolve it through mediation.

6. Your Case Would Be Better Off in Small Claims Court

For some disputes, you may be better off filing in small claims court than initiating mediation. The speed and low cost of small claims court—and the fact that you don't need a lawyer—make it fairly comparable to mediation at a community mediation center. Small claims courts are particularly good at handling disputes where the facts and the law are clear, including cases in which each party's legal rights are plainly spelled out in writing, as in a lease or other contract. Disputes between landlords and tenants involving nonpayment of rent or return of security deposits, for example, are routinely handled in small claims court. The maximum amount for which you can sue in small claims court varies from state to state. In most states, it's between $2,500 and $5,000.

But small claims judges—like most other judges—have neither the time nor the authority to help disputing parties resolve personal differences, which means that interpersonal disputes often are not successfully resolved in small claims court. In addition, crowded small claims courts are not usually good at dealing with complicated fact situations that can take a long time to sort out. If you're planning a long argument over what the general contractor told your spouse about whether the electrician would move the electrical jacks before installing the radiant heaters, small claims court is probably not the place to do it.

In addition, small claims court offers no privacy from the public or the press, meaning that even small disputes can sometimes be blown way out of proportion. And some small claims courts require the parties to at least try some form of alternative dispute resolution—such as mediation—before their lawsuit can proceed. This means that you may decide to take your case to small claims court, only to find yourself mediating. For more on information on bringing a case in small claims court, see *Everybody's Guide to Small Claims Court* (California and National Editions), by Ralph Warner (Nolo).

7. You Can Easily Win in Regular Court or Arbitration

Few disputes are so clear-cut that either side can confidently predict a pure victory in court. Even if a party wins, the costs and attorneys' fees can take a big bite out of the spoils. But occasionally, it will clearly pay off to go to court. If you find yourself in that situation, it does not make sense to mediate, unless there are other compelling reasons to do so (to preserve a family, business, or social relationship, for example). As long as you are willing to tolerate the delays, loss of privacy, and other drawbacks of a lawsuit, you might as well take a route that will get you a decision 100% in your favor. Arbitration can also provide this type of absolute victory if the other side is willing—or required—to arbitrate.

Factors favoring mediation	Factors opposing mediation
No legal remedy	Wanting test case
Preserving a relationship	Wanting jackpot
Maintaining privacy	Party refuses, is absent, or incompetent
Avoiding high fees	Serious crime
Avoiding delays	Need court order to prevent harm
Avoiding legal precedent	Better off in small claims court
Unable to negotiate	Real court victory is assured ■

CHAPTER 3

Choosing a Mediator

If you decide to file a lawsuit (or you are sued by someone else), detailed rules dictate the state, county, and courthouse where you'll have to wage your court battle. In contrast, you will often be free to choose where and by whom you will have your case mediated. Depending on where you live and what kind of dispute you are involved in, there may be several mediators or mediation services available. This chapter will help you choose the right mediator for your dispute.

As you evaluate the available options, you might have some or all of these goals in mind:

- **Convincing the other party to mediate.** You can't mediate alone. Therefore, if the other party is reluctant to mediate, you'll want to select a mediator or mediation service that will be able to get that party to the table. Often, mediation services do a better job than independent mediators at getting reluctant parties to mediate. These services usually have staff members (often called "case managers") whose job includes explaining mediation to the parties and persuading them to give it a try. Services are also more likely to have printed materials available that will explain the process and assuage the concerns of a reluctant party.

- **Finding a mediator with the right combination of skills.** The success of your mediation may well be determined by the skills your mediator brings to the table. Two types of skills are necessary: process skills (the ability to conduct an effective mediation) and subject-matter knowledge (an understanding of the particular issues in dispute, sometimes including technical information). In complex cases, such as business disputes involving multiple issues and parties, you'll want a mediator with the process skills to handle a complicated case and the subject-matter know-how to understand the legal and technical aspects of the dispute. Often, a private mediation service is the best place to find mediators who specialize in particular subjects (such as intellectual property or employment issues).

- **Getting the most bang for your buck.** Obviously, you will want to pay as little as possible for the services you need. If you will mediate at a community mediation center or through a court-connected program, cost won't be an issue—these services are generally available free or for a nominal fee. But if you hire an independent mediator or use a private mediation service, you should compare prices and quality of service. For example, if the same mediator works occasionally for a mediation service and also has a private practice, you'll probably find that you can hire the mediator directly for a much lower rate than you would pay to use the same mediator through a mediation service. The smaller your case, the more you need to worry about cost—after all, you don't want the costs of mediation to eat up all of the money you hope to gain (or stand to lose).

    This chapter will help you meet these goals while finding a mediator who can help you resolve your dispute. Here, we explain the types of mediators and mediation services available (Section A), how to gather leads to mediators and services you may want to use (Section B), how to choose the right mediation service (Section C) and how to choose the right mediator—either a mediator in private practice or one of the mediators available through a mediation service (Section D).

A. Mediators and Mediation Services

To choose a good mediator for your dispute, you first have to know what your options are. This section explains the various types of mediation services or mediators that are available in many communities and the kinds of cases each is most experienced in handling.

1. Community Mediation Centers

Most community mediation centers are independent, nonprofit organizations that receive funds from state and local governments. Services are generally provided free or at low cost (perhaps $25) and are available to anyone in the community. These centers provide a cost-effective way to resolve relatively minor cases that often get lost in, or otherwise are not well served by, the local courts and criminal justice system.

There are hundreds of these centers nationwide. They are called by various names—such as "dispute resolution center," "neighborhood justice center," "community mediation program," or "center for dispute settlement." To find out if there is a center in your community, check the Yellow Pages under "mediation," call the general information number at city hall, or contact your local bar association. If this doesn't produce results, contact the National Association for Community Mediation, 1527 New Hampshire Ave., NW, Washington, DC 20036, 202-667-9700, or visit their website at www.nafcm.org and click "Mediation Center Directory."

Community mediation centers typically have a no-frills "public service" look. This works just fine; all you need for a successful mediation is a quiet room, a table with a few chairs, and a good mediator. Indeed, the modest look may help disputants relax—you know you're not paying for circular stairways or Persian carpets.

Many cases heard at the centers are referred there by judges, police, and social service agencies. But these days, especially when it comes to small consumer claims and disputes between neighbors and between landlords and tenants, the centers are also seeing lots of cases brought to them directly by the parties involved. Most centers are prepared to handle disputes involving charges of assault without injury, personal harassment, consumer claims, disputes between spouses, housing disputes, neighborhood disputes, and disputes among coworkers.

Some centers have also developed special mediation programs to meet local needs. For example, disputes between roommates may be a common occurrence in a college town, and centers in rural areas may specialize in mediating disputes between farmers and food storage companies or bankers, as well as disputes between mobile home park owners and tenants.

Usually, cases at community mediation centers are mediated by trained volunteers from the community (the state laws that establish community mediation centers also set minimum training standards for the mediators who work there). Most community mediation centers do not give the parties much choice in who their mediator will be. Instead, the case manager will consider various factors, such as subject matter, complexity of the case, and mediator availability, and then assign a mediator from the pool of volunteers available. But sometimes you can choose your mediator, or at least influence the assignment (see Section D, below).

THE OLD WOMAN AND THE FAST CAR: A TYPICAL COMMUNITY CENTER MEDIATION

In Delaware County, Pennsylvania, an elderly woman was at the end of her rope when she called the Community Dispute Settlement Center. She complained of a young couple next door who came and went at all hours of the night in a high-performance Porsche, with motor roaring and radio blaring. So intimidated was she by her neighbors that she asked for police protection at the mediation (a center staff member assured her it wouldn't be necessary).

At an evening mediation session, the woman and the young couple reached a settlement. The couple agreed to operate the Porsche quietly while in their driveway or on their street (not shifting above second gear, and with the radio off, for example) and the woman agreed to call the couple at their home or offices (they exchanged phone numbers) if she had further complaints. The woman was so relieved, she later told the mediation center's staff, "I didn't believe in miracles until the night of my mediation."

Adapted from Anne Richan, "Developing and Funding Community Dispute Settlement Programs," *Mediation Quarterly*, No. 5, 1984, p. 86.

2. Private Dispute Resolution Companies

An increasing number of for-profit firms now compete to mediate cases such as contract disputes between businesses, construction cases, employment disputes, and disputed insurance claims arising out of auto accidents and other mishaps.

Private dispute resolution companies provide a panel of trained and experienced mediators for the parties to choose from. However, they serve other functions as well, including:

- explaining the benefits of mediation to all parties (and convincing reluctant parties to give it a try)

- administering the mediation, including all paperwork, scheduling, and billing, and

- following up with the parties after the mediation ends, if further dispute resolution services are needed.

There are hundreds of private dispute resolution firms. Some operate at the national level, with branch offices in major cities, while others are mid-sized or smaller firms that operate regionally or locally. One of the largest national outfits is Judicial Arbitration & Mediation Services or JAMS, headquartered in Irvine, California. This company has more than 25 offices nationwide and maintains an impressive roster of mediators—mostly lawyers and retired judges. To learn more about JAMS and to find a location near you, check out their website at www.jamsadr.org.

Other national firms include Resolute Systems, Inc., headquartered in Milwaukee, Wisconsin (www.resolutesystems.com), and U.S. Arbitration & Mediation, Inc. (www.usam.com). The American Arbitration Association, Inc., in New York, New York (www.adr.org), is a well-established nonprofit corporation that handles many of the same kinds of large, complex disputes as the newer, for-profit companies. (You can find a list of some of the larger national and regional dispute resolution firms in Appendix C.)

Fees at most of the private firms start at a minimum of about $500 per party for a half-day mediation session. Costs can rise to thousands of dollars, depending on the complexity of the case and the length of time needed to resolve it. Many private firms also charge an administrative fee—a one-time charge to cover the costs of opening and managing the case. This fee might range from $150 to $300 or more.

Most of the larger private firms, and many of the smaller ones, maintain a list of people available to mediate disputes, usually referred to as "mediation panels." The panel is simply a list or roster of mediators available through that firm. Most panel members are former judges and practicing attorneys, or others with expertise in subjects such as engineering, health care, construction, and land-use.

Private firms can differ hugely in terms of how much training and skill their mediators have. At one extreme they often provide the most highly skilled career mediators. Yet, paradoxically, it is also in these firms where you are fairly likely to run into problems with inexperienced mediators. One reason for this is that these firms often hire big-name judges who have recently retired. Judges with little background or training in mediation may believe their role is just to "knock people's heads together" until they settle, as they did when they were on the bench. Similarly, you may encounter a lawyer-mediator with great specialized knowledge and reputation in a particular area of the law—but little training or experience in mediation.

3. Independent Mediators in Private Practice

Independent mediators in private practice work on their own, unaffiliated with private dispute resolution companies or other mediation providers. Whether they practice locally or nationally, independent mediators set their own fees, handle their own paperwork, keep their own schedules, and often develop and use their own rules. Fees range from $100–$300 an hour and up for independent mediators who work at the local level and handle a variety of cases, to $2,000–$5,000 or more a day for those who operate nationally and specialize in large, complex disputes in areas such as business and construction. Some local mediators use a sliding fee scale based on size and complexity of the case, the parties' ability to pay, and how much the mediator wants the work.

It's wise to consider using an independent mediator when you don't need or want to pay for the extra services that a mediation service typically provides—perhaps all parties readily agree to mediate and you're willing to set up the date, time, and place yourself. But an independent mediator usually won't get involved in trying to persuade reluctant parties to mediate. So if you anticipate any reluctance on the part of the other side to mediate, you should probably choose a mediation service rather than an independent mediator.

You also should consider using an independent mediator when your case will require a mediator who is highly knowledgeable in a particular field. For example, if you are involved in a complicated construction dispute, an independent mediator who specializes in this type of case can bring to the table a great deal of knowledge about construction law and experience in working out creative settlements.

To find an independent mediator with a specialty in your field, ask lawyers or business owners who work in that area. For example, if your case involves a construction dispute, a local lawyer who specializes in construction litigation is likely to have a list of independent mediators, both locally and nationally, who specialize in construction cases. A lawyer who specializes in health care—or the president of the local medical society—may have names of mediators who handle medical disputes. Similarly, if your dispute involves a particular area of business—printing, scrap metal, or injection molding, for example—state or national offices of trade groups representing these fields may have lists of mediators with those specialties. You may also get help in locating independent mediators qualified to handle your case from the various mediator professional groups listed in Appendix C.

4. Court-Connected Mediation Programs

State trial courts all over the country are initiating mediation programs in order to reduce their caseloads and operating costs. Some of these programs are for civil cases; others are for minor criminal offenses.

a. Civil Cases

Some court programs handle a variety of civil (noncriminal) cases. Under these programs, people who file lawsuits are required or strongly encouraged to try mediation before they can proceed. Nearly every state today has some kind of court-connected mediation program. Some states require parties to try mediation; others require only that parties receive information about the availability of mediation, but do not require them to pursue it.

In some states, the court itself provides the parties with conference rooms and mediators. In others, judges or court clerks simply instruct the parties to pick a mediator from a list of "qualified" mediators or to go out and find their own mediator.

If your case is already in court, call the clerk of the court to find out if there is a mediation program available, or ask your attorney to check on this. If your case is not in court, a court-based program won't be an option for you.

Don't file a court case just to be referred to mediation. It's ordinarily not worth incurring the hostility, fees, and delays that come with filing a lawsuit just to have access to a court-connected mediation program. Sometimes, however, you won't have any other choice. If the other party refuses to negotiate or mediate (which means that you must either sue or forget about pursuing your case), you may want to go ahead with your lawsuit—and plan to ask the judge to refer your dispute to a court-connected mediation program. For more on this option, see Chapter 4.

Typically, mediators in programs run by the courts are practicing lawyers who volunteer or are paid a small stipend for occasionally mediating cases. These lawyers probably have had some minimal mediation training but most do not handle enough cases to develop really good skills. If the court refers parties to local mediation services rather than trying to run the whole program on its own, you may have better luck. In some situations, you may even have your pick of anyone in the local mediation field, including panels of mediators put together by private firms as well as independent mediators. In some states, you can even use a nonlawyer mediator in a court-connected program.

If a court requires you to mediate, it will sometimes pick up the tab, at least for the first couple of hours, as long as you use a mediator connected with the court's program. If you and the other party decide to choose your own mediator, you will probably have to foot the entire bill.

COURT-SPONSORED DIVORCE MEDIATION

In many states, divorce courts will send parties who have children to mandatory mediation to work out custody and visitation issues. This court-sponsored mediation is usually free to the participants (although there may be a fee for missed appointments). The mediators are full-time employees of the court, and they are often experienced social workers or therapists who are trained to deal with complex family issues. Some court programs require the mediator to report to the judge after the mediation and make a recommendation about custody or visitation; in others, the mediation is confidential and the mediator doesn't make a recommendation. For more on court-sponsored divorce mediation, see Chapter 10.

b. Criminal Cases

Mediation programs established by local public prosecutors or district attorneys are fairly similar to those established by courts. But unlike court programs, which usually focus on civil disputes, prosecutor programs are designed to resolve minor criminal complaints.

Programs around the country differ, but typically the mediators will be either full-time court employees with backgrounds in social services or criminal justice, or part-time mediators with legal backgrounds. Mediators who work at this type of program usually handle a high volume of cases, most of which present intense personal grievances. If they are able to continue mediating these kinds of cases successfully for more than a few months without burning out, they probably have developed pretty good mediation skills.

5. Federal and State Government Mediation Programs

Lots of federal and state agencies have implemented mediation programs as a way to improve services and reduce administrative and litigation costs. If you have a dispute with a government agency (or a dispute with a private party that a government agency is supposed to handle), ask whether mediation is available. For example, at the federal level, if you file a workplace discrimination claim with the Equal Employment Opportunity Commission, you can try to resolve it through a mediation program offered through the agency's district offices. Or, if you are a farmer who is having trouble with a lender, several Midwestern states offer mediation services through the state agency that deals with agricultural concerns. And Medicare is just beginning a mediation program to resolve disputes between Medicare patients and health care providers.

6. Trade and Professional Group Mediation Programs

Some trade groups and professional organizations, such as realtors and lawyers, have created specialized programs to try to mediate their own disputes. For example, lawyers in some cities and states have set up mediation programs to handle fee disputes with clients. And the National Association of Realtors requires its member associations to offer mediation when disputes arise after the sale of a home.

Consumers should approach these programs with caution. Although they are free or very low-cost, they often aren't really neutral. The purpose of these programs, at least in part, is to reduce the number of lawsuits against members. The mediators are often members of the trade or professional group and may be more inclined to push for solutions that favor the organization.

Despite these potential problems, you may wish to try mediating with one of these groups. After all, you can always withdraw if you believe the process is unfair. For example, let's say you hired a real estate sales agent to handle the sale of your home, and you believe the agent disclosed confidential information about your negotiating position to a prospective buyer, resulting in a lower offering price. After the realtor refuses to pay you the money you believe you lost on the sale, you agree to mediate the dispute through a program run by the local real estate board. Under the program, the board pays supposedly neutral local real estate agents a small stipend to sit as mediators. Can a realtor-mediator really be neutral as between you and your former agent? Probably not. But because the process is free and the realtor has no authority to impose a decision you don't agree to, it may be worth a try. Also, some trade groups want their mediators to be pro-consumer in order to head off any potentially bad publicity directed at their group as a whole. In other words, the mediator may push for a settlement in your favor to keep you from contacting "60 Minutes."

7. Specialized Mediation Services

As mediation gains in popularity, some groups that serve particular communities have begun to develop their own networks of mediation services. Here are just a few of the specialized programs available:

- **Arts Resolution Services.** Developed by California Lawyers for the Arts, this nationwide program provides mediation for arts-related disputes, including disputes over copyright, ownership of artistic work, payment for work, contracts, board and artistic control, and more. Fees are based on a sliding scale. To find out more, check out the website of California Lawyers for the Arts at www.calawyersforthearts.org.

- **Institute for Christian Conciliation.** If you would like your dispute mediated based on Christian biblical principles of conflict resolution, you may want to contact the Institute for Christian Conciliation, a national group with members and affiliated organizations around the country. The Institute trains and certifies its own mediators, who come from many professional and work backgrounds, including lawyers, mental health counselors, clergy, homemakers, and business people. For information, contact: Institute for Christian Conciliation, 1537 Avenue D, Suite 352, Billings, MT 59102 406-256-1583; www.Hispeace.org.

- **Asian Pacific American Dispute Resolution Center.** This organization provides mediation and conciliation services in Asian Pacific languages, including Chinese, Korean, Japanese, Vietnamese, and Tagalog. The Center handles ethnic disputes as well as domestic, housing, neighborhood, employment, and business conflicts, and matters involving race relations. Disputants are asked to pay nominal processing and hourly fees, but fees are waived for those unable to pay. The Center primarily serves Los Angeles County, but can assist those outside the area by conducting telephone mediation and by making nationwide referrals to mediators or translators fluent in Asian Pacific languages. For information, contact the Center at 1145 Wilshire Blvd., Suite 100, Los Angeles, CA 90017 213-250-8190; http://pages.sbcglobal.net/apadrc.

In addition, many lesbian, gay, bisexual, and transgender community centers offer mediation services, as do some social services agencies that work with the elderly and other specific communities.

Common Types of Disputes and Where They Can Best Be Mediated

Case Type	Best Choices	Fees	Reasons
Assault, harassment	Community mediation center; court or prosecutor's program, if available	$0–$50 sliding scale	Low cost; subject matter expertise; experience mediating this type of dispute
Contract dispute	Dispute resolution company; independent mediator with this specialty	$100–$350 an hour per party	Subject matter expertise; experience mediating this type of dispute
Consumer complaint	Community mediation center	$0–$50 sliding scale	Subject matter expertise; experience mediating this type of dispute
Divorce	Private divorce mediator; court program, if available	$80–$400 an hour per couple; sliding scale may be available	Subject matter expertise; experience mediating this dispute
Employment	Dispute resolution company; independent mediator with this specialty	$100–$350 an hour per party	Subject matter expertise; experience mediating this type of dispute
Environmental	Dispute resolution company; independent mediator with this specialty	$100–$350 an hour per party	Subject matter expertise; experience mediating this type of dispute
Interpersonal	Community mediation center	$0–$50 sliding scale	Low cost; subject matter expertise; experience mediating this type of dispute
Intrafamily	Private family mediator	$50–$175	Low cost; subject matter expertise; an hour experience mediating this type of dispute
Landlord/ tenant	Community mediation center	$0–$50 sliding scale	Low cost; subject matter expertise; experience mediating this type of dispute
Neighbor	Community mediation center	$0–$50	Low cost; subject matter expertise; sliding scaleexperience mediating this type of dispute
Small Business	Dispute resolution company	$100–$350 an hour per party	Subject matter expertise; experience mediating this type of dispute

B. Gathering Leads

Now that you know what types of mediators and mediation services might be available to you, it's time to start your search. The first step in finding a good mediator is to gather the names of some mediators or mediation services in your area. Once you've got some leads, you can consider the strengths and weaknesses of each option. This section explains where to find out about local mediators and services.

1. Your Own Private Information Network

No matter where you are or what kind of dispute you face, you should be able to get some useful leads by simply picking up the phone or logging on to the Internet. For example, depending on the specifics of your dispute, a local woman's organization, gay-lesbian organization, or business trade group (or their key members) may be able to make a knowledgeable referral. Lawyers are often another excellent source of referrals. Even if you have few professional contacts, you probably know someone who knows a decent lawyer, and that lawyer, in turn, may know just the independent mediator or mediation center to help you.

Try making a short list of the people you know who are in the best position to advise you about a mediator or refer you to someone who can. You may end up calling your son's financial advisor or your mother's minister. But so what? If you get results, that's all that matters.

2. State and National Organizations and Directories

There are lots of state and national groups you can contact for help in locating mediators and mediation services. The Association for Conflict Resolution, for example, will provide lists of divorce and family mediators in your area. (For contact information on this and other national groups, see Appendix C.) Also, many states now have government-sponsored offices that keep track of mediation programs within their states. For contact information, see the list of "Statewide Mediation Offices" in Appendix D. You can also check out the "ADR Locator" on the website of Martindale Hubbell (a legal publishing company), at www.martindale.com (click "Dispute Resolution" to get to a nationwide list of ADR practitioners, searchable by state, specialty area, and languages spoken, among other things).

3. Bar Association Listings

Your local bar association—the professional organization of lawyers in your area—may keep a list of lawyers who mediate cases. Proceed with caution, however. Most bar associations don't screen the lawyers on their rosters—they just give you the name of the next person on the list, without evaluating or commenting on the person's skill level. Also, lots of busy, in-demand mediators won't bother to list with the bar, because they don't need any extra work.

4. Yellow Pages

Check under "mediation" or "dispute resolution." Most mediation services, as well as some independent mediators in private practice, will have some kind of brochure to send you with descriptive information about their services.

C. Selecting the Right Mediation Service

If you have decided that you want to use a mediation service and have located one or more services you might want to try, the next step is to call them and ask for a brochure describing their services. Nearly all services have a brochure—many services have made their informational materials available online (ask if the service has a website when you call).

Once you've had a chance to look over their materials, call them back to ask some or all of the following questions. The answers you get should help you figure out whether the service can handle your case.

 If you won't be using a mediation service, you can skip ahead to Section D.

1. How Extensive Is the Case Management?

"Case management" is industry jargon for handling preliminaries and administrative details, such as:

- getting a reluctant party to mediate

- selecting a particular mediator from a service's panel

- agreeing on a date for the session, and

- agreeing on how fees will be split.

If the other party is reluctant to mediate, the skills of a mediation service's case managers will be the key to getting the other party to the table. If you're facing this situation, you'll want to know the following information: How will they work to get the other side to agree to mediate? Will they contact the other side by letter only, or will they follow up with phone calls? How long will they keep at it? Some services close files after a certain period of time or charge a processing fee to keep a case open. Others will keep working on a case for a long time without a fee in hopes of getting an agreement to mediate.

2. Who Are the Mediators?

Ask about the people on the mediation service's panel to make sure you will be able to work with a mediator who is competent to handle your case.

For example, does the service use only retired judges? Only lawyers? Or do they have a mix of mediators, including some full-time career mediators? Are their mediators trained? Who trains them? Is the training minimal (they read a pamphlet and watch a videotape) or extensive (25-40 hours)? How many cases a year does a typical member of their panel mediate: just a few, or dozens? For how long have most of them been mediating?

Do they have mediators available with special areas of knowledge and expertise (if applicable to your case) such as engineers (mechanical, electrical, civil), physicians, business people, real estate experts, or family counselors?

3. How Will the Mediator Be Chosen?

Many private dispute resolution companies allow the parties to jointly select a mediator from their panel, while most community mediation centers simply assign a mediator or panel of mediators to your case. Does the mediation service you are considering give you the opportunity to pick? If so, how does the selection process work?

4. Are the Fees Reasonable?

Is there a published fee schedule? If so, ask to see it. If you are the one initiating mediation, do you have to pay a filing fee simply to have the case opened? Or are fees due only if the mediation service is successful in getting the other side to agree to mediate, and then from both sides equally? If your dispute settles before the mediation, will you owe them a fee? (It might be reasonable for a service to charge a closing fee, if you didn't have to pay a fee to open the case and the service did substantial work on your case before it settled.) Is there a fee to reschedule the mediation? (Again, this may be reasonable if the fee bears some relation to the amount of administrative work that has to be done to reschedule the case.)

5. Can You Mediate Without a Lawyer?

You can handle most mediations without having a lawyer represent you, and most mediation services will not require you to bring a lawyer. A few, however, may have policies on this. You should find out whether the service has any rules about bringing a lawyer (or not bringing one). Sometimes having legal advice available during mediation is a good idea. The pros and cons of bringing a lawyer with you to mediation or even having one available to consult with by telephone during the session are discussed more fully in Chapter 5, Section E.

6. Are There Written Mediation Rules?

Though mediation is a relatively informal process, a good mediation service will have written rules and procedures, to avoid needless disputes about the process itself. Even independent mediators in private practice—including those who handle divorce and family matters—usually have a set of written rules or procedures for the parties to follow. Ask to see the mediation rules. Are they in plain English, or will you need a lawyer to decipher them for you? Do they cover procedures to be followed before, during, and immediately after your case? A sample set of mediation rules appears in Appendix A.

7. How Will Confidentiality Be Protected?

Will the mediation service preserve the confidentiality of the mediation? How? For example, is the confidentiality of the mediation process part of the rules or do the parties have to sign a separate confidentiality agreement that specifies exactly what the parties and the mediator must keep confidential? Ask to see a copy of their standard confidentiality agreement.

8. Will the Process Be Convenient?

Are you dealing with a "user-friendly" mediation service that will treat you like a valued customer? For example, will they schedule your mediation after work hours or on a weekend, if necessary? Where are mediations held? If their offices are highly inconvenient for you, will they arrange another location? If so, is there an extra fee? How quickly could they schedule your mediation if both you and the other party were ready to start? A day or two? A week or two? It shouldn't take much longer than that.

9. Are References Available?

Are there past users of this mediation service whom you can contact? Most services will start by saying that their client list is confidential (that's appropriate—you'll probably want your name kept confidential, too). Still, you can often press them a little to see if they will call one or two former customers and ask if you can call to talk—not about the details of their case, but about their experience using the mediation service.

10. Are There Any Conflicts of Interest?

Does the mediation service have any conflicts of interest with you or the other side that would prevent it from handling your case in an impartial manner? For example, are any relatives or business partners of either party connected in some way with the mediation service? Or does the mediation service have an ongoing contract with the other side—as it might with a bank, brokerage firm, or insurance company—to mediate a large volume of cases? If so, can the service satisfy you that the arrangement does not in any way encourage the mediators to push for settlements favorable to the other side? It's the mediation service's duty to be aware of and disclose any potential conflicts of interest to you, but it doesn't hurt to ask a few questions of your own to uncover problems early on.

D. Selecting a Mediator

Whether you are using a mediation service or a mediator in private practice, you will want to select a mediator who has the necessary skills, techniques, training, and demeanor to help you resolve your dispute. This section describes some common selection methods, qualities you should look for in a mediator, and questions to ask prospective mediators that will help you make your choice.

Using more than one mediator. Many mediators prefer to work alone, and are well able to handle cases by themselves. Some mediators will offer you the option of involving an additional mediator in your case—often a therapist or someone with mediation skills and expertise in a subject relevant to your situation.

There are pros and cons to using a second mediator. On the negative side, using a second mediator can increase costs and complicate scheduling. On the positive side, two heads can definitely be better than one when it comes to working with difficult personalities and using different methods to move things forward, or when your case is particularly complex or involves a large number of people. In some types of cases, having two mediators can even be more efficient and cost-effective—for example, in a case involving difficult interpersonal relationships as well as business concerns, a lawyer-mediator and a therapist-mediator working together can help resolve the practical business matters and also address patterns of communication and emotional dynamics that contributed to the conflict. In this situation, although the mediation sessions might be more expensive, the process may also move more quickly, and the resolution may last longer and prove more satisfying.

1. Methods of Selecting a Mediator

The method you use to select your mediator will depend, in part, on whether you are using a mediation service or a mediator working in private practice.

a. Selecting From a Mediation Service's Panel

Many mediation services maintain lists of mediators (often called "panels") who are available to handle their cases. Private dispute resolution companies typically invite the parties to select one mediator from the panel. At community mediation centers, the staff often appoints the mediator who will handle a case. This subsection describes some of the most common ways a mediator is selected or appointed to handle a case; Sections D2 and D3, below, will help you decide which mediator to choose, if you have the opportunity to do so.

By Appointment

At some community mediation centers, the staff will simply appoint a mediator (or more than one) from their panel without asking for your input. Many court-connected mediation programs also run this way.

Typically, the case manager will look over the file to determine whether your case presents any special requirements for a mediator, such as foreign language skills or technical knowledge. If you think your case requires a mediator with special expertise, make this request to the staff. The case manager should try to pick someone from their panel who has the qualifications you need.

You could also request a mediator of a particular ethnicity or gender, if you can reasonably show that this would help facilitate your mediation. For example, if two African-Americans or two gay people involved in an interpersonal dispute felt strongly they could only discuss the intricacies of their dispute with someone from their community, many mediation services would appoint a mediator who has the appropriate background.

If the case presents no special mediator needs, the case manager will assign someone from the panel, either at random or in rotation, in an effort to give every mediator on the panel an opportunity to handle some cases. Before making the assignment, the case manager will probably call the mediator to ask if there are any reasons he should not be assigned the case, such as a conflict of interest or a scheduling problem.

Although it may appear that the case manager's selection of a mediator is final, you do not always have to accept this person. If you can show a valid reason for rejecting the mediator—an overlooked conflict of interest, for example, where the mediator has a family, social, or business connection with you or the other party—the mediation service will make a new assignment.

Striking Out Names

In the "strike-out" method, each party is sent a list of mediators and asked to strike (cross out) the names of one or more mediators they do not want. You don't have to give a reason for striking a name—it can be because you know one of the mediators and think she would not be a good mediator, or because someone else advises you not to use one of the mediators. From the names remaining, the case manager will appoint a mediator. This selection method has traditionally been used by the American Arbitration Association and other organizations that help resolve labor problems and other disputes between organizations; some private dispute resolution companies also use it to choose mediators for individual disputes.

Ranking by Preference

Some mediation services will ask you to rank, in order of preference, the four or five people on the list whom you would most like as a mediator for your case. The case manager then appoints the one ranked highest by both parties. This method is favored by some private dispute resolution firms because it is customer-friendly—it gives both parties some measure of control over mediator selection. On the other hand, this process can be more cumbersome than others: If the names you and the other side select do not overlap, you may have to repeat the process.

Combining Strike-Out and Rank by Preference

Some mediation services combine the strike-out and rank-by-preference methods. Following this approach, you may be presented with a list of ten or so mediators' names, with the following instructions:

"Line out any names that are unacceptable and rank the remaining names in order of preference, with #1 representing the most preferred. Subject to availability, the most mutually acceptable mediator will be selected."

Staff members often make good mediators. At some mediation services, staff members mediate cases in addition to helping run the business. In our experience, staffers are often more experienced and skillful mediators than many of the part-time mediators on the service's panel. Other things being equal, you may wish to choose a staff mediator to handle your case.

b. Selecting an Independent Mediator

If you and the other party prefer to select an independent mediator in private practice, how you decide on a mediator will depend largely on how well you are getting along. For example, if you and the other party are on relatively good terms, you could both make calls to find a few independent mediators and then jointly interview them—either in person or by conference call—to decide which one you want to use.

More typically, you and the other party may prefer to work cooperatively, but with less direct contact. For example, if you and your business partner are breaking up, you might agree that one of you will identify three independent mediators who have a specialty in disputes involving small business. The other can then check out all three and choose the one to mediate your case.

If the other party is reluctant to mediate and/or the two of you cannot agree on a private mediator for your case, you are probably better off using a mediation service.

2. Mediator Qualifications

Here are some of the factors you should consider when deciding which mediator to choose, whether you are looking at mediator in private practice or considering the mediators on a mediation service's panel.

a. Skill Level

Generally, a mediator's skill at helping people work through problems depends on training, experience, and the mediator's own intuitive peacemaking abilities. While it's tough to measure someone's intuitive ability, you can learn whether a mediator has adequate training and experience—and these should be the first questions you ask of any mediator.

Some people who call themselves mediators have little training or experience. This is particularly likely to be true of former judges and lawyers, some of whom see mediation as a sort of quasi-retirement from the legal profession. These mediators may be quite skilled as litigators or decision makers, but often lack the special abilities and people skills necessary to mediate cases. If you are considering using a retired judge or lawyer as a mediator, be sure to ask about mediation training and experience—not just prominence in the community or experience in the courtroom.

Training

Most good, basic mediator training programs involve between 25-40 hours of classroom time and include lectures, demonstrations, videos, and role-playing exercises. Training topics include the psychology of human conflict and conflict resolution, negotiation theory, laws of mediation and confidentiality, mediator ethics, and the practical steps involved in conducting a typical mediation session. Of course, training quality varies with the skills of the trainer, the sponsoring organization, and the group of people being trained. But if the mediator you are considering attended a training program of 25 hours or more, you can probably assume—regardless of the specific training organization—that the course adequately covered the basics.

Mediation doesn't require a degree or certificate. These days, many colleges and universities offer degree programs in conflict resolution. However, many of these programs teach theory rather than practical skills. You shouldn't favor a particular mediator for possessing such a degree, nor rate one lower for lack of one. Similarly, a mediator who claims to be "certified" won't necessarily have the skills or training to handle your dispute. Certification usually means only that a person has received a certificate from a mediation training program—not that he is skilled or likely to do a good job in your case. Unfortunately, certification also does not mean a person has lots of mediation experience; nor does it normally require any continuing education, advanced training, or minimum level of practice.

Beyond the basic 25-40 hour programs, mediators who specialize in particular types of disputes often participate in advanced training programs. For example, a divorce mediator may have taken a program established by the Academy of Family Mediators. Similarly, mediators who specialize in areas such as construction, health care, business, and intellectual property may have further training in these fields.

Experience

It takes practice to mediate well. This is not to say that a person who has successfully completed a mediator training course could not do a good job for you right out of the box, but all things being equal, it makes sense to pick a mediator who has some experience.

Some people mediate full time and have handled hundreds of cases; others—such as practicing attorneys whose names appear on mediation panels—may only mediate one or two cases a year. Those are the extremes, of course. In between, there are many well-trained people who mediate with some regularity; even mediating one case a month will let a person build up skills over time.

You should also find out how much experience the mediator has had with cases like yours. For example, if you are ending a relationship and have to work out property division, child custody, and ownership of a business with your former partner, you will want a mediator who has considerable experience handling family disputes. A mediator who has handled hundreds of cases may be a poor choice if most of those cases involved monetary disputes between auto accident victims and insurance companies and yours is a family matter.

Similarly, special skills are required to mediate a case with multiple parties. A mediator who is dealing with three or more parties will have to work harder to maintain order, give everyone an opportunity to speak, and keep the discussion moving forward. If your case involves multiple parties, you should select a mediator who has experience with these kinds of cases.

Take a look at mediator settlement rates, if possible. Some mediation services keep statistics on settlement rates for each mediator on their panel. For example, "Joe Doaks mediated 17 small business disputes last year; 12 of those cases settled either at the session or within a short time afterward." While settlement rates are no guarantee that a mediator will be able to settle your case, it can be a useful indicator of experience and skill level.

b. Professional Affiliations

Another way to size up a mediator is to ask about membership in professional mediator organizations. Because most professional groups have no fixed requirements for membership (other than paying dues), membership by itself won't tell you how skilled a mediator is. However, a person who is willing to pay for memberships in two or three professional groups probably wants to keep up with developments in the field.

One mediation group, the Association for Conflict Resolution (ACR), has an additional membership requirement. This national organization requires those who join as "practitioners" to have at least three years (or more than 200 hours) of experience as a mediator or arbitrator *and* at least 40 hours of training (or the equivalent). Those who join as "members" don't have to meet these requirements. ACR and other professional mediator groups are listed in Appendix C.

c. Expertise

For some types of cases, such as small claims, simple contract matters, or neighborhood disputes, any well-trained, experienced mediator should be able to handle the problem adequately. But for more involved cases, you will usually be better off with a mediator who knows about the issues and options available in that type of dispute. For example, if your case is against a bank over the way finance charges were levied on an overdue portion of a commercial real estate mortgage, it will be helpful to have a mediator who has a basic understanding of the financial aspects of the dispute. This way, you won't have to spend the beginning of your mediation educating the mediator. Similarly, if your dispute involves the breakup of a small business partnership, you should look for a mediator who is experienced in helping small businesses arrive at creative solutions. Subject areas in which mediators often specialize include:

- divorce and family

- business

- employment

- construction, and

- intellectual property (patents, trademark, and copyright).

The case manager at your mediation service can tell you which, if any, of their panel members are up to speed in the subject area of your dispute. If you are considering an independent mediator, ask about the mediator's expertise. If the mediator doesn't specialize in disputes like yours, ask for referrals to mediators who do.

PAIR A GOOD MEDIATOR WITH AN EXPERT

If a mediator whom you really like lacks the necessary expertise in the subject of your dispute, don't despair. You can ask the mediator to pair up with another mediator or professional who has the necessary expertise.

With a co-mediation team, you can choose one mediator with strong mediation process skills and a second mediator with subject matter expertise. Co-mediation teams are especially good with large, multiparty cases; the mediators can divide up to meet with the parties separately, which will keep things moving along. But a co-mediation team is likely to be nearly twice as expensive as using a single mediator.

Another option, which is less expensive, is to use one mediator but hire another person (not a mediator) who is an expert in the subject area of the dispute. The parties or the mediator can choose the expert. The expert will be available to help the mediator understand the issues and to suggest possible solutions. For example, if your dispute involves a building project in which the basement flooded during construction, you can hire a good general mediator and a civil engineer with a specialty in subsurface construction issues. The mediator can consult with the engineer as needed during the mediation. You and the other side would pay the engineer by the hour—much less, probably, than you would have to pay a full-time co-mediator.

d. Mediator's Style and Philosophy

The general goal of every mediation is the same: to resolve a dispute. However, how the mediator goes about trying to reach that goal will vary greatly, depending on the mediator's philosophy and approach.

Facilitative or Evaluative?

Some mediators are traditional, almost purist, in their approach to mediating. They see themselves as "facilitators" whose primary job is to be good and patient listeners who can help the parties (1) communicate, (2) see the strengths and weaknesses of each side's position, and (3) think creatively about ideas for settlement. These mediators will not tell the parties what a case is worth or how they think it should be settled.

"Evaluative" mediators, on the other hand, will take a more direct, or activist approach. For example, they might tell the parties how they think a judge or jury would decide a case, and they may propose concrete settlement proposals for the parties to consider.

Do you want a mediator who is more facilitative or one who will plunge in and propose a specific resolution? In many cases, it won't matter; either type will do a good job. But in some cases, you may sensibly have a preference. For example, many business executives seem to favor evaluative mediators; because the executives themselves are used to weighing alternatives and making decisions, they often have little patience for long drawn-out proceedings. On the other hand, if your dispute concerns an interpersonal problem—such as a painful feud with a relative, long-term friend, or neighbor—you may want a mediator who will be patient enough to help you arrive at your own solution, not one who will presume to suggest how you should resolve things.

If you are selecting a mediator from a mediation service's panel, discuss your preference with the case manager. Because the terms "facilitative" and "evaluative" are not universally used, you may need to describe the type of mediator you want either as one who will actively appraise the case and propose solutions, or one who will refrain from giving an opinion and instead focus on helping you and the other party work toward your own solutions.

Willing to Make a Specific Recommendation?

Going a step farther, you might want a mediator who, if your case appears unlikely to settle, will make a recommendation as to how you and the other side might resolve it. Sometimes called a "mediator's proposal," a recommendation is entirely different than a mediator's efforts to advance a mediation by evaluating the strengths and weaknesses of each party's case. See Chapter 8, Section A, for more on asking a mediator to make a recommendation.

If you think that you and the other party might want your mediator to make a recommendation, tell the case manager.

Willing to Intervene to Protect the Weaker Party?

In some disputes, one party may, for a variety of reasons—a poor education, language difficulty, emotional fragility, or past abuse—be subject to intimidation by the other. This could lead to the weaker party accepting an unfair settlement in mediation.

In general, a mediator has no duty to protect the interests of a weaker party; it is just not part of the job description. The rules of some mediation programs even spell this out. As a result, many mediators will never intervene to help a weaker party, even one who is about to agree to what seems like an unfair solution.

Nevertheless, there are times when some mediators will intervene to protect a weaker party, if they believe the proposed settlement is grossly unfair or likely to lead to problems down the road. If you want a mediator who will be willing to intervene to steer you away from making a bad deal, discuss this preference with the case manager or the independent mediator.

Impartiality

You want an impartial mediator, not one who will favor one party or the other. You need not be as concerned about mediator bias as you might be with an arbitrator or judge, who has the power to impose a decision (unless the mediator has the authority to make a recommendation to a judge). Nevertheless, a biased mediator could steer you toward settlement terms tilted in the other side's favor.

What would constitute bias or partiality? It can be any relationship, experience, or set of beliefs that might cause the mediator to favor one side over the other. For example, you probably would not want a mediator who has a social, family, or business relationship with the other party, or a lawyer-mediator who works in the same law firm as the one that represents the other party on this or other cases.

There are other types of biases you may wish to consider. For instance, if you are a tenant in a landlord-tenant dispute, you may have qualms about a mediator who is a landlord. Or, if you are a homeowner mediating against a contractor, a contractor mediator may be suspect in your eyes. Although you should feel free to raise these types of concerns with the case manager or mediator, remember that a mediator with a good grasp of the subject matter can often work much more efficiently, and that such a person will generally have to come from one side of the dispute or the other. On balance, the most sensible approach is to assess the mediator's character rather than worry about these types of side issues—especially because you, rather than the mediator, are in control of the final decision.

The best source of information about possible mediator bias is your case manager or, if you are using an independent mediator, the mediator himself.

Don't worry too much about a lawyer-mediator's legal background. Most lawyers specialize to some degree—and this means that many of them represent only plaintiffs or defendants. If you have a dispute with your employer, for example, you may not wish to use a mediator who usually represents employers. However, we have generally found that lawyer-mediators who are otherwise well-trained and experienced can take off their other professional hats and be impartial as mediators. In fact, it can be an advantage to have a mediator who usually does legal work for the other side. These mediators will be particularly perceptive of the weaknesses in the other side's case, and their opinions will carry special weight with the other side. If your opposing party has really dug in his heels and refuses to give an inch, using a mediator from the same side of the fence may be the only way to make any progress towards settlement.

Mediator's Personality

You may be spending many hours in private and sensitive discussions with your mediator. It follows that, if possible, you'll want to select a mediator with whom you feel personally comfortable. Working with a mediator can be like working with a music teacher, therapist, or clergyman—if you don't connect with the person on an intuitive level, you're better off picking someone else.

3. Checking Out Prospective Mediators

By this point, you probably know whether you want to use a mediation service or a private mediator, whether your mediator should have any special expertise or training, and whether you want a mediator with a particular philosophy or approach. Now you have to do some research on the mediators you're considering (or the ones the mediation service has recommended) to decide which one would be best for your dispute.

This section explains some good ways to find out more about prospective mediators.

a. Interview Case Manager at Mediation Service

If you are using a mediation service that allows you to have some say in choosing your mediator, a big part of what you're paying for is the case manager's help in setting things up—including selecting an appropriate mediator. You can ask the case manager for information about each prospective mediator, including the factors discussed above (training, experience, subject matter expertise, style, and so on).

b. Ask for a Resume

Many mediation services will provide you with a one- or two-line statement about each mediator listed on the panel, which often includes degrees the mediator holds and current employment. Obviously, this doesn't tell you much. To get more information, you can ask to see a more detailed resume for mediators who interest you. The resume should outline the mediator's professional background. It may even reveal possible conflicts of interest of which you were unaware.

c. Check References

You can learn a lot about a mediator's style and demeanor from talking to past clients, particularly those who had a dispute similar to your own. Some mediation services and independent mediators may hesitate to provide names of past customers out of concern for their privacy. In practice, however, most satisfied mediation customers will be glad to discuss their experience as long as no confidential information about their case is disclosed. When you ask for references for a particular mediator, explain that you just want to discuss how the mediator conducted the mediation, not the details of the case. With this understanding, the case manager should be willing to find a few past users who will talk to you.

d. Talk to Professionals Who Know the Mediator

Another way to learn about mediators is to ask others in your local dispute resolution community. For example, if you are interested in a particular mediator who works as a lawyer, you may be able to get a knowledgeable opinion by calling another lawyer you know. Even if that lawyer doesn't know the mediator, he will probably know someone who does. But as with any personal evaluation, you'll want to consider the source. For example, if your brother-in-law is the lawyer you talk to and he has often proved to be a blundering fool, you should probably take his opinions about the mediator with a grain or two of salt.

e. Interview the Mediator

When you can't get information about a mediator from any of the sources listed above, you might consider going straight to the source and talking to the mediator directly.

If you are using a mediation service, ask the case manager to arrange a phone or face-to-face interview with one or two of their panel members. The case manager should be willing to cooperate, but will probably want to invite the other side to participate in the interview. Having a private conversation with just one party could compromise the mediator's neutrality—or at least make the other party suspicious.

Most independent mediators will engage in a brief initial conversation about their practice with whoever contacts them. But, if you or the other party wants to have an in-depth interview about the mediator's background, philosophy, and possible approach to handling your case, the mediator is likely to suggest that all parties participate in the conversation. Again, the realistic concern is that a private conversation between a mediator and either party to a dispute may jeopardize the mediator's neutrality.

A good way to set up an in-depth interview with an independent mediator is to ask the mediator to arrange a conference call during which you and the other party can do the interview together. A joint, face-to-face meeting can sometimes be arranged, but the mediator may be reluctant to make this greater time commitment (especially when you have not yet decided to hire the mediator).

INTERVIEW QUESTIONS FOR A POTENTIAL MEDIATOR

When you interview a mediator directly, you'll want to ask questions that will yield information about the mediator's training, experience, impartiality, approach to mediation, and ability to help you resolve your case.

Here are some sample questions to consider:

- What kind of mediation training have you had?
- Tell me about your experience as a mediator.
- How long have you been mediating? How many disputes do you typically mediate in a week, month, year?
- What types of disputes do you mediate? Do you have a specialty? Do you have experience in [the subject matter of your dispute]?
- Do you mediate full time? What did you do before you began mediating? If you don't mediate full time, do you hold another position or do other work?
- Do you belong to any professional organizations?
- Do you have any personal, family, or business contacts with either party?
- How do your mediations typically proceed?
- How do you see the role of a mediator? Will you help us value our claims? Will you offer a recommendation or mediator's proposal if we can't reach a resolution through mediation?
- Describe your mediation style. What do you think are your strengths as a mediator? Are there particular issues or problems that you feel especially well-equipped to handle? ■

CHAPTER 4

Starting Your Mediation Case

This chapter discusses when and how to begin your mediation. For the most part, we assume that you will be the person initiating the effort to mediate, which means it will be up to you to start the process with a mediator or mediation service.

➡ **If mediation is required:** If you are required to mediate by a court or other agency, as part of a court-connected mediation program, or under the terms of a contract, many issues discussed in this chapter obviously won't apply (and it makes sense to skip or skim them). However, if the court order or contract gives you the right to participate in selecting your mediator or mediation service, the information in Section C will be useful.

A. Is Your Case Ready for Mediation?

In theory, mediation can occur at any point in a dispute. The fact that a court case has been filed, or even that a trial is about to begin, doesn't rule out mediation—in fact, a looming trial can be a powerful incentive to give mediation a try. As long as both parties agree, you can always mediate.

As a general rule, however, the sooner you can bring a dispute to mediation, the better. Not only can an early mediation mean a quick end to uncertainty and anxiety (especially when litigation has begun or is seriously threatened), but it also can mean significant savings of money, time, and energy.

On the other hand, parties sometimes try to mediate too soon. This can occur when people are still extremely angry (some mediators inelegantly refer to this as "the frothing at the mouth stage") and thus not yet ready to participate in a rational discussion. Mediation can also be premature when one party does not yet have enough information to know what would constitute a reasonable settlement. For example, if someone is hurt in a car accident and doctors have not yet determined the full extent of her injuries, it makes sense to postpone settlement discussions until the injured person has a better sense of what her medical bills, time lost from work, and other effects of the injury will be.

Here are several factors that will help you decide whether your case is ripe for mediation.

1. Settlement Talks Have Failed

Direct negotiation between disputing parties is the most efficient way to resolve most disputes. Not only do one-on-one negotiations save time, they also eliminate the expense and delay of getting third parties (including mediators) involved. Whenever you have a dispute, your first step should be to contact the other party to see if you can work things out. If you have not tried to settle your dispute directly with your opponent, it is probably too soon to mediate. For example, if you hired a contractor to put a new roof on your house and now the roof leaks, your first call should be to the contractor, not the mediation service.

2. Emotions Have Had Some Time to Cool

Emotions run high in many disputes, even those over seemingly dry business matters. Although mediation can accommodate people with strong emotions, there may be an initial period when one party, or even both parties, are so angry that rational discussion is difficult. If your dispute has left you feeling intensely angry, hurt, or even full of rage, you should give yourself some time to deal with these feelings before trying to mediate. Similarly, if you recognize these emotions in the other party, it may be wise to slow things down.

3. You Have Enough Information to Evaluate Settlement Options

In order to mediate intelligently, you need enough information about your dispute to know how to settle it to your advantage. Sorting out all the facts that underlie a dispute can take time. For example, a boundary dispute with a neighbor usually can't be mediated until a survey is completed. A period of delay will also be useful if you want to do some legal research or get a lawyer's opinion about the important legal issues in your dispute and the value of your claims. Until you and the other party have enough information to evaluate your settlement options intelligently, it's probably too early to mediate.

4. The Parties Are Not Too Set in Their Positions

Some disputants wait too long to begin mediation. In the jargon of mediators, their case has become "overripe." The usual result of trying to bring an overripe case to mediation is either that one side refuses to participate or that the mediation fails to produce a settlement.

Your dispute may be overripe if any of the following are true:

- Preparations for trial have proceeded too far. A party who has invested heavily in preparing for trial—in terms of legal fees, time, and effort—may be much less willing to settle for anything less than a full court "victory."

- The people personally involved in the dispute no longer control it. It might be too late to mediate a dispute if the original disputants— who might have been willing to give mediation a try—lose control of their own decision making. This can occur when lawyers become intensely involved and strongly advocate fighting it out in court. Or, it might happen when senior managers or owners take a dispute away from lower-level employees, who might have been more likely to settle it.

EXAMPLE: *Peter, the sales manager of a computer-parts manufacturer, and Rosamund, the purchasing agent for a computer manufacturer, get into a dispute over the quality (or lack thereof) of certain parts Peter's company has delivered to Rosamund. These two have been doing business together for years, and though they disagree about this job, they have a history of working things out so as to not jeopardize their mutually beneficial relationship. As long as they can keep in sight the mutual advantage of continuing to do business together, a mediator can probably help them solve their immediate dispute. But if the matter gets "bumped upstairs" to their respective bosses or company lawyers, each side's position may harden. Now, instead of being motivated to compromise so as to make future business dealings possible, both companies may make it a priority to try and get as much money out of the other as possible.*

Sometimes, it's a good idea to bring in a more objective person. If the original disputants feel extremely bitter towards each other or have really gotten stuck in their bargaining positions, they may find it difficult to mediate successfully. In these situations, a manager or lawyer may take a more dispassionate view and be better able to work out a reasonable settlement in mediation.

- Emotional links among disputants are "dead." Disputes involving close interpersonal relationships between friends, spouses, and relatives are particularly likely to become overripe. This can happen when hurt feelings have been allowed to fester so long that the parties would rather live with the situation as it is than risk opening up old wounds. For example, a brother and sister fighting bitterly over their mother's estate may be open to mediation for a couple of months or more after the mother's death. But if a couple of years pass without any resolution, their relationship may be so compromised that neither is motivated to resuscitate it through mediation. Still, if either person wants to try for a resolution, it's worth the effort—many mediations that look hopeless at the start end in a surprisingly successful way.

B. How to Propose Mediation

Mediation doesn't just happen—usually one party has to propose it. It's then up to the other party to say yes or no. (Of course, no one has to propose mediation if a judge or government agency orders it, or a contract requires it—see Chapter 3 for more on this situation.) Here, we present a strategy that will help you propose mediation in a way that is most likely to persuade the other party to give it a try.

1. When to Propose Mediation

Unless you know that the other party is willing to mediate, start by assuming that she will be at least somewhat reluctant (in fact, she might oppose it simply because it was your idea). To increase the chances of reaching an agreement to mediate, try to make your proposal at a time when the other side is most likely to say "yes."

This isn't as hard as you might think. In the course of any dispute, there are usually events, such as a fact-finding hearing or court appearance, that promise to be expensive, scary, or risky. It follows that a proposal to mediate just before one of these events is scheduled may be especially appealing to the other side.

a. If Your Dispute Is Not Yet in Litigation

If your dispute has not yet resulted in a court filing or other official proceeding, you can often convince the other party to mediate by presenting mediation as a way to avoid a formal action. For example, if you have an employment-related claim against your employer that is scheduled for a fact-finding hearing under your company's internal grievance procedure, your proposal to mediate shortly before the hearing date may be welcomed as a way to possibly settle your claim before it escalates.

Similarly, if your dispute is with a small company that you know is trying to go public, the owners may be eager to clear up all possible disputes rather than risk a lawsuit at a critical time.

Particularly with smaller disputes, you can often make mediation more appealing to the other party by proposing it at one of those predictable times during the year when many people like to get disputes out of the way and make a fresh start. Of course, the beginning of the new year is one of these times. Many mediators find, for example, that early December is one of their busiest periods; people want a clean slate for the new year (and may be motivated by the approaching holiday season to try to make peace). Therefore, you might want to propose mediation in the late fall, when the other party might be interested in getting the dispute resolved before the holidays.

Similarly, you can propose mediation just before some personal event in the other party's life that may put him in a mood to "clear the air." It's hard to know exactly what events will trigger such a mood in another person, but common ones include an upcoming marriage, birthday, birth of a child, anniversary, change in employment, or even a visit from a relative.

b. If Your Case Is in Litigation

If your dispute has already resulted in a lawsuit, it can make sense to push for mediation just before an expensive or otherwise unpleasant stage of the litigation is scheduled to occur. For example, you might propose mediation just before the other side has scheduled the deposition of a physician or other expensive expert witness. Similarly, you might suggest mediation just before the deadline for exchanging sensitive documents, or before an important pretrial motion (for example, one considering whether key evidence will be admissible at trial). Sometimes, it's even possible to head off a fast-approaching trial date by proposing a last ditch effort to mediate—judges will sometimes agree to delay (continue) the trial to give mediation a chance.

Timeline of Strategic Points to Initiate Mediation

| before lawsuit filed | → | date when answer due | → | before deposition | → | before document exchange | → | before pretrial motions | → | before trial date |

---

2. Contact the Mediator or Mediation Service

You may be tempted to call and ask the other party directly to give mediation a try. This might work if you have a history of trust and goodwill that remains at least somewhat intact. Unfortunately, if that's not the case, the other party may suspect that your request to mediate is some kind of trick or strategy to get the upper hand.

If the other party has had experience with mediation, he might be more likely to accept your proposal. For example, if you propose mediation to a home repair contractor who is a member of a builder's trade group that supported the creation of a community mediation center in your town, you could reasonably anticipate a more positive response.

The best way to keep distrust from scuttling your efforts is to ask a mediation service to extend the invitation to mediate. Mediation services have lots of experience in convincing reluctant parties to give mediation a try. After all, a mediation company or organization that can't get people to the bargaining table won't stay in business long. This holds true even for nonprofit, community mediation centers; they must conduct a large number of mediations to justify continued support from the public agencies that fund them.

⚠ Many independent mediators prefer not to "sell" a party on mediating. As discussed in more detail in Chapter 3, many independent mediators prefer not to try to talk people into mediating, in part because most of them don't have trained staff to do the job. And they are reluctant to do it themselves, because the conversation might give the appearance of compromising their neutrality. For this reason, if the other party is likely to be reluctant to mediate, you are better off using a mediation service rather than an independent mediator.

Should you just contact the mediation service without even bringing up the subject of mediating with the other party? This may be tempting, but it overlooks an important fact of human behavior: people don't like to be surprised. If you call a mediation service without telling the other party, she may be extremely suspicious of your having initiated a process without her knowledge. For example, she might jump to the conclusion that you have said negative things about her or that you have "influence" with the particular mediation service. If she is unfamiliar with mediation, she may even accuse you of plotting to bypass her legal rights. That's why it's a good idea to at least let the other party know that you'll be contacting a mediation service.

3. Send Your Opponent a Letter

A short, polite letter is usually the best way to notify another party that you want to mediate and will be contacting a mediation service. (An exception to this general rule might occur if you and the other side have had such a close relationship in the past that, despite your dispute, even a friendly letter would seem too formal.) Why is a letter usually better than a phone call? In writing, you can simply state that you want to mediate, with no need to discuss the merits of the dispute. Personal contact, such as a phone call, might invite an argument about the merits of mediation or of your case, exactly the sort of interaction you probably want to avoid at this point.

Your letter should let the other side know that you want to mediate, without saying anything that is likely to trigger a defensive response. Here are some suggestions that will help you set the right tone:

- State that you would like to try mediation and list some reasons why. For example:
    - ✓ "If mediation works, we can both save a lot of time, aggravation, and money."
    - ✓ " Mediation is quick and inexpensive, and we can do it without lawyers."
    - ✓ "Mediation carries no risk because the mediator is neutral and has no power to impose a decision on us."

- Do not try to persuade the other person to mediate—leave that up to the mediation service.

- Do not presume to say what the other person thinks or wants. For example, it's fine to say, "I want to mediate because I believe mediation is an excellent way to solve disputes." But it's a mistake to say, "You probably don't know much about mediation" or "I doubt you will agree to this...." A good way to steer clear of this problem is simply to avoid using the word "you."

- Never threaten the other person. For example do not write, "If you don't agree to mediation, I will have no recourse but to commence a lawsuit."

- State clearly that you have no personal connection with the mediation service, other than contacting them for the purposes of this mediation. The other party may not believe you, but at least you will have raised the issue and stated the facts. If the other person wants more input in the selection process, you can offer to use another mediation service.

- Let the other person know that the mediation service will be in touch.

- Let the other person know that you are using this book and offer to provide a copy so that you can both be on the "same page" regarding mediation. If the cost of the book is a problem, find out whether it is available in your local public library.

Here's a sample letter that will give you some ideas for drafting your own:

EXAMPLE: *Mike and Ron are co-owners of Big Slice Pizza, Inc., a restaurant. For some time, they have had serious arguments over various aspects of running their business, including pricing meals and dealing with employees. Each owns half the company. If they can't work out their differences or decide who will buy the other out, the business may fail. They have had several face-to-face conversations in an effort to negotiate a settlement, without success. Mike has read several books on dispute resolution and believes the time is right to mediate. After some investigation, he has identified a local private dispute resolution company, Settle It Now, Inc., as a good mediation service to handle the case. Mike and Ron have never discussed mediation and Mike doesn't know if Ron will be willing to give mediation a try. To start the process, Mike writes the following letter to Ron:*

October 24, 2004

Dear Ron:

I am writing to let you know that I have given our situation at Big Slice Pizza a lot of thought and have decided that one way we can both try to get this thing resolved without spending a huge amount of time and a fortune on lawyers is to try mediation.

I have read that mediation is a simple and straightforward way for people to try to work out a solution to many different kinds of disputes. As I understand it, mediation is quick, we don't need lawyers, it's fairly inexpensive, and no decisions or actions can be imposed on either of us unless we both freely agree. For starters, we don't need to make any commitment short of showing up and sitting down with a neutral third person who will try to help us work out a solution. I'm willing to give it a try if you are.

As a first step, I've asked Settle It Now, Inc., a private dispute resolution company here in town, to send you some information about their service. I don't have any personal connection with this company; they just seem to have experience working with businesses like ours. If for any reason you don't like Settle It Now, I'm open to your suggestions for another mediation service for us to try.

Incidentally, I am reading a book published by Nolo called *Mediate, Don't Litigate*. I find it very helpful, and if you would like your own copy I will be happy to find you one. If both of us are using the same resource it may help this entire matter go more smoothly.

Yours,
Mike

C. Starting Your Case With a Mediator or Mediation Service

To initiate your case with a mediator or mediation service, you will probably have to fill out a one- or two-page "submission" or "intake" form. Some services may charge you a filing fee to open and begin processing your case; others charge no fee until everyone has agreed to mediate and a date for the mediation is scheduled. This section explains some of the forms you may need to complete and choices you may face as you start your case.

1. Completing the Submission Form

When you call a mediation service, you will typically be asked to complete a short submission form, giving some basic information about your dispute. You can ask the office to mail the form to you; some offices will just take your information over the phone and fill in the form themselves. Either way, it shouldn't take more than a few minutes to complete. (If you call an independent mediator, the initial contact may be less bureaucratic.)

The submission form requests basic information about your case, such as the names and addresses of the parties and attorneys (if any), what type of case it is, whether a lawsuit has been filed, and what solution you are seeking. The mediation service may communicate the information you put on the form to the other party, as part of its efforts to convince the other party to mediate.

> ### WHAT'S IN A NAME?—"CLAIMANTS" AND "RESPONDENTS"
>
> Some mediation services—particularly community mediation centers—call the person who submits a case the "claimant" and the other person the "respondent." This can create a problem when both sides feel they have something to complain about. Some services avoid the term "claimant" by calling the party that initiated the case the "submitting party" or the "initiator," and some simply call the parties "Party 1" and "Party 2."

2. Describing Your Dispute

To avoid revealing any sensitive information to the other party (and to avoid saying anything that would make him reluctant to mediate), it is usually best to describe your dispute in a fairly general and noninflammatory way. Let's look at how to do this in the context of the types of questions you are likely to be asked on the submission form.

a. The Nature of the Dispute

Most forms include a question like, "What is the nature of your dispute?" Your response should be brief and general. For example, you might write "My insurance company has refused to pay for injuries I suffered in a car accident," "My employer put me on probation after I complained about unsafe working conditions," or "My neighbor and I cannot agree on who should pay to repair the fence between our properties."

When describing your dispute, it's best to use ordinary—not legal—words. Remember, the mediation service's case might quote you to the other side. For example, if you have a beef with your landscape gardener because the shrubbery that was guaranteed for three years died after three months, it's better to describe this as "dispute over shrubbery plantings" than as "breach of contract." Plain words are not only easier to understand; they are also less likely to push the other side away from the bargaining table and into a lawyer's office.

b. Desired Remedy

When describing the result you wish to achieve, it's best to be straight-forward. These statements are all fine, assuming the dispute involves money or property:

- "Return of the following property" (include a list with clear descriptions)

- "Fair payment for my injuries suffered on 1/7/04," or

- "My job at Racafrax International back."

If your case is about the way someone is behaving toward you or your family, it's particularly important to be diplomatic as not to anger or affront the other person. For example, if you are complaining about a neighbor who drives dangerously on your street, you might say "Remedy sought: Mr. Adams to drive carefully on Hickory St." However, it would be a mistake to say, "that Mr. Adams stop speeding [or driving recklessly]…so he doesn't run over my kids."

Perhaps it will help you modulate your tone if you imagine yourself as Mr. Adams for a moment. You receive a call from a mediation service's case manager telling you a neighbor is seriously concerned because you drive so recklessly as to endanger his children. What would your response be? Chances are that you would tell the mediation service and your neighbor to take a hike.

c. Amount of Money Sought

How much money, if any, do you really want the other side to pay you? Unlike in litigation (and sometimes even negotiation), where it's common to establish a "strong bargaining position" by claiming a much higher amount than you really want—sometimes by a factor of ten or more—in mediation, it's usually wise to claim an amount much closer to what you really want. Remember, your first hurdle is to get the other side to agree to mediate. If a demand for money appears too outrageous, it's likely to drive the other person away.

Some people worry that offering to compromise in mediation could jeopardize their right to go for the jackpot in court if mediation fails. However, because efforts to settle a case (including statements made in mediation) are not admissible in court, your efforts to be reasonable won't come back to haunt you.

d. Additional Parties

The form may ask if there are additional parties whom the mediation service should contact. This is an important question. To be successful, mediation needs to be inclusive—that is, everyone with a significant stake in the outcome of the dispute should be invited to participate. An agreement that excludes an important stakeholder will be of little value if that person is in a position to undermine it. For example, assume you are a real estate agent who lost a commission when your clients backed out of a signed purchase offer after cracks were found in the home's chimney, even though your clients' offer was not contingent on an inspection. Legally, your clients might be obligated to buy the house. However, to avoid cost, delays, and damage to your client relationship, you instead would like to go to mediation to see if the deal can be put back together—maybe by you, the seller's agent, and the sellers all contributing some money towards repairing the chimney. For this to work, you will need everyone at the mediation—not only your former clients, but also the sellers and their agent.

e. Type of Dispute Resolution

The intake form may also ask what type of dispute resolution services or help you want (some mediation services offer many options—see Chapter 1, Section D, for more information). Indicating a preference for one type of dispute resolution does not prevent you from changing your mind later; however, your initial preference may determine what the mediation service says in its introductory letter to your opponent.

WHAT IS "BINDING" MEDIATION?

Mediation is, by definition, nonbinding. However, some mediation services may ask if you want "binding" or "nonbinding" mediation. What they mean is this: If you settle your case in mediation, do you want the mediator to write the terms of the settlement in the form of a legally binding contract that will be enforceable in court? Otherwise, the settlement just expresses the parties' intentions—and it is not legally enforceable.

Some mediation services offer this option; others do not. If it's available, you should choose the binding option. If the other party reneges on the settlement, you can go to court to have the agreement enforced as a contract. (For more on writing your mediation agreement as a binding contract, see Chapter 7.)

D. Securing an Agreement to Mediate

The mediation service will usually start by sending the other party a form letter asking her to agree to mediate, and follow up by telephone if she doesn't respond.

If you and the other party are required to mediate under the terms of a contract or court order, the other party has no legal choice but to mediate. Even so, she may still drag her feet or try to avoid it. In this situation, the mediation service should be particularly persistent in sending letters and making repeat phone calls to set a firm date for the mediation. (If you show up and the other side doesn't, at least you've fulfilled your obligation under the contract or court order and can go on to pursue other legal remedies.)

1. How a Mediation Service Works to Overcome Resistance

The initial letter and supporting materials that a mediation service typically sends to the other party will emphasize the benefits of mediation, stating the advantages in terms of low cost, privacy, and speed. Letters from private dispute resolution firms often go on to point out the high quality of the people on their mediation panels, their "user-friendliness," and their competitive pricing.

Some community mediation centers go beyond this "soft-sell" approach. In an effort to get people to the table, they sometimes play up their affiliations with courts or government agencies, coming fairly close to making a subtle threat that negative consequences may result from a failure to mediate.

⚠️ **Don't be intimidated by a tough contact letter.** If you are the recipient of a heavy-handed contact letter, there is no reason to be pressured into doing something you don't want to do. Unless a contract or court order requires you to mediate, you are under no obligation to do so. Whether you choose to mediate should depend on how you assess what is in your own best interest, not on the tone of a mediation service's letter. (See Chapter 2 for a discussion of factors that favor and oppose using mediation.)

If the mediation service gets no response to its initial letter within a week or two, the staff person—often called "case manager" or "case coordinator"—will usually follow up with a phone call (or series of phone calls) to answer the other side's questions about mediation and review mediation's potential benefits. If the party declines to participate based on a lawyer's advice, the staff person may ask permission to call the lawyer directly to discuss the situation.

How successful a case manager is likely to be in overcoming a person's resistance to mediation will depend on the facts of your case, the other party's personality, and the case manager's own skills. For example, some of the better private dispute resolution companies have very well-trained case managers who are quite skilled at turning a party's "no" (about mediating) into a "yes."

2. Working Out an Agreement to Mediate

After proposing mediation, you should expect to hear from your mediation service within a week or two about the results of their contact with the other side. If not, call to check on your case. Often, politely reminding the case manager or other person whose job it is to set up the mediation that you are eager to get into mediation may help move things along.

If all goes as you hope, the case manager will soon report good news: the other side is willing and ready to mediate. If so, you can now select a mediator and schedule the mediation. Often, however, the case manager will report that the other party's response is a pretty firm "maybe." Here is a short list of objections or issues the other party might raise:

- "I might mediate, but only if you pay all the fees, since it was your idea."

- "I might mediate, but only with a certain mediator."

- "I might mediate, but I want to limit (or expand) the issues to be discussed."

- "I might mediate, but I want to use a different mediation service."

- "I won't mediate, but I might consider another type of dispute resolution (such as binding arbitration)."

- "I need more time to think about it [or, investigate my case, or talk to my lawyer, or take care of personal business]."

Although this type of conditional response may seem disappointing, it's actually quite positive—it means that you and the other side (with the help of the mediation service) are now negotiating about resolving your dispute. Chances are excellent that a competent case manager will be able to guide you and the other party through these preliminary negotiations so that mediation can take place."

Depending on the other side's position, here are some strategies you and/or the case manager might adopt in response:

IF THE OTHER PARTY SAYS	YOU CAN RESPOND
Might mediate, but won't pay	• If fees are low, offer to pay them all. • Agree to split fees, but during the mediation you can discuss dividing up payment differently. • Offer to pay the entire administrative fee, but split the hourly fees. • Offer to pay up to some fixed amount, after which you each pay half.
Might mediate, but only with a certain mediator	• Agree to the other party's choice of mediator. • Suggest that you each submit a short list of preferred mediators from the service's panel. If you both name the same person, that person will be selected. • Agree that the case manager may appoint an available mediator on the basis of skills, knowledge, and availability. • Suggest that the case manager propose three possible mediators; you and the other party each get to eliminate one name.
Might mediate, but wants different mediator	• If fees are a problem, find out whether the service you chose may be willing mediation service or independent to lower them. • Agree to the change, unless the other party gains some unfair advantage by using the other service or mediator. • If you don't like the service or mediator the other party has proposed, suggest some other possibilities and allow him to choose from the list.
Might mediate, but wants to limit or expand issues	• Agree, unless the list of issues excludes important items or is so long that the mediation will be unfocused.
Won't mediate, but might arbitrate	• Suggest advisory (nonbinding) arbitration (see Chapter 1). • Suggest mediation followed by a written recommendation (see Chapter 1).
Wants more time to think it over	• Agree, but set a reasonable deadline to begin mediation. • Agree, but ask the other side to agree to an interim solution if appropriate (for example, "Neither of us will cut down any trees on our property line until we mediate").

Mediation services vary in how long they will keep trying to get a reluctant party to agree to mediate. Community mediation centers, with limited funding and staff, may make just one or two follow-up calls to the other party before marking your case "party refuses to mediate" and closing the file. Private dispute resolution companies, on the other hand, may keep a case manager working much longer to try to bring a dispute to mediation. They are highly motivated to do so because private firms generate most of their income from hourly fees charged during the actual mediation. Independent mediators in private practice, as noted earlier, generally prefer not to get involved in trying to persuade a reluctant party to mediate. Faced with hesitation from the other side, most independent mediators will probably ask you to try on your own to bring the other person to the table.

3. If the Other Party Refuses to Mediate

If the other party refuses to mediate, there are still a few things you can try. Remember, there are strategic times in every dispute when a person is likely to be more inclined to mediate than others—for example, just before or after a lawsuit has been filed. Consider when the next "strategic point" will occur and prepare to reintroduce your proposal to mediate then.

If no obvious "strategic points" are coming up soon, you may want to try to create one. For example, if no lawsuit has been filed in your case, you can threaten to file one. One way to do this is to have a lawyer prepare the summons and complaint (if your case can be taken to small claims court, you can prepare the papers yourself) and send them to the other party with a letter stating that you plan to file them if he refuses to mediate. Be cautious with this approach, however; preparing the paperwork could get expensive—and if you hire a lawyer, you may be persuaded to undertake more aggressive legal action than you originally had intended. There is also the danger that you threat will turn the other party off (or convince her to launch a preemptive strike and sue you first)! And in some states, it's illegal to threaten someone with litigation for failing to agree to certain demands.

If you file a lawsuit but still want to mediate, tell the judge that you would prefer to try resolving the dispute through mediation. (In some courts, your case may be sent to mediation automatically.) Many judges will be glad to get your case off their docket and will strongly suggest that the other party try mediation. Sometimes the judge will even go a step farther and refer you both to a local mediation service. In this context, it will often be difficult for the other side to resist the judge's suggestion—after all, the same judge will decide the case.

There are some obvious disadvantages to this, however. First, you have to pay court filing fees, which may amount to several hundred dollars, plus an attorney's fee (unless you represent yourself). Second, a party who agrees to mediate only under great pressure may not come to the mediation with an open mind. Third, a contested court case might result in both parties becoming too angry to mediate. Despite these drawbacks, if you are intent on going to mediation, this tactic might get you there.

A variation on this tactic can also be used in disputes involving minor criminal offenses. Let's assume, for example, that you are troubled by excessive noise from a neighbor's house, and your neighbor has refused your invitation to mediate. At this point, you can file a complaint about the noise with the police, and tell the responding officer (or the prosecutor, if you get that far) that you would like to mediate. There is a good chance the police will be delighted to divert the case from the criminal justice system to a court-connected mediation program or community mediation center. Now, when the mediation program contacts your neighbor, the letter will state that the dispute has been referred by the police. Your chances of getting your neighbor to mediate should markedly improve. ■

CHAPTER 5

Preparing for Your Mediation

This chapter explains how to prepare for your mediation session. While mediation isn't nearly as complicated as a full-scale court trial, there are still many things you can do to improve your chances of achieving a positive result. How much preparation you do will depend on the facts of the dispute and how significant it is to you. A small consumer dispute worth a couple of hundred dollars, for example, is unlikely to require nearly as much preparation as a work-related sexual harassment claim involving a lot of money and the future of your business or career.

To get ready for your mediation, you'll usually want to:

- review the mediation rules

- gather documents and other items you want to present in the mediation

- decide whether anyone should attend the mediation with you (and make the necessary arrangements)

- identify your goals, including both what you hope to achieve and the minimum you will accept, and

- write a memorandum for the mediator, outlining your version of the facts and the issues involved in the dispute.

 For information on preparing your opening statement and figuring out how best to present your case, see Chapter 6.

A. Review Paperwork

Begin your preparation by carefully reading the rules that will govern your mediation. Most mediators or mediation services will give you a set of written mediation rules. You may also receive a "Notice of Mediation" and an "Agreement to Mediate."

1. The Mediation Rules

Many mediators and mediation services will send you a set of rules when you schedule your mediation. If you have not yet received a set of rules, call and request one.

Mediation rules cover things like when and how fees are to be paid, procedures to be followed during the mediation, and the degree to which the mediation proceeding will be considered and kept confidential. Fortunately, mediation rules are usually just a few pages long and are almost always written in plain English. (Sample Mediation Rules appear in Appendix A.)

Because mediation rules don't vary much from place to place, chances are good that yours will cover the following points:

- **Sending Notices.** If you need to inform the mediator or the other party of something—for example, that you plan to bring someone to the mediation who has special expertise—the rules may tell you how to do so. For example, can you call on the telephone or send an email, or do you have to send a fax or letter? Can you send the letter by regular mail, or must it be certified? Do you have to send copies to the other party?

Leave a paper trail for important messages. If the rules do not tell you how to send an important notice to the mediator or the other party, play it safe and put the notice in writing. For example, if you use the telephone or email, be sure to follow up with a fax or letter. This will give you written proof that you sent the notice.

- **Pre-Mediation Memorandum.** This is a written statement you prepare for the mediator, explaining your version of the facts and issues involved in your dispute. The rules should tell you whether you will be required (or allowed) to submit a memorandum before the mediation. They should also explain any requirements relating to the memorandum (for example, when it is due, whether you must send a copy to the other party, and what it should include). Section D, below, explains how to prepare a memorandum.

- **Mediation Procedures.** The rules will probably explain how the mediation will be conducted. Will the mediator hold only joint sessions where everyone meets together, or will the mediator also have separate meetings with each party (called "private caucuses")? Caucuses are common in business mediation, but less frequent in divorce and family mediation. (For more on caucuses, see Chapter 6, Section D.) Knowing whether caucuses will be used can help you plan your strategy. For example, if you have an idea of how your dispute could be settled, you might want to try it out on the mediator during private caucus before telling the other party at a joint session. But if you know you won't be having caucuses, then you will have to think about how and when to present the idea to the other side directly.

- **Evidence Rules.** Strict courtroom rules that limit the types of evidence you can use don't apply in mediation. This makes sense—after all, the mediator is not a judge but simply a person trying to help you reach an agreement. Nevertheless, because parties sometimes want to offer testimony from witnesses, or present or refer to documents or other written reports (lawyers call these "exhibits"), mediation rules typically address this issue. Some leave it up to the mediator to decide what sort of outside information is and is not appropriate, while others set more definite rules. (For more on different types of evidence, see Section C, below.)

- **Bringing a Lawyer, Law Coach, or Friend.** It's unusual to bring lawyers to mediations involving small consumer disputes and interpersonal matters, but more common to have a lawyer involved in business disputes and cases involving complex legal issues. And if you're already involved in a lawsuit and have hired a lawyer, your lawyer will probably want to attend the mediation. Mediation rules will usually tell you whether there are any restrictions on bringing a lawyer or other adviser or friend to the mediation. (For more on bringing someone to the mediation, see Section E, below.)

- **Deadlines.** Most mediation rules include deadlines for doing certain things, such as:

    ✓ submitting a written memorandum to the mediator prior to the mediation; often, the memorandum will be due at the mediator's office a week or two before the mediation

    ✓ rescheduling or canceling the mediation without a fee—mediation services may charge a fairly steep fee to cancel or reschedule on only one or two day's notice (the amount they charge will depend on how high their regular fees are), and

    ✓ notifying the other side if you plan to bring an expert witness, such as a physician or accident investigator, to your mediation session; this deadline is usually a couple of weeks before the mediation, to give the other side time to find its own expert.

2. Other Paperwork

After your mediation has been scheduled, the mediator or mediation service will probably send you a document called a "Notice of Mediation" (sometimes "Hearing Notice") confirming the date, time, and place of your mediation. Be sure these details are as you agreed. If you did not set a date, make sure that the assigned date is convenient for you; if the date won't work, contact the mediator or service right away to reschedule.

Reschedule the mediation, if necessary. Typically, a mediation service will schedule your mediation within a few weeks or a month after a mediator has been selected. Unlike in court, where scheduling is at the convenience of the judge and civil servants, your mediation can be scheduled at the convenience of the parties and the mediator. Don't be afraid to ask to reschedule, especially if you are using an independent mediator or private dispute resolution company, who will want to treat you well as a customer. If the other party's schedule permits, your request will probably be accommodated.

You may also receive and be asked to sign an "Agreement to Mediate." The purpose of the agreement is simply to commit the parties in writing to mediate their case in good faith, to follow the rules, and to pay the fees. Check it carefully to make sure your name is spelled correctly, your dispute is accurately described, and the mediator assigned is one whom you have agreed to use (if you were permitted to select). Also, be sure the fees are as you agreed.

3. Confidentiality Protections

During a mediation, you may want to make deeply personal statements or share confidential information. For example, if you're a business owner mediating a claim of sexual harassment with a former employee, you might be tempted to share information about exciting new products the company is about to introduce, to encourage the person to settle and take a new job with your company. Or in a case in which you and a business partner are trying to rebuild trust and save the company, you may be called on to acknowledge your own past mishandling of company finances or business opportunities. (Disclosing secrets can be an especially relevant issue in divorce cases. For more on confidentiality in divorce and family mediation, see Chapter 10.)

Confidentiality is essential to a successful mediation. Without it, many people would sensibly not agree to mediate (and certainly would not want to confide in the mediator). Accordingly, as the practice of mediation has grown, so too have the legal and ethical protections designed to make mediation as confidential as possible. These protections include:

- **Mediation Rules.** Most mediation rules require the mediator and the parties to keep private everything said during the session. These rules often provide that if the case ends up in court, neither party may call the mediator to testify about what was said in the mediation. Unfortunately, the consequences of breaking these rules— particularly by the disputants themselves—are not entirely clear. For example, there's really no practical way for you to prevent the other party from telling his neighbor or brother-in-law what went on during your mediation.

- **Ethical Rules for Mediators.** Most mediators voluntarily follow ethical rules, which usually require the mediator to maintain confidentiality. (See "Standards of Conduct for Mediators," in Appendix B.)

Some states have laws or court cases addressing confidentiality as well. However, because mediation is not a licensed profession, there are few professional sanctions for violating these ethics.

- **Privilege Laws.** Many states prohibit mediators from testifying in court (or in an arbitration) about what was said in mediation. But these so-called "privilege laws" vary greatly in terms of what they cover, and some apply only to mediators working in specific types of programs (for example, nonprofit mediation centers).

- **Evidentiary Rules.** Federal Rule of Evidence 408 and comparable laws in most states make settlement offers, responses to them, and general settlement discussions confidential, whether they occur in or outside mediation. These statements cannot be presented in court (or arbitration) to prove the validity or value of a claim. These laws have generally been interpreted to exclude much of what is said in mediation from later court or arbitration proceedings.

EXAMPLE: *Jim broke his back and leg when he fell on a rotted stair at a restaurant. Jim and the insurance company for the restaurant went to mediation. During mediation, Jim offered to settle if the insurance company would pay him $40,000 for his injuries, but the insurance company refused and the mediation ended without a settlement. Now, Jim is suing the insurance company and asking a jury to award him $100,000. Under a state law that is comparable to Federal Evidence Rule 408, the insurance company may not tell the jury that Jim was willing to settle for less than half that amount in mediation.*

Some mediators have a duty to report criminal activity. Some federal and state laws require people in helping professions (such as therapists, social workers, and often mediators) to report information they learn about felonies, family abuse, and other serious crimes.

PROTECTIVE ORDERS

In some cases, you may need to get an order from the court to protect trade secrets or other confidential business information that is critical to your mediation. This usually comes up only if you already have a court case going and your case involves proprietary information that you want to keep private (so business competitors don't get hold of it), but the information absolutely must be revealed and discussed in order for the mediation to be effective. In this situation, you can agree in advance that information you share during the mediation will be subject to a court order of confidentiality, and that there will be penalties for disclosing it outside of mediation. You can then submit the agreement to the judge where your lawsuit is pending. After the judge signs the protective order, everyone involved in the mediation will be legally required to maintain the confidentiality of the information covered by the order.

So how confidential is mediation? From a practical viewpoint, confidentiality is not usually much of a problem in mediation. Generally, you can safely rely on most mediators to keep quiet about your session(s). But if someone else—such as the other party—decides to disclose what is said in a mediation, there's very little you can do about it. The bottom line is this: If you have a secret that you really don't want known, get a binding protective order or don't reveal the information in mediation. If you have particular concerns about confidentiality, discuss them with the case manager at the mediation service or the independent mediator.

B. Set Your Goals

Before you take a seat at the mediation table, you'll want to have some idea of what you hope to accomplish. Remember that the purpose of

mediation is to find a solution that you and the other party both find
acceptable—not to prove that you are right or to sell your point of view.
Unlike a courtroom trial, mediation allows you flexibility to come up
with creative, workable solutions.

EXAMPLE 1: *House painter Tom paints the interior of homeowner Sally's house
but is not paid for his labor. Tom sues Sally. The law would usually require
Sally to pay Tom according to the terms of their contract—unless, of course,
Tom had seriously breached the contract. In court, Tom's goal would be to
prove that the contract had been carried out and to get a judgment for the
money owed. In other words, Tom's goal is to establish what happened in the
past and then rely on the law to reward him appropriately.*

EXAMPLE 2: *Same circumstances, but now Tom and Sally decide to mediate.
Here they face an entirely different situation. Because they are not limited by
the law or legal procedures, there are any number of ways they can resolve the
dispute. For example, if Sally didn't pay because she believes that Tom did a
poor job, she might agree to pay Tom if he does some of the work again. Or,
Tom might agree to accept only part of what he is owed, if Sally agrees to let
him photograph her living room to use in his brochure. Or, Tom and Sally
might agree that Sally will pay Tom in installments, or that part of the
payment will be in cash and the rest will be in services (for example, if Sally
owns a car repair garage, she might agree to repair Tom's truck).*

Your goals in mediation are essentially forward-looking—what will
work best for both of you in the future—and need not be as limited as
they would be in court. The sections that follow review several methods
for figuring out your mediation goals. Each section includes a short
exercise to help you apply the method to your particular dispute.
Although completing the exercises will take a few minutes, it will help
you think creatively about what you want to get out of mediation.

1. Consider Potential Legal Outcomes

One way to define or limit your mediation goals is to consider what you could get (or lose) in court. What the law requires may turn out to be a less imaginative or less efficient solution than you and the other party end up devising, but you shouldn't ignore it altogether. For example, if you were injured in a car accident and are preparing to mediate with the company that insures the other driver, it would be helpful to know what a judge or jury in your area might award for your injuries. If your case went to court, would it most likely be worth $10,000, $100,000, or nothing at all? To find the answer, you may need to consult briefly with a lawyer. (See Chapter 13 for information on how to find a reliable and experienced one.) Some lawyers will provide this type of information as part of an initial consultation for which they don't charge a fee. Generally, however, it's a poor idea to try to get good advice for free—sometimes, you end up getting exactly what you pay for.

Once you find a good lawyer, lay out the facts of your case and ask, "If this case went to court, how much would I be likely to get?" Although many lawyers will be reluctant to give you an exact figure, they should be able to predict a range of likely outcomes. Also with the help of the lawyer, consider how long the legal process would take, what you would have to pay for court costs and other expenses, and how much of your award would go towards legal fees.

If you need more than a consultation, consider hiring a law coach. If you want a lawyer to help you figure out what your case is worth, help you prepare for mediation in other ways, and be available for consultation during your mediation, consider using a self-help law coach. A law coach is a lawyer who does not represent you but is willing to provide you legal advice as you handle the case on your own. The coach should charge you only for time spent consulting with you. Some lawyers are willing to coach self-helpers; others are not. (For more on finding and using a self-help law coach, see Chapter 13.)

Exercise 1: *Legal Rights and Remedies*

What could you win (or lose) if your case went to court?_____

_____

_____

If your dispute involves money, how much might a judge or jury award to you—or require you to pay?_____

_____

How much might it cost, in legal fees, court costs, and other expenses, to bring or defend a lawsuit?_____

_____

2. Consult With Experts

Experts in various fields can provide useful information and opinions that will help you identify your mediation goals. For example, if you and your business partner are coming to mediation to dissolve your partnership, an accountant with training in business valuation and/or a broker who specializes in selling businesses could estimate how much the business is worth, either sold as is or carved up in different ways. Or if your dispute is with a person or business in a particular field—electrician, gardener, or tile layer, for example—you could ask another person in the same field for an impartial opinion about the validity of your complaint and ideas about how it could be resolved.

How to overcome professional courtesy. Some professionals might be reluctant to consult with you once they realize that you have a claim against another person in the same profession. You can probably lessen these concerns by explaining that you are mediating with the other professional to try to work out a settlement, not taking the other person to court. If you have trouble finding a practitioner to consult, think about who else has expertise in that area. For example, if you can't find an electrician to evaluate problems with a wiring job, try someone who teaches in that field—possibly at a local trade school or union-sponsored accreditation program.

Depending on the facts of your dispute, there will be a variety of experts you can consult concerning possible goals and likely outcomes. Here are just a few who are often consulted as part of preparing for mediation:

- **Accountant or business broker.** Often useful to deal with problems concerning the breakup of a small business. For example, you might want to know the value of a partner's share of the business, whether you can afford to buy a partner out, and what tax implications a buyout might have.

- **Builder or skilled tradesperson.** Valuable in helping you decide whether a contract for building or repair has been properly carried out and, if it hasn't, how the problem should be valued and/or remedied. For example, if a carpenter you hired to redo your stairs botched the design for the handrail and newel post, you might ask how a reasonably skilled carpenter would have handled the job, how the problem could be fixed, and what the repairs would cost.

- **Architect.** Can provide a second opinion as to the quality of another architect's work, whether too many or too few drawings had been made in response to your original request, and whether fees charged were fair based on local practice. For example, if an architect charged you for a preliminary sketch you thought was part of her bid, you might ask if that is customary in the field. You might also want suggestions for working out a compromise.

- **Prosecutors.** Though they generally won't give legal advice, prosecutors (also called district attorneys) sometimes will tell you what procedures they would typically follow in a given situation, or how they recently responded to a similar situation. For example, if you were mediating with a local nightclub owner over excessive noise, you might want to ask what would happen if you filed charges against the club for violating the noise ordinance, or whether others have succeeded in forcing clubs to turn down the volume.

- **Acoustics expert.** Helpful in suggesting a range of practical solutions to a variety of noise situations. For example, you might want to ask how to deal with noise from a restaurant or a neighbor who has frequent late parties, and how much it would cost. You might also ask about ways to measure noise levels.

- **City official.** Local government employees may be willing to advise you in the areas they help regulate, such as zoning, trash collection, roads, property maintenance, and the like.

Exercise 2: *Ask the Experts*

What information could an expert provide that might be helpful in understanding or resolving your dispute?_____

_____

What types of experts could provide this information?

_____

_____

List all experts consulted and their opinions on your dispute.

_____

_____

3. Create a Timeline

A useful way to help identify goals for mediation is to examine your dispute in terms of time—past, present, and future. This approach can help you understand your dispute from different perspectives and prompt you to think of a range of possible remedies that might satisfy your needs.

EXAMPLE: *An office secretary is so emotionally stressed by her boss's sexual harassment that she quits and threatens her company with a lawsuit. Now she doesn't have to put up with her boss's dirty jokes and lewd behavior any more, but she's also out of a job and is worried about her chances of finding a new one. Before filing her harassment lawsuit, she agrees to mediate with her former employer. Here are her goals for the past, present, and future:*

- **Past:** *To settle what happened in the past (the boss's inappropriate behavior), the secretary might want cash compensation for her mental suffering and a written apology from the boss.*

- **Present:** *To deal with the fact that she is currently without income, the secretary might want a consulting position with the company for several months to cover living expenses while she looks for a new job. In addition, she might want temporary use of a company desk, phone, and fax to help with her job search (or the company can rent space for her elsewhere).*

- **Future:** *To be sure that the dispute will not affect her future job prospects, she might want the company to remove any critical material from her personnel file and provide a favorable job reference.*

Exercise 3: *Timeline*

My goals for dealing with what happened in the past:

_____

_____

My goals for handling ongoing problems in the present:

_____

_____

My goals for avoiding or coping with the effects of the dispute in the future:

_____

_____

4. Analyze What Each Party Wants and Needs

Another way to look at your mediation goals is to do what's often called a "wants vs. needs analysis." People in the midst of a dispute generally think they know what they want: "I want my job back with full pay," "I want the money you owe me for the work I did," or "I want your dog to keep quiet and let me sleep." But long-time participants in the mediation field know that what people say they want is not necessarily the same as what they really need. The truth is that people's needs are often different from, and easier to satisfy than, their desires.

EXAMPLE: *Ted wants to erect a six-foot solid wood fence between his backyard and Joan's, a plan that Joan opposes for aesthetic reasons. Ted's desire (want) for a fence reflects a need for privacy. But privacy can be achieved in many ways. A hedge, a stone wall, or perhaps even a porch or patio screen can also provide privacy. If Ted and Joan can see past Ted's wants (a fence) and focus on his needs (privacy), they may be able to come up with alternative, aesthetically pleasing ways to separate their backyards.*

It's usually fairly easy to identify your wants: think of the demands or requests you made in your last phone call or impassioned letter to the other party—for example, a sum of money, the right to live in a rental house, or getting your old job back.

Your real needs may be harder to identify. To help you get started, here is a short list of needs that are often reflected in disputes:

- emotional security

- financial security

- respect and self-esteem

- safety

- privacy

- recognition

- vindication

- protecting your reputation

- avoiding needless expense, aggravation, or stress

- preserving stability and predictability in your life, and

- keeping your options open for the future.

Many disputes involve the very common (but sometimes over-looked) need to maintain a relationship. You may need or want to have a long-term relationship with one or more people involved in your dispute, such as a customer, boss, co-worker, fellow church-member, sibling, parent, relative, friend, or the parent of your child's playmate. For example, if your father's will left management of the family business to you and your sister and the two of you can't agree on how to run the company, you need to resolve this in a way that preserves your relation-ship, or you and your respective families risk losing something far more valuable than the business itself.

Fortunately, mediation offers the best chance to meet this need while resolving your dispute. Unlike a lawsuit, where the very process of creating a winner and loser will probably weaken or destroy any under-lying relationship, mediation offers you the chance to work together to solve your problem—an experience that can make your relationship stronger and better able to weather problems in the future.

Wants and needs are both legitimate goals to pursue in mediation. It's fine to get your wants met, but it's important not to lose sight of your needs as well. Some apparently simple disputes (such as our example of the neighbors and the privacy fence) can be resolved only when the disputants understand what they really need and why. By knowing both what you want and what you need, you stand the best chance of coming up with a solution that will work in the long term.

It is also useful to try to identify the other party's wants and needs and then compare them with your own. (See the exercise below.) You may discover, for example, that some of your needs overlap (avoidance of legal fees, protecting reputations, working together in the future) and that others don't necessarily conflict (economic security for one; recognition for the other). This information can provide a more realistic sense of possible outcomes for your mediation.

As the Rolling Stones once said, "You can't always get what you want… but if you try sometime, you just might find, you get what you need."

Exercise 4: *Wants & Needs Analysis*

List your stated wants. (What have you said you want out of this dispute?)

_____

_____

List the economic, emotional, relational, and other needs that underlie your stated wants in this dispute. _____

_____

What are the other party's wants? (Do the best you can with this one. One good place to start is with any formal written or oral demand or offer to settle the other side has made.)

_____

_____

What do you think might be some of the other party's important underlying needs?

_____

_____

In the table below, list your own and the other party's wants and needs.

Comparison of Wants & Needs

What I Want	What I Need	Other Party's Wants	Other Party's Needs

Are any needs—yours and the other side's—the same?

_____

_____

Can any of the other party's needs be satisfied without harm or cost to you?

_____

_____

WHAT DOES A TODDLER NEED?

Anyone who has had a two-year-old knows that they sometimes cry when you leave the house. Why do they cry? Because they want you to stay with them. But what are the needs underlying this want? Of course, every toddler is different, but they all need:

- **Emotional security:** someone to protect them and make them feel loved and cared for.
- **Responsible care:** someone to help keep them safe, to make sure they don't pull any lamps over on their heads or tumble down the stairs (or, if they do, to give them care and comfort). Most two-year-olds also like a nice lunch and a good nap afterwards.
- **Playful companionship:** someone with whom they can play, talk, sing, learn, walk, and explore the world.

The only way their desires can truly be satisfied is by you staying home. Nevertheless, responsible and loving caretakers, relatives, or grandparents can do a good job meeting their underlying needs.

5. Find Your Bottom Line

Once you have identified your goals, your next step is to determine the minimum for which you would be willing to settle—your bottom line.

Knowing your bottom line is important because mediation is a fluid, ever-changing process where compromise is encouraged. While it is almost always in everyone's interest to maintain a conciliatory and collaborative mood, you will also want something firm to hold onto—some way to make sure that any solution you come up with, no matter how creative, clever, or completely unexpected, meets your minimum goals. In other words, you don't want to be bamboozled into agreeing to something that you'll later regret.

One way to determine your bottom line is to take all of the information you have gathered as part of the written exercises above and then consider what would be 1) the best possible outcome, 2) an adequate outcome, and 3) the minimum acceptable outcome. The last one is your bottom line.

EXAMPLE: *Edna was hired to do some interior painting at a private home. The contract called for Edna to do $5,000 worth of painting, but as the work began, the homeowner kept insisting on small changes that took extra time and required a different kind of paint. Then, when just over half the work was done, the homeowner criticized Edna's work and refused to pay. Edna thinks that her work was fine and wants full payment. After several acrimonious conversations, Edna and the homeowner agree to mediate.*

After checking with a friend who is a lawyer, discussing the situation with a couple of other painters, and doing both a timeline (Exercise 3) and wants & needs analysis (Exercise 4), Edna identifies the following major goals:

Money: *$3,000 for work completed, plus $750 for extra labor and materials required by homeowner's changes; be allowed to finish job and be paid balance of $2,000 as per contract.*

Future Work: *Be allowed to bid on painting for Phase II of homeowner's remodeling plan later in year.*

Reputation and Future Opportunities: *Maintain good professional reputation so this problem does not hurt word-of-mouth referrals.*

Relational Needs: *Avoid major feud with homeowner, as we belong to same church and know lots of the same people.*

Edna then breaks these goals down into "best," "adequate," and "minimum acceptable" results.

Best possible outcome: *I get paid $3,750 immediately for work already done; I'm allowed to finish job with no further hassle (maybe half the money up front and a written agreement on how the homeowner wants the new work done); I get to bid on Phase II; the homeowner acknowledges that the work I've done is of high quality and is willing to recommend me to others who may call for a reference; and this dispute ends in a friendly way so that we can see each other at church without feeling awkward or uncomfortable.*

Adequate outcome: *I get paid $3,000 immediately for work already done; I'm allowed to finish the job (maybe half the money up front and a written agreement on how the homeowner wants the new work done); and a chance to bid on Phase II (if I decide after the mediation that I am willing to do more work for this person). We agree not to badmouth each other in the future.*

Minimum acceptable outcome (Bottom line): *I get paid $3,000 immediately for work done. We agree not to badmouth each other in the future.*

A solution may emerge that does not exactly meet Edna's bottom line. For example, suppose the homeowner adamantly refuses to pay anything for the work Edna did because he claims she used the wrong color. However, because Edna otherwise did excellent work, he will agree to pay her promptly if she redoes the painting (the prep wouldn't have to be redone) and hire her for the much bigger job of painting the interior of the office section at a new factory he owns. Painting at the factory would be done during the coming winter, Edna's slow season, and she would receive a generous up front deposit. If the factory painting goes well, she would stand to make $15,000—way more than the $3,000 in immediate cash she had identified as her bottom line. Obviously, in this case, Edna may choose to change her bottom line and consider doing the required repainting.

Even though Edna may ultimately choose to change her bottom line, that doesn't mean it was wasted effort to determine it in the first place. It will provide her with a clear and thoughtful measurement against which to evaluate any new proposal, and act as a useful brake on any tendency she might have to agree to a solution that doesn't really meet her needs.

C. Gather Evidence

Before the mediation, you'll want to spend some time thinking about what types of evidence you can use to make your points. If the word "evidence" conjures up images of Perry Mason shouting "Objection!" set your mind at ease. The technical legal rules that judges use to decide what evidence can be admitted at trial do not apply in mediation. Each party is expected to speak in ordinary English, and no information will be banned as irrelevant or immaterial, or for some other technical reason. In short, pretty much anything is grist for the mediation mill.

Because no evidence is excluded, you might think this would make mediations go on endlessly. Just the opposite is true. With no technical objections and arguments over what can and can't be discussed, the parties say what they want, show what they want, and usually, with the mediator's help, move on fairly quickly to try and craft a mutually acceptable solution.

1. The Role of Evidence

As you consider what types of evidence you might bring to the mediation, think about why you want to use it. A piece of evidence is worth bringing if it will:

- help you tell your side of the story in a clear and persuasive way

- help show the other party that her position on an issue is based on a mistake or misperception

- help establish the extent of losses or injuries you've suffered, or

- help you reach a settlement by showing that your proposed resolution is fair and workable, or by showing that you are likely to win in court if you don't settle.

On a strategic level, bringing evidence to the mediation can increase your bargaining strength by showing the other party you have a strong case. It says, in effect, "You should settle with me in mediation, because if I am forced to take you to court, this evidence will convince a judge that I should win." (In some cases, you may want to hold back evidence, to keep part of your strategy secret in case you do end up in court. For more on this, see Section C3, below.)

Unless your mediation rules say otherwise, you are free to bring to the table almost anything and anybody that will help you present your case. This can include:

- witnesses or letters from witnesses

- photographs

- drawings

- maps

- tape recordings

- medical bills

- pay stubs

- receipts

- apartment or condominium rules

- repair estimates, and

- letters from friends and neighbors.

As long as the particular item will help demonstrate that your position is fair or your proposed solution is reasonable, you should bring it along. Here are some examples:

- At a California mediation program that handles disputes about noise from barking dogs, owners often bring in the offending beast, especially if it's relatively benign looking.

- A man who wanted to show that his basement was damaged by water pouring off his neighbor's roof brought photographs, taken during a rainstorm, of the neighbor's gutter angled at his house and water running onto his basement wall. He also brought photos of his water-filled cellar.

- When the owner of an auto repair shop wanted to show that a customer should have clearly understood that he would have to pay a storage fee if he didn't pick up his car, he took a huge sign off the front of his building and brought it to the mediation. The sign said, "Storage Fee: $1 per day after 30 days."

- When the co-owner of a "quick print" printing business wanted to illustrate what he claimed was irrational behavior by his partner, he brought to the mediation copies of memos from the partner that contained disjointed, contradictory, and ranting statements.

2. Types of Evidence

To best present your position in mediation, you should bring the most persuasive evidence. The best evidence is objective and unambiguous. Much of this is just common sense. Think about it—are you more likely to believe your opponent, who says "My back hurts when I bend kind of like this," or a doctor's report detailing the damage your opponent suffered to his sixth and seventh vertebrae? In the same way, an invoice documenting how much you paid to fix your car—and marked "paid" by the repair shop—will be more persuasive than your statement that you paid $500 to get your car repaired.

Here are some common types of evidence, from most persuasive to least:

- **Real or Demonstrative Evidence:** The actual item in dispute. For example, the BB gun you claim your neighbor's child used to shoot your dog; the shutter with bubbled paint you claim the painter forgot to prime; the suit from the cleaners, with bleach stains. If you can bring in the physical item at the heart of the dispute and its condition supports your argument, it will help others understand the problem from your point of view.

"YOU SHOULD HAVE BROUGHT THE BASSOON"

A college music student, injured in a car accident, sustained damage to her shoulder muscles. This was especially troublesome as she was a bassoonist and hoped to play professionally as well as teach. Her shoulder injuries prevented her from holding the bassoon in proper playing position for more than a few minutes at a time before the pain forced her to stop. Among other things, she sought money from the other motorist's insurance company for lost future wages if she remained unable to play her instrument.

At the mediation, she described the bassoon, how it rests against the shoulder, and the importance of strong shoulder muscles to hold it. After a mediation session that lasted eight hours, the case finally settled and the woman got a reasonable amount of money for her lost ability to play. After the mediation, the mediator told the music student, "If you'd really wanted to show the insurance people how hard it is to hold your instrument, you should have brought the bassoon. If you had, I think we would have been out of here hours ago."

- **Live Testimony by a Witness With Knowledge of the Facts:** Someone who actually saw or heard the incident underlying the dispute. For example, in a dispute with an insurance company over whether a faulty wiring system might have caused a fire in your home, testimony from one of the firefighters who responded to your 9-1-1 call and saw that the problem came from a short in your wiring system would be highly effective.

- **Documentary Evidence:** Written or printed evidence. Here are the most important types of documentary evidence:

  ✓ **Public Records:** Government documents carry a lot of weight because of their official status. Examples include police reports, copies of your town ordinance (usually available from the local public library or law clerk) showing allowable noise levels in your community, or a brochure distributed by the city explaining rules for putting trash in front of your house.

  ✓ **Business Records:** Unless contradicted, a record routinely made in the ordinary course of business is usually considered to be reliable. Common examples include a hospital's or doctor's medical report; your receipt for a purchase at a hardware store; the organization chart drawn by your company's personnel department; the rules of your apartment building issued by the building manager when you signed your lease.

  ✓ **Photographs, Maps, and Other Reliable Written or Printed Materials:** Obviously, these are more believable if the maps or other materials come from reputable companies, or if something else about them helps show their authenticity. For example, if the photos have a date of printing on the back (ask the developer to date the paper on the back so you can prove they are current photos), it helps to show they were taken before that date.

Your own photographs can be convincing evidence. Your photos of the matter in dispute (an ugly fence, for example), can often be a big help. But be sure to take them from the point of view that matters most to you. In one case, for example, a homeowner complained of a junked car parked on his neighbor's lot. At the mediation, he presented color photos of the old, rusted car that he had taken from his kitchen window, the vantage point from which he had to look at the car every day.

✓ **Private Writings:** These include written statements from family, colleagues, or neighbors about your dispute, such as a neighbor's written statement that "the Gallaghers' dog barks at all hours of the night." These writings carry less weight than other types of evidence because the writers are not present at the mediation, but they can still be very effective. And you can make them more persuasive if the writers will have them notarized, proving that they really wrote them. Alternatively, writers might provide daytime phone numbers so the other party can call if verification—or additional explanations—would help.

• **Expert Testimony:** A witness such as a doctor, auto mechanic, or carpenter—anyone who, by training or experience, has special knowledge in a field and can render an opinion on some important aspect of the dispute. When the mediator has no special knowledge of the subject in dispute (such as a major engine repair or replacing a bearing wall), this kind of witness can be especially helpful—the better informed the mediator is about the subject of the dispute, the more creative he can be in helping the parties reach an acceptable solution.

Evidence Examples

The Problem	Good Evidence to Bring
Harassment	Your ex-boyfriend grabbed, pushed, and threatened you in public. You feared for your safety and called the police. The police report on the incident; a notarized statement from a friend who was with you and saw the incident; a notarized statement from you current roommate, who has heard your ex-boyfriend call you repeatedly, late at night; a letter from your doctor describing how the past incidents of harassment you reported to him and fear of future problems have affected you (loss of sleep, anxiety, difficulty concentrating).
Personal Injury	While you were backing out of your driveway one morning on your way to work, a speeding car struck the rear of your car. You suffered injuries to your back and neck. Photographs showing your injuries; the police report saying that the other driver was at fault; a live witness or a notarized statement from a witness who can confirm that the accident wasn't your fault; a doctor's report describing the extent of your injuries; your medical bills; a written statement from your employer showing wages you lost due to your absence from work; a copy of your own health insurance statements showing medical expenses that weren't covered by insurance.
Property Damage	During a high wind, a neighbor's tree fell onto your house, damaging the roof, wall, and windows on the upper story. Your neighbor disputes the extent of the damage, as well as the state of your roof and windows before the tree hit. Photographs of the damaged areas of your home before and after the incident; actual repair bills or estimates from contractors who specialize in home repair; a police report (if you called the police) affirming your version of events; a statement from your insurance carrier stating or affirming the cost of repairs.
Business Contract Dispute	Your company received a contract to make one million widgets. Halfway through the job, the buyer told you to change the sizes, then later refused all shipments. A copy of the original contract and specifications for the widgets; subsequent memos from the buyer changing the specifications; handwritten log entries by your assembly supervisor attesting to the quality of widgets as they came off the line; records of shipment of widgets to the buyer.
Neighborhood Noise	A noisy neighbor, who throws loud parties and keeps a barking dog, is driving you crazy. Tape recordings of the neighbor's dog barking and of the rock band that played at the neighbor's most recent backyard party (recorded from your bedroom window); a written, notarized statement from other neighbors about the level of noise; a copy of the page from the town ordinance stating the noise limits in residential areas during evening hours; a report on the decibel level reading by an acoustics expert.
Landlord/Tenant	Despite repeated requests, the landlord has refused to repair the stairway leading to the basement in your apartment. Every time you go down to check you things in storage, you believe you are risking your life. A photograph showing the dangerous condition caused by rotted boards on the stairs; a sample rotted board; a copy of your lease stating the landlord's duty to repair; a copy of a report by a city housing inspector who responded to your complaint.

Evidence Examples, continued

The Problem	Good Evidence to Bring
Employment Dispute	Two days after your 55th birthday, you were summarily dismissed from your office job. You believe that the primary reason you were fired is your boss's negative attitude toward older workers. The termination letter from your boss; a copy of your employment contract; copies of state and federal laws prohibiting age discrimination; a copy of the company manual; one or more coworkers who can confirm that the boss made unflattering remarks concerning your age; an internal company memo, written by your boss, disparaging the value and contributions of older workers.

These are just a few examples and suggestions—the general rule is that it's a good idea to bring anything that might be helpful to the parties and/or the mediator.

3. Holding Back Evidence

Once you've figured out what evidence will best help you tell your story, you have a strategic decision to make: Should you reveal it all at the mediation, or hold some of it back, in case the dispute ends up in court? As a general rule, your best strategy is to bring everything to the mediation, to enhance your chances of reaching a good settlement. Even if the mediation proves unsuccessful, the evidence you held back may have lost some of its power by the time you get to court. The other party may have found out about the evidence through pretrial investigation and prepared ways to counter it. And of course, if a live witness is involved, that person may have died, forgotten the incident, or moved away.

However, there are a few situations in which it makes sense to hold back evidence in mediation, particularly if revealing it would help the other side in litigation later without moving your dispute closer to a settlement. For example, if you have a claim against a manufacturer for making an unsafe product and someone from the company has leaked you an internal memorandum showing that the company knew the product was unsafe, you might want to keep it secret. If the case does not settle, you can use it at trial to undercut the company's legal position. Disclosing it now would allow the company plenty of time to prepare a defense against it. If your case involves an issue of this importance, you should probably get some advice from a lawyer or law coach about what to do.

You may also choose not to divulge some evidence because of the reaction it would trigger from the other side. For example, say your claim is for wrongful termination against a former employer. You have evidence that your boss occasionally used drugs at work, but you know that she knows of an affair you had with a married coworker. In this case, maybe you shouldn't cast the first stone.

If you are hesitant about divulging evidence, talk to your lawyer or law coach before the mediation. (See Section E, below, and Chapter 13.) Or, you can ask the mediator (during a private caucus) how the other side might react if you reveal a particular piece of evidence at mediation, or later at a trial or arbitration. The mediator can probably give you an educated opinion, based on the case and the other side's position, and you can make your decision accordingly.

D. The Pre-Mediation Memorandum

A pre-mediation memorandum or brief outlines the facts and issues of your dispute for the mediator. If a case involves substantial amounts of money or property or significant legal issues, many mediators require or encourage the parties to submit a memorandum. On the other hand, community mediation centers often do not allow the parties to submit briefs because many of their cases concern relatively minor disputes and parties might not have the time or resources to prepare a memorandum.

The mediation rules will probably tell you the procedures and deadlines for submitting the memorandum; if not, look in the notice of mediation or the mediation agreement. If you can't figure out whether you have to submit a memorandum, ask the mediation service or mediator. If you have the opportunity, it is almost always worthwhile to submit a memorandum, even in small disputes—you can adjust the length and complexity of the memo to fit your situation.

1. Purpose of the Memorandum

The purpose of the memorandum is to tell the mediator about the basic facts and issues that will be addressed in your case. The memorandum can be especially useful if the dispute involves legal or technical issues, or complicated facts. You can attach copies of legal statutes, technical papers, contracts, or other important documents—like building codes or project specs—with relevant sections highlighted. This will help bring the mediator "up to speed" before the mediation begins, which will save you time and money (if you're paying by the hour).

2. Submitting the Memorandum

If a memorandum is required or allowed, the parties typically have to submit it a week to ten days before the mediation. In some cases, you will be writing your memo for the mediator's eyes only. Under some mediation rules, however, disputants are required to exchange copies of their memos. If you will be exchanging memos, be especially careful to use neutral, noninflammatory language. Mudslinging or needless accusations may trigger an equally nasty reply from the other side—and doom the mediation before it even gets started. Even if the other party won't see your memo, it's still a good idea to state your position calmly and objectively—you will seem more credible and reasonable to the mediator.

Don't exchange memoranda if it isn't required. If the rules don't require you to exchange memos, we recommend that you don't. While you do want to educate the mediator, there is no sense in showing the other side exactly how you intend to present and support your point of view before your session even begins. If you want to keep your memo confidential, write at the top that you are submitting it in confidence to the mediator and do not want it shared with the other party.

If you do exchange memos with the other party, the contents are subject to the mediation rules on confidentiality. Under most rules, the other party would not be able to use the information in your memorandum against you in any other proceeding, such as an arbitration or trial.

3. Contents of the Memorandum

A good memorandum is short, usually just a few pages in length, unless it concerns a very large and complex case. (Remember, if you are paying hourly fees for your mediation, this will usually include the time a mediator spends reviewing materials before the session—including time spent reading your memo!) Your memo should give the mediator a sense of what the dispute is about and highlight any technical issues that may require some advance study. Because the mediator doesn't have the power to decide anything, there is nothing to gain by arguing your points in detail or including lengthy legal-sounding discourses. (If you have a lawyer who will prepare and submit the memorandum for you, ask the lawyer to keep it short; you don't want to pay for the preparation of a court-style memorandum or brief.)

Think of your memorandum as a terrific chance to make a good first impression on the mediator. Present your information clearly and with some passion, but without sounding strident or unreasonable. Don't lie or overstate your case. As one mediator put it, "If I find I can't have confidence in what one of the parties says to me, if I have to be skeptical, then just as a human being, my heart won't be in it and it becomes that much more difficult as a professional to do my best for that person."

There is no official format you have to follow in preparing the memo. You can print out or type your memo on plain white paper. You should include the following information:

- **Undisputed facts.** Begin by giving the mediator a quick overview of what your dispute is about, starting with the facts everyone agrees on. For example, "ABC Manufacturing Company makes wood furniture for residential and commercial customers. From 1997-2004 (May), I was employed at ABC as a lathe operator. My immediate supervisor was Mr. Gene Dowl. On May 3, Mr. Dowl informed me in writing that I was being terminated in ten days because of 'sloppy work.'"

- **Disputed facts and issues.** Clearly explain what the dispute is about. For example, "When I asked Mr. Dowl what he meant by my work being 'sloppy,' he said I made too many errors on the Royal Oak account (1,000 lots of sculpted chair legs). However, my work is always good and I wasn't sloppy on the Royal Oak job. I think his real reason for firing me is that he overheard me talking with other employees about how we didn't like working with the cheaper wood the company has been buying and how it's unsafe to make furniture with wood that could easily crack and break. I think I was fired to keep me from talking about this problem." After you have explained the dispute from your point of view, don't provide a series of arguments and justifications as to why you are in the right and the other party is a dishonest so-and-so. Again, the purpose of your memo is simply to tell the mediator what your dispute is about, not to show that you are correct and the other side is wrong.

- **Desired result.** State in general terms what you hope to achieve from the mediation. For example, "I am coming to mediation because I want my job back at ABC. I am willing to sue over this if I have to, but I am willing to try to work out a settlement as long as (1) I get my job back with no penalties, and (2) Mr. Dowl is no longer my supervisor." There is no need to go into great detail or to disclose your bottom line.

- **Attach key documents.** To help the mediator prepare for your case, include copies of any documents that are especially important. These might include laws, court decisions, contracts, company rules, insurance policies, leases, and so on. Use a yellow marker or similarly readable highlighter to mark the important passages.

E. Who Should Attend the Mediation

In some situations, you may want to bring others—such as a witness, a friendly supporter, or a lawyer—along to the mediation. This section will help you decide who should come (and who should stay home).

1. Decision Makers

There must be someone at the mediation who has the authority to agree to a settlement for each side. Obviously, if this is your personal dispute, you are that person. But in disputes involving businesses or public entities, it's not always clear who has the power to sign off on an agreement. It's important to find this out before the mediation begins. You don't want to spend hours working in good faith toward a solution, only to find out that the people on the other side of the table aren't authorized to settle the case. In fact, if the other party does not have the authority to make a settlement on behalf of whatever company or organization he represents—and cannot quickly get in touch with someone who does—you should be hesitant to continue the mediation.

If the person's recommendations are routinely accepted by the powers that be, then you may wish to proceed. However, if you are unable to get such an assurance, it makes very little sense to continue. If you are mediating because of a contractual provision or court order, you can argue that the other side has not mediated in good faith because it failed to send someone with the authority to reach an agreement.

EXAMPLE: *Richard Wagner, a claims representative of the Racafrax Insurance Company, comes to the mediation of a personal injury claim with authority to settle only for an amount up to $10,000. He does not inform the other parties or the mediator of this limitation. After several hard-working hours, everyone—including Richard Wagner—agrees that a fair settlement would be $15,000. Only now does Wagner reveal that he cannot agree because he lacks the authority. The mediation must adjourn with the dispute at least temporarily unresolved while the claims rep goes to consult with his supervisor.*

If you don't have ultimate authority, stay in close touch with someone who does. If you are coming to a mediation as the representative of a large organization or company, be sure that you have adequate authority. If not, at least arrange for a decision maker to be available by telephone during the time the mediation is expected to last (and get a home telephone number, in case the mediation extends after normal working hours).

2. Others Involved in the Dispute

If your dispute involves an organization, such as a business, nonprofit, club, or government agency, think about whether particular people in the organization have such a strong emotional involvement in the dispute that they might find it hard to agree to a rational settlement. If so, these people may not be able to negotiate successfully, and it's often best that they not attend the mediation. On the other hand, if they are in a position—and have the ill will—to undermine a settlement, they should probably attend the mediation. Repairing this relationship may be an essential part of finding a workable solution.

EXAMPLE: *A computer maker and a parts supplier have a contract dispute about the quality of manufactured parts. At first, the decision makers for each company planned to come to mediation alone to try to work out a settlement that would not only solve the contract problem, but also pave the way for the two companies to do business together in the future. But in this case, a strong personal distrust had developed between the computer maker's director of engineering and the parts maker's chief engineer. The decision makers realized that if the antagonism between these two men was not resolved, either would be in a position to sabotage future relations. Therefore, both were invited to attend the mediation—even though they were not decision makers—in order to say their piece to the mediator and to each other. Hopefully, once the air is cleared, both companies can work out a settlement that won't fall apart.*

3. Witnesses

In some mediations, disputants are permitted to bring any witnesses they wish. The purpose of bringing a witness is primarily to support your version of the facts and your opinion of what a reasonable solution might be. For example, if your complaint involves a neighbor who keeps a rusted car in his front yard, you might bring another neighbor to confirm the unsightly condition of the car and help the other side see that it really is an eyesore.

In a mediation, you usually do not ask questions of your witnesses. Instead, the mediator simply invites witnesses to tell what they know about the dispute. The mediator and the other party may then ask your witness questions, but the process looks and feels far more like a conversation than a cross-examination.

If you plan to bring a witness, take some time to prepare the person. Review the points you would like the witness to cover, and be sure that statement will be helpful to you. Also explain a bit about how mediation works—knowing that the proceeding is not adversarial should help your witness avoid coming across as too angry or strident.

Although a good witness can help you arrive at a good settlement, there can be downsides to bringing witnesses. Even if your witness is not an "expert" and does not charge you a fee (see below), witnesses usually slow down the mediation, which increases the mediator fees (if you're paying by the hour). In addition, no matter how much time you spend preparing your witness, you still cannot be sure what will happen if the mediator or the other party asks a question that you did not anticipate. The witness could even end up saying something that undermines your position. For example, if the neighbor says that rusted car in your neighbor's yard, though it isn't pretty, is not as much of a neighborhood problem as the two old pick-ups you park on the street, you won't be too pleased. Also, bringing witnesses can make the other party feel "ganged up" on, which could reduce the chances for a settlement.

Make sure your neighbor is really your supporter. Talk to any neighbors whom you plan to bring as a witness about other possible issues the other side might raise, as these come up fairly often in mediation. Make sure that the neighbor supports your broader perspective—that is, that the other party to the mediation is the cause of a neighborhood problem (and that you are not).

Before you invite a witness to attend, consider whether you can present the evidence in some other way, to avoid the delay and risk (and sometimes, cost) of bringing a witness. For example, you might get a written statement from the witness (notarized if possible) and offer it instead of the live testimony. Because you are only using the witness to try to better explain your position and convince the other side that you can prove it if necessary, you don't lose that much by using the statement instead of the person. Also, if you don't like what the witness says, you don't have to use it at all. For example, instead of bringing a neighbor to support your complaint about the neighbor's rusted car, you might bring a notarized statement from the witness to that effect, and also include some color photographs of the car taken from different angles.

a. Expert Witnesses

Expert witnesses, such as doctors, accountants, investigators, and others can help show that you would have a strong case if you were to take your dispute to court or arbitration. This type of witness can be extremely valuable in situations where a major issue is the dollar value of an economic loss, but less valuable in neighborhood disputes where convincing someone to change their conduct is your primary concern. For example, if your claim is against an insurance company for injuries involved in a car accident, you can bring your doctor to talk about the extent of your injuries and how they affect your ability to work. (But it is much more common just to bring a written report from the doctor. This saves a lot of money because you don't have to pay the doctor for time spent attending the mediation, nor the mediator for the time it takes to sit and listen to the doctor.) If you do plan to bring an expert witness, find out whether your mediation rules require you to notify the other party; the purpose of this notification requirement is to give the other party a chance to find an expert on the same topic.

b. Should Your Witness Become a Party to the Mediation?

Sometimes, it might be better to ask a person you would consider bringing as a witness to join you as a party to the mediation. For example, a tenant in an apartment building who agreed to mediate a dispute with the landlord over poor trash collection in the parking lot might want to bring other tenants to the mediation as witnesses. It may be better, however, to ask them to join the mediation as parties.

One reason for this is that a mediated agreement only applies to the parties in a dispute, not witnesses. Thus, if the mediation agreement said, in effect, "The landlord agrees that rent can be withheld unless parking lot dumpsters are emptied once a week," this might be a good agreement for the original tenant activist, but it would not let the other tenants in this situation withhold their rent. A better solution would be to sign any willing tenants on to the case. Then they could come to the mediation as parties (or, if the group was too large, they could designate one or two tenants to represent them) and share in the benefits of the mediated agreement. Their participation would also give them added bargaining power at the mediation, and possibly help them achieve more favorable settlement terms.

4. Supportive Friends or Relatives

When you come to mediation, you sit face to face with the other person(s) involved in your dispute. For some shy or easily dominated people, this encounter can be intimidating, even though mediation is informal and most mediators will try to make sure that neither party gets steamrolled by an aggressive adversary. This problem typically occurs when the disputants were in a personal relationship (such as a marriage or living-together relationship) and one of them was far less forceful or dominant. However, it could also come up between coworkers, neighbors, or friends. A similar problem can occur when one party doesn't speak well in front of other people, has a speech problem, or is not fluent in English.

Any significant power imbalance—no matter what causes it—not only threatens the position of the weaker person; it also affects the entire mediation process. For example, many people who perceive themselves at a disadvantage are extremely reluctant to agree to anything, even a fair solution.

If any of these circumstances apply to you, consider bringing a friend or relative to the mediation to support you and, if necessary, to help you articulate your point of view during the mediation. This not only allows you to prepare and plan together, but also lets you appoint your friend as the keeper of your bottom line.

Your "helper" can be a friend, relative, lawyer, or other professional such as a teacher, social worker, or member of the clergy. But be careful not to let your "helper" become your advocate. Even if the mediator permits it, this would most likely make the other party more defensive and reduce the chances for a settlement.

WITH A LITTLE HELP FROM MOM AND SISTER...

Rebecca, a college student, had worked extremely hard as a part-time advertising salesperson for a magazine and was disputing the amount of commissions she was paid. Only 18 years old, Rebecca felt shy and intimidated by the prospect of facing the publication's advertising director. To help counter this, she brought her older sister and mother with her to the mediation.

Rebecca still did most of the talking, but her family was there to remind her of points she wanted to make and dates that escaped her mind, and to put in a few words now and then about the extent of her work on the magazine's behalf.

Thus supported, Rebecca was able to represent herself adequately in the mediation and to agree with the magazine ad director on what both considered to be a fair settlement.

5. Lawyers

Nearly all mediation rules give you the right to bring a lawyer to the mediation. Lawyers might already be involved in your dispute—for example, if the dispute has progressed to a lawsuit and you are represented by counsel, your lawyer may attend the mediation. Or, you may want to consult with a lawyer during the process, to make sure that any settlement you reach is fair. In general, however, you don't need a lawyer to mediate. In fact, bringing a lawyer can sometimes undermine the process.

For mediation to be most effective, disputants need to deal with each other directly, air their differences, learn to perceive the dispute from each other's point of view, and work together to find a resolution. Against this background, bringing a lawyer, who is trained to function in the more adversarial atmosphere of the courtroom, can sometimes be self-defeating—especially in interpersonal disputes involving family, friends, neighbors, or business colleagues. This is particularly likely if a disputant lets the lawyer do most of the talking (bringing and relying on the help of a lawyer is likely to be less of a problem in disputes between more distant parties over money or property).

However, there are times when it makes sense to bring—or at least consult—a lawyer.

a. When Your Lawyer Should Attend

There are some circumstances in which you probably should have your lawyer attend the mediation, such as:

- When complex legal issues are involved and it would be impractical to conduct the mediation without a ready source of legal advice. For example, a town government and a building contractor have a dispute over the contractor's work on the town hall. Any settlement would have to take into account the company's compliance with complicated provisions of local building codes and historical preservation rules.

- When substantial amounts of money or property are involved. For example, if your dispute concerns a claim that your former boss sexually harassed you, and you are seeking a $200,000 settlement, you should probably have a lawyer.

- When you lack self-confidence, are intimated by the other party, or need help articulating your position. Bringing a lawyer is one remedy for a "power imbalance," but this problem can often also be solved by bringing a strong-minded friend or other adviser. In any situation like this, you will have to weigh the benefits against the costs of bringing a lawyer. If a lawyer will charge $200 an hour to represent you, is the dispute big enough to justify that expense?

If you do want to bring a lawyer, try to use one who is experienced in mediation and supports its methods and goals. (For more on finding a lawyer to work with in mediation, see Chapter 13.) Be sure to work out the lawyer's fee in advance. Many lawyers charge one hourly rate for office work and a higher rate for time spent in court. Because mediation is a lot less work than a trial, a rate somewhere between the "office rate" and the "court rate" would probably be fair.

Ask your lawyer to stay in the background. Your lawyer doesn't have to play the lead role at the mediation. For example, you might ask your lawyer to simply sit quietly and listen. Occasionally, you can have a private conference to be sure that you haven't left out anything important and that you are considering all of the legal implications of any proposed settlement terms.

b. Consulting With a Lawyer

If you want formal legal help with your mediation, or you simply want to make sure that your legal information or conclusions are accurate, you can use a lawyer as a consultant or information specialist. Under this model, the lawyer becomes your law coach, providing helpful insights into the more technical legal aspects of your dispute before, during, or even after your mediation sessions.

- **Before the mediation:** Consult with your lawyer about the issues in dispute. In order to use the law as a benchmark in determining your goals, ask what might happen if your case went to trial or arbitration. For example, in a personal injury case, a lawyer can give you a pretty accurate high and low estimate of how much a judge or jury might award for your type of injuries. Or in a case where you believe someone plagiarized an article you wrote, a lawyer could advise you about how various settlement options might affect your ability to stop others from plagiarizing the same work.

- **During the mediation:** You can ask a lawyer to remain on call during the session, in case you need immediate help on a particular point. For example, in a business mediation, if you are moving toward a settlement in which you will buy your partner out, you can take a break to call your lawyer and ask about the personal tax consequences of various ways of structuring the deal.

- **After the mediation:** Successful mediation doesn't always result in an agreement on all the details; sometimes, it provides a sound framework for an agreement. Your lawyer can help later with hashing out the fine print. Even if you do reach a detailed agreement, you can condition it on your lawyer's approval. One way to do this is to have the mediator insert a clause stating that the agreement will take effect one week after it is signed, unless either party objects in writing before that date. During that week, you can ask your lawyer to review the agreement to make sure that it says what you want it to say and that it does not impair your legal rights in any way you did not intend. If you want your written agreement to have the binding effect of a contract, your lawyer can handle this as well. (For more on conditioning an agreement on your lawyer's review and drafting an agreement in the form of a contract, see Chapter 7.) ■

CHAPTER 6

The Six Stages of Mediation

The bailiff bangs three times and says, "All Rise! This Court is now in session, The Honorable Thomas A. Watson presiding! You may now be seated."

That is how a typical courtroom hearing begins. Mediation begins differently.

"Hello. Are you Elizabeth Ferraro? Are you Richard Rafferty? I'm Tom Watson, the mediator. Will you both follow me into the conference room, please?"

The mediator's low-key opening sets a tone of sensible informality that will continue throughout the proceedings. But it is also a little deceiving, because it is such a casual overture to the compelling drama about to unfold. Mediation can be so dramatic because you and the other side—your former business partner, your annoying neighbor, the boss who fired you—play the starring roles. In just a few moments, you will sit face to face, with the chance to say what is on your mind, wrangle over the issues, and if all goes well, arrive at a solution.

Although mediation is conducted informally, it is a process that usually moves from one defined stage to the next, giving the disputants time to speak and listen to each other, sometimes meet privately with the mediator, and work together to find a solution to their dispute.

EXAMPLE: *You are mediating a dispute over noise with the upstairs neighbor in your co-op apartment building. The mediator begins by explaining the purposes of mediation and the procedures to be followed. Then, you and your neighbor each have an opportunity to make an opening statement, explaining how you see the dispute. A short joint discussion follows, during which the mediator* *reviews the issues raised by both of you and helps you sort out the key concerns. Next, the mediator probably asks to meet with each of you privately to discuss your positions on the issues and your ideas for solving the problem. After shuttling back and forth to conduct several rounds of these private meetings (called "caucuses"), the mediator calls you back together to try to work out the details of a settlement in another joint discussion. Finally, if both of you agree to the same settlement terms, the mediator outlines the agreement, reads it to you for your approval, and declares the mediation closed.*

Mediators agree that mediation usually proceeds through these stages (or some version of them), but disagree on how many stages there are and what they should be called. As you have doubtless gathered from the title of this chapter, we divide the process into six stages, which we refer to as follows:

1. Mediator's Opening Statement

2. Disputants' Opening Statements

3. Joint Discussion

4. Caucus

5. Joint Negotiations, and

6. Closure.

WHERE'S STAGE FOUR?

Some mediators omit stage four, the private meeting or "caucus" between the mediator and each of the parties. Divorce and family mediators are particularly likely to omit the private caucus, preferring instead to keep family members together in order to help them jointly rebuild at least a measure of trust. (See Chapter 10 for more on divorce mediation.) Some community mediation centers also do not hold private meetings in cases that involve interpersonal disputes, fearing that separate caucuses may make one or both sides worry that the mediator is being unfairly influenced by the other.

The sections that follow will describe each of these stages in detail, using these three fictional cases as illustrations:

- **CASE 1—The Noisy Neighbor.** This is a neighbor dispute involving Ms. Ferraro, who is complaining of noise from late evening pool parties hosted by her backyard neighbor, Mr. Rafferty.

- **CASE 2—The Missing Security Deposit.** Ms. Sherman leased space in her industrial park to United Tea Bags, a company that sells tea whole-sale to local restaurants. The company has moved out, but Ms. Sherman has refused to return its security deposit because of dam-age she claims the company's employees did to the offices before they left.

- **CASE 3—Business Owners Fall Out.** Mike Woo and Ted McDonald are co-owners of Big Slice Pizza, Inc., a restaurant. They have had a falling out over various issues of running the business, including pricing and employee relations. Each owns half the company. They have come to mediation either to work out their differences or to decide to end their partnership.

A. Stage One: The Mediator's Opening Statement

The first lines in the mediation drama are known as the "opening statement." The mediator will usually start things off by making a short speech describing, in simple terms, the procedures and rules of media-tion. Listen carefully so you'll understand exactly how things will proceed—even if you are an old hand at mediation. The mediator's rules and procedures may be slightly different from those you've used before. When the mediator finishes, you will have a chance to ask questions.

WHERE TO SIT

Typically, the mediator will come to greet you and the other parties in a waiting area. He will introduce himself to everyone and then escort all of you together to the conference room or other room where the mediation will be held. He does it this way to protect his image of neutrality. If the mediator brought one side into the room before the others, the party entering last might wonder if the other party had said anything to influence or prejudice the mediator.

Once in the conference room, the mediator will invite you to take a seat at the table. There is no strategic advantage in jockeying for table position; the mediator usually knows where he wants you to sit and, much like a host at a dinner party, will direct you to a seat. A typical seating plan places one party on one side of a rectangular table, the other party directly across, and the mediator at the head. A lawyer or witness who comes with you will usually be seated next to you, or perhaps just behind you if there isn't room for everyone to fit at the table. If for some reason you are uncomfortable with the seating arrangement, speak up and the mediator should be willing to accommodate you.

1. The Purpose of the Opening Statement

The mediator will use the opening statement to achieve two important goals: to explain the mediation process, and to gain control of the mediation. The mediator has temporary control just by virtue of making the opening statement, but that is not the same as earning the trust of both you and the other party. This temporary control can be lost if the mediator doesn't act quickly to hang onto it. For example, if one party calls the other a rotten liar, things can quickly get out of hand; the other person might leave, take a punch at the other, or more likely, make the same type of accusation, which could bring the mediation to an early adjournment.

Only by gaining and keeping control can the mediator keep the mediation on track and moving forward. Everything your mediator says and does is designed with this goal in mind, including meeting you in the waiting room, presenting a neat appearance, and speaking politely and respectfully. The mediator will try to continue in this fashion during the opening statement, by speaking confidently, answering your questions fully, and otherwise demonstrating intelligence, sensitivity, and lack of bias—in short, by proving to be someone in whom you can and should place your trust.

2. Sample Opening Statement

The opening statement below is adapted from those typically delivered by a mediator at a community mediation center. But no matter what the mediation setting, you're likely to hear something very similar. In this example, the parties are neighbors who have come voluntarily to a community mediation center to try to resolve a dispute involving noise, among other problems. Neither has brought an attorney.

Introduces Self: "Good morning, my name is Tom Watson. I'm the mediator who has been assigned to your case." (Or, if you selected the mediator, "I'm pleased you selected me as the mediator to hear this case.")

Introduces Parties: "Before we go any farther, I want to make sure I have everyone's correct name and address. On my left is Elizabeth Ferraro of 112 Bristol Ave. And on my right is Mr. Richard Rafferty, 644 Eastbrooke Drive. Mr. Rafferty, the witness you have brought with you is Mr. Robert Medden of 206 Savannah Boulevard."

Commends Parties: "I would like to start by commending each of you for choosing mediation as a way to resolve your dispute. By doing so, you have given yourselves the opportunity to solve this problem in a cooperative, rather than an adversarial, way and with greater flexibility, speed, and privacy than you would likely have in court."

States Goal: "This community mediation center is a nonprofit organization set up to help people in our town resolve their disputes. Our goal is to help you find a solution to your problem that will be fair to both of you and workable in the long run. Our experience is that disputants who work in good faith during the mediation have a very high success rate in reaching an agreement and sticking to it. My job is to help you do this."

Explains Mediator's Role: "As a mediator, I have been trained and certified by this center to handle disputes such as yours. I have no authority to make a decision about your dispute or to recommend one to a judge. I can't send anyone to jail or impose any fines. My only job is to help you find your own solution to this dispute.

"I am completely neutral. I don't know either of you, and I know very little about your dispute except its general nature as you described it on your submission forms." (Rules of this community mediation center did not allow disputants to submit a memorandum prior to the mediation. If they had, the mediator would know more about the case and the positions of the parties and would refer at this point to the memos. See Chapter 5, Section D.)

No Time Pressure: "One of the advantages of mediation is that we are under no time constraints. This room is available to us for as long as we want it, and I am prepared to stay here as long as our effort appears to be productive. If, as we go along, you want to take a break, just let me know and we'll do that." (Some mediating programs, particularly those run by court systems, do impose time limits.)

Explains Procedure: "We'll begin today by having each of you make an opening statement, telling us what this dispute is all about from your point of view.

"Ms. Ferraro, because you were the one who initiated mediation, you will go first, and then Mr. Rafferty will have his turn. While one of you is speaking, I'll ask the other to just listen without interrupting, no matter how much you disagree with what you hear. You will have a chance to speak as well. If you need to make notes to remind yourself of comments you want to make later, there are pads and pencils on the table for you to use.

"While each of you is speaking, you may notice me taking notes. If I write something, it doesn't mean I agree or disagree with what has been said. I am taking notes just to help me keep track of the facts."

Use of Evidence: "While you are speaking, you can show us any evidence you have brought with you, such as bills, letters, photographs, or whatever. The purpose of evidence is to help us understand your side of this dispute. The technical rules of evidence followed in court are not followed here, so I am willing to look at anything you want to show me. The other person will be able to look at it, too."

Discussion Stage: "After the opening statements, we will begin to discuss the issues in dispute, and hear from any witnesses you have brought today. During this discussion phase, you can each say whatever you like, but I will stop you if you use profanities or other inappropriate language, and ask you to find a different way to make your point."

Caucusing: "At some point, I may want to talk to each of you separately in what is called a caucus. If that happens, I will ask one of you to leave the room while I speak with the other. I will keep everything you tell me in a caucus confidential and I won't reveal it to the other side, unless you give me specific permission to do so. If I spend longer in caucus with one of you than the other, it doesn't mean I am partial to one side, it just means that it may be taking me a little longer to understand all the facts and the options available."

Confidentiality: "You have both signed a pledge to keep everything said and revealed in this session confidential." (This pledge usually appears in the mediation agreement both parties signed before the mediation. See Chapter 5, Section A.) "I have taken a similar pledge to keep secret everything you say or show me. In fact, when this mediation is over, I will even throw away my notes." (At community mediation centers it is common practice for mediators to destroy their notes after a case concludes. Private mediators handling business disputes often keep their notes in case the parties want to come back into mediation to address related disputes.) "The mediation center considers this rule of confidentiality the most important rule of mediation and expects each of you to uphold it strictly."

Consent Agreement: "As I said, our goal today is to find a solution to your dispute that both of you feel is fair and workable in the long run. If we can find such a solution, I will help you write it up in the form of what we call a consent agreement." (See Chapter 7 for more on writing an agreement.) "This will be an official document, which will be notarized after each of you signs it. It will be a binding contract and may be legally enforceable in court." (In disputes involving large sums of money, property, or legal rights, the parties will often want a lawyer or business advisor to review an agreement before signing. Chapter 7, Section E, explains how to arrange for this. Especially in this situation, the agreement reached in mediation may not be the final, detailed agreement between the parties, but just provide a solid basis for further negotiations.)

Questions: "Now, before we begin with your opening statements, are there any questions? If not, then Ms. Ferraro, let's begin with you. Please tell us what this case is all about."

B. Stage Two: The Parties' Opening Statements

After the mediator's opening statement, it will be time for you and the other party to speak. You will each have a turn to make an opening statement. Typically, the party who initiated the mediation goes first.

1. How to Make Your Opening Statement

This is your chance, finally and without interruption, to tell the other party and the mediator exactly how you see the dispute. Consider how delicious this opportunity is: Even if you have previously tried and failed to negotiate a settlement, you probably never had the chance to tell your side of the story without being interrupted. Even if you had taken your case to court instead of mediation, you would be constrained by court rules to limit your testimony to the narrow legal issues in dispute, and you would probably face constant interruptions in the form of objections from opposing counsel.

But in mediation, the floor is yours. No one will stop you (unless you just ramble on too long). No one will object or try to twist your words. If the other party does try to say something, the mediator will quickly remind him to let you make your presentation without interruption. If witnesses are in attendance, some mediators may ask them to leave the room during the opening statements so their views are not influenced by what the disputants say. They will be asked to return later to speak.

Here are some guidelines for making your opening statement.

a. Speak to the Mediator

Stay seated, use a conversational tone, and speak directly to the mediator. Unless the mediator invites you to use first names, address the mediator and the other parties as Mr. or Ms. (Later, if the mediation is going well, you may begin speaking directly to the other party, using a first name.) Addressing your remarks to the mediator has at least two benefits: It helps you keep calm by avoiding having to look directly at the other party, and it helps you establish a rapport with the mediator. Of course, if the other party is a member of your family or a former close friend, you should look at them as you speak (if you are comfortable doing so).

b. Start at the End

Your task in your opening statement is to tell the mediator and the other side what the dispute looks like from your point of view and how it has affected you. The best and simplest way to do this is to start at the end of the story—that is, to explain the event that triggered the mediation. If this was a loud party or a dog bite or a fender bender, start with that, so the mediator knows what the dispute is about. Then go back and fill in important preliminary facts that will help the mediator understand how your dispute developed.

Opening Statement for Neighbor Dispute: *In Case 1, described in the introduction to this chapter, Ms. Ferraro starts at the end of her story: "I'm here today because my backyard neighbor, Mr. Rafferty, keeps me up at night with noise from his parties. The trouble began in July of 2003. Before then, the neighborhood was very quiet. I could sleep with the windows open and never be disturbed by noise. But that summer is when I first started being woken up at night by noise from parties that Mr. Rafferty had at his backyard pool. Our houses back up to each other."*

Opening Statement for Lease Dispute: *In Case 2, Mr. Nehru begins by saying: "I'm here because my company, United Tea Bags, Inc., rented space from Ms. Sherman. After we vacated the building last month, she didn't return our security deposit, which, according to our written agreement, was refundable. Our company represents several nationally known tea manufacturers and sells tea bags by the case to restaurants, hotels, and some convenience stores. A couple of years ago when we were looking for local office space, we met Jane Sherman, who had space to rent in the Four Corners Office Park."*

Opening Statement for Business Ownership Dispute: *In Case 3, Mike Woo starts this way: "We're here today to resolve—one way or the other—a problem between Ted McDonald and me that has been growing for nearly three years. We've either got to figure out how to run our restaurant together, or one of us has to* *buy the other out. I started Big Slice Pizza by myself in January of 2002. We were doing okay, and then my brother-in-law introduced me to Ted McDonald, who was looking for a new business to get involved in. We didn't know each other at all, but he seemed capable and was really eager, and frankly, I was a little overwhelmed to be starting up this business on my own. So I sold him 25% and later another 25% of the stock, so that we owned the business 50-50. That's when our troubles began."*

c. Use Dates Carefully

As you tell your story, pinpoint when important events happened as accurately as possible. This will help the mediator place everything that happened in correct chronological order. (If you submitted a Pre-Mediation Memorandum, you have already begun this process.)

Neighbor Dispute: *Ms. Ferraro: "The first time I was woken up by noise from a pool party was one night around the middle of July 2003 at about 2 a.m. I remember the incident because the next morning I had to be up at 6 a.m. for an early flight to Chicago for business."*

Or, looking again at the lease dispute:

Lease Dispute: *Mr. Nehru: "We signed a lease for 1,800 square feet of office space in Ms. Sherman's building to begin on January 1, 2001 and run for two years, until December 31, 2003. We left the premises on schedule, on December 31st."*

Mike's recollection of his problems with Ted in the pizza business are keyed to an important date:

Business Ownership Dispute: *Mike: "I signed over 50% of the stock to Ted around October 12, 2002—I remember the date because it was right around Columbus Day and we had a big special on deep-dish Sicilian-style pizza. The next night was when we had our first big argument in front of the employees."*

Showing the mediator that you can be reasonably accurate with dates is also a good way of demonstrating that you will be reliable when relating other information, too. This can be a big help in arriving at a settlement later on—the other party is likely to be more forthcoming if you appear reliable enough to do what you promise.

d. Display Evidence as You Tell Your Story

To help illustrate and support your point of view as you tell your story to the mediator, you may want to present photographs, receipts, medical reports, and other evidence. (See Chapter 5, Section C, for more on evidence.) A display of compelling evidence may also prompt the other side to change position, or at least show that you have the evidence necessary to take your case to court or arbitration if you can't reach a settlement.

⚠ Think twice before you present evidence likely to anger or embarrass the other party. Your goal is to solve the problem, not to win a court case. That's why it's counterproductive to present evidence that is likely to upset the other party—you will only scuttle your efforts to reach a settlement. For example, in the neighbor dispute, Ms. Ferraro, the neighbor complaining of loud pool parties, might have found bits of roll-your-own cigarette paper that wafted onto her lawn. She may believe this is evidence that her neighbor and his guests have been using marijuana, but it would be a mistake to introduce this at the mediation. It is not relevant to the noise dispute, and accusing her neighbor of drug use will only increase the level of animosity, possibly ruining any chance of working out a settlement.

Display your evidence as it comes up in your story, rather than all at once at the beginning or at the end. Here are some examples:

Neighbor Dispute: *Ms. Ferraro: "I tape-recorded what I often hear from my bedroom window when Mr. Rafferty has one of his work-night parties. The recording on this cassette I brought today was made from a tape-recorder placed on the ledge of my bedroom window at 1:30 a.m. on a weekday morning in July. I am playing it at the same loudness that I hear when trying to get to sleep. You can clearly make out the shouting and the loud music."* [With permission of mediator, she now plays the tape.]

Lease Dispute: *Mr. Nehru: "Here's a copy of my company's lease with Ms. Sherman, and here's a copy of my letter to her written two months after we vacated the building, requesting the prompt return of the security deposit."*

Business Ownership Dispute: *Mike: "We've been unable to keep any chief cook employed in our restaurant for more than six months at a time because they always end up having problems with Ted. Here are resignation letters from two of them, in which they clearly state that they are leaving because they find it too difficult to work with him."*

The mediator will look at any documents and other evidence you present, then pass them to the other side to view. Because the floor is still yours, the other party will usually not be allowed to comment or ask questions at this time. To avoid interrupting your presentation, the mediator will also probably hold major questions or comments about your evidence until later.

e. Do Not Conclude Your Opening Statement With a Demand

When you have finished explaining your version of the dispute, stop talking. Resist the urge to conclude with a strong demand, such as, "I insist Mr. Rafferty not have any guests in his backyard after 10 p.m. or I will call the police."

Making a demand or proposing a solution at this stage not only risks needlessly annoying the other party, but it also locks you into a settlement demand you may wish to change later. Better to find out what the other side wants and is willing to give up before you reveal what you want. As the mediation proceeds, you may learn that you could have asked for more—and gotten it.

f. What to Do If Your Lawyer Is Present

Unless a case involves complicated legal issues or lots of money, you won't need to bring a lawyer to mediation. If you do decide to bring a lawyer, you will probably want to do most of the talking yourself and have the lawyer advise you about the legal implications of proposed settlement terms. If your case raises complicated legal issues, you could have the lawyer share the opening statement with you. You could start by stating the facts of the dispute; then the lawyer could present the legal theory on which you base your position. Finally, you could explain how the dispute has affected you personally.

g. Making an Impression on Your Mediator

In theory, what your mediator thinks of you as a person should not affect the outcome of the mediation. After all, the mediator doesn't have the power of a judge, so personal likes or dislikes should not enter into the picture. This is why parties to a mediation are best served by focusing on the other party—not on the mediator—as they make their opening statement and participate in negotiations.

However, mediators may sometimes be influenced in their work by their personal impressions of the disputants. A mediator who sees you as reasonable and reliable will take your position seriously. A mediator who clearly understands your point of view will also be better able to help the other party see where you're coming from, if this opportunity comes up in a private caucus. And as part of the caucus process, the mediator may share impressions of you and your case with the other party. If the mediator understands the strength of your position and convinces the other party that you would make a strong adversary in court, this might encourage the other party to agree to a compromise.

⚠ Sometimes, the mediator has the legal power to influence the decision. In some states, when judges refer particular kinds of cases to mediation, the mediator has some legal authority to influence the judge's ultimate decision if mediation is unsuccessful. In California, for example, where divorcing couples are required to mediate child custody and support issues, the mediator may recommend how the judge should decide these issues if the parties can't agree. Or, if you are participating in "med-arb" (a hybrid process that combines mediation and arbitration; see Chapter 1, Section D, for more information), the mediator will decide the issues as an arbitrator if the parties cannot reach an agreement. If your mediator has the legal power to influence the outcome of your dispute, you will obviously want to work very hard to impress the mediator with your sincerity, your integrity, and the strength of your case.

h. What the Mediator Is Up To

Some mediation participants feel that no one (outside their family and closest friends) has ever listened to them quite as attentively as the mediator does during their opening statement. These mediators are doing a good job demonstrating, through gestures, facial expressions, and body language, concern both about the facts of your problem and about your emotional reaction to it. This is called "empathic listening," an important skill mediators draw upon to help build trust and maintain control of the mediation.

Don't dismiss your mediator as a phony. Just as some people are put off by therapists, some mediation participants have a negative reaction to a mediator's effort to convey interest and concern. Here is our advice: Give the process a chance. Although occasionally a mediator will come across as being just a little too sincere, the great majority have an honest desire to help people solve problems. Even if your mediator's style doesn't quite work for you, it might work for the other party—and therefore, create greater possibilities for settlement.

In addition to listening attentively, the mediator should also be ready to help you tell your story. For example, if—like many disputants under the pressure of making a statement—you stumble on one or more details of your story or mix up names or dates, the mediator should ask some clarifying questions to straighten things out. Sometimes the mediator accomplishes this by summarizing what you have covered, which gives you the chance to make any needed corrections or additional points.

2. The Other Side's Opening Statement

When the other party makes an opening statement, your job is to listen carefully. You will often hear things about your dispute that you didn't know, such as a fact you weren't aware of or the other party's emotional reaction to your conduct. You might also hear some clues about the type of settlement the other party might accept.

a. Do Not Interrupt

Keeping quiet and calm may not be easy, especially if the other party is prone to exaggeration or just plain lying. Perhaps it will be easier to refrain from interrupting if you remember three things. First, you're not in court, where the judge has the power to make a decision based on misinformation. Second, the mediator will have lots of experience dealing with people who exaggerate or lie. And third, you will have a chance to say whatever you want during your uninterrupted time. Make a note of the statement that upsets you and raise it later if it still seems important.

b. Listen for Wants and Needs

In Chapter 5, we noted the importance of understanding the difference between "wants" and "needs." Your wants are the positions you've staked out—for example, a demand for a sum of money, the right to live in a rental house, or getting your old job back. Your needs are your underlying interests, such as emotional and economic security, respect and recognition, avoiding needless expense, aggravation, or stress, and maintaining important relationships. As we noted, people's needs are often different from, and easier to satisfy than, their wants.

During the other party's opening statement, try to differentiate between wants and needs. For example, your business partner may insist on being named president of the company; this want reflects a need for power and recognition. Or, a bank officer may demand (want) that you pay a loan back immediately, but what the bank "needs" is to make a profit and protect its assets. Even if you agree to pay the loan back gradually, its needs will be met.

The point of trying to distinguish between wants and needs is simple. If you can see past the other side's stated "wants" and instead focus on underlying "needs," you may be able to think of alternative ways of satisfying everyone and ending your dispute in a mutually satisfactory way.

c. Look for Bargaining Chips and Opportunities

By listening carefully to the other party's opening statement, you may also discover some bargaining chips you didn't know you had. Your opponent may, for example, refer to a problem or dispute separate from the one you are discussing. Your first reaction may be to get angry, because you are now faced with another "unfair" accusation. This would be a mistake. Far better to treat the new subject as an opportunity. For example, you may find that the new issue involves something you can easily eliminate or control, and therefore is a perfect trade for an issue you care more about. In short, you've picked up a bargaining chip that may be useful later in the mediation.

Neighbor Dispute: *Mr. Rafferty: "You know, I would like to feel I can enjoy my own yard without having neighbors rushing to call the cops the second things get a little loud. And if she's so concerned about being a good neighbor, why doesn't she keep her dog on a leash like she's supposed to, and out of everyone's trash?" [Possible bargaining chips for Ms. Ferraro include a promise not to call police without advance warning, and a promise to leash her dog.]*

Lease Dispute: *Ms. Sherman: "I have no interest in withholding a tenant's security deposit if I'm not entitled to it. It doesn't do me any good to have my former tenants running around this town badmouthing me." [Here, a possible bargaining chip for Mr. Nehru might be to promise not to discuss the dispute with other business owners.]*

Business Ownership Dispute: *Ted: "I thought when we got into this business I could help out my sister's husband by buying our imported cheese from him. But because of all the problems between Mike and me our business has been extremely uneven—do you know how embarrassing it is to continually place and then cancel cheese orders from my own brother-in-law? Instead of helping him out, I've actually ended up costing him money!" [A possible bargaining chip for Mike in trying to get Ted to sell him back his stock in the restaurant would be an agreement to have the restaurant continue to buy imported cheese from Ted's brother-in-law.]*

You should always be listening for new information—and not just to discover bargaining chips. Sometimes, you might learn something that causes you to rethink your own position. Look for these openings and use them as a path to compromise.

C. Stage Three: Discussion

After opening statements are concluded, your mediator will likely move the mediation into a discussion stage, during which you and the other party can start talking directly to each other. The starting point for the discussion is often a comment one disputant wants to make about something the other said during the opening statement.

Neighbor Dispute: *Ms. Ferraro: "Mr. Rafferty, I don't know where you got the idea that I have a reputation in the neighborhood for being a complainer, but I can tell you that's just not true. I'm a quiet person and mind my own business. Since I moved into my house five years ago, you are the first person who has given me any reason to complain about anything."*

There is a tendency for things to get out of hand during these early stages of discussion, so the mediator will be working hard to keep the discussion under control. The mediator may have to remind one or both of you not to use uncivil language or make personal attacks. Beginning at this stage, your mediator will likely use one or more of the following techniques to control and advance the mediation:

- **Investigation:** In considering the evidence and statements of each party, the mediator might find information that demonstrates potential holes in a party's argument. For example, in a dispute over property rights, by examining a map brought by one of the disputants, the mediator may discover an error in measurement that casts new light on the position of the complaining party.

- **Empathy:** By showing a willingness to hear and discuss matters that concern the parties (even if those issues are not technically relevant to the dispute), the mediator builds trust and helps engender a cooperative attitude. For example, in a case where the president of a subsidiary of a large conglomerate terminated an employee, the mediator could listen patiently as both the president and the former employee complain about heavy-handed tactics used by the parent company.

- **Persuasion:** Slowly at the beginning, then more intensively as the session progresses, the mediator may encourage disputants to embrace one or more possible terms for settlement. During private caucus, for example, the mediator may say, "John, I can't tell you what to do, but I think this plan will satisfy many of the needs you've expressed." You are more likely to see this technique used by a mediator who has a more evaluative approach to mediation, as opposed to a mediator who seeks to facilitate the parties' ability to arrive at their own agreement. (For more on mediator styles and philosophy, see Chapter 3, Section D.)

- **Distraction:** The mediator may try to relieve tension during the session by use of humor, anecdotes, or just plain diversion. "You know," the mediator might say, "this reminds me of a story...."

- **Invention:** If no workable options for settlement emerge from the disputants, the mediator may propose some of his own. As with "persuasion," you are more likely to see this technique from a mediator who takes an evaluative approach to the job.

1. How the Mediator Organizes the Issues

Once things are on a fairly even keel, your mediator may attempt to put the issues in some kind of order. A common practice is to tackle the easiest ones first. This helps build up the disputants' confidence in the mediation process and in their own ability to address their dispute in a reasonable and productive way.

Lease Dispute: *Mediator: "Well, from everything you two have told me, it sounds like we need to focus on this question of whether United Tea should be repaid the $7,000 given to Ms. Sherman's real estate firm as a security deposit. Ms. Sherman says employees of United Tea damaged the reception area of the office, and therefore some or all of the deposit should be used for cleaning and repairs. Before we talk about that, however, let's see if you both can agree about the condition in which United Tea left the other rooms in the space it rented."*

Often, your mediator will try to narrow the number of issues in dispute. For example, the mediator may probe to see if any complaints discussed in the opening statements can be dismissed because they are no longer relevant or were based on misinformation. (If so, it will be easier now to focus on the other issues.) On the other hand, the mediator will also try to figure out whether any of the issues raised need to be broadened to include underlying issues—such as hidden interpersonal conflicts—not disclosed by the parties.

HOW THE MEDIATOR LOOKS FOR HIDDEN ISSUES

Often, disputants do not reveal an important issue to the mediator, either because they do not want to or because they honestly do not recognize it. In disputes between business partners, for example, it is often easier for the parties to focus on "nuts and bolts" business matters like sales, profits, and control of decision making than it is to examine underlying issues such as personal habits and styles, career goals, personal financial needs, self-image, recognition outside the company, or pride.

Through gentle but direct questioning and careful listening, a skilled mediator can often find clues to these types of underlying issues. For example, in one dispute between co-authors of an Italian cookbook over who owned several key recipes, it didn't take long for the mediator to figure out that one side needed money and the other side had money. Even though the parties were convinced that they were arguing over the principle of who developed the secret recipe for killer garlic bread, it turned out that a little cash moving from one to the other made the problem disappear.

In neighborhood disputes, particularly, there are often hidden issues. For example, in our neighborhood case, if Mr. Rafferty (who hosts the pool parties) hadn't mentioned the concern he has with Ms. Ferraro's unleashed dog in his opening statement, the problem nevertheless might have been festering in the background, waiting for a skilled mediator to discover it through active listening. In that case, the mediator might ask the parties about their relationship as neighbors, or ask whether there are any other issues either would like to raise.

2. Your Chance to Question the Other Side

You probably feel that the other party failed to address some important issues—or answer some of your questions—in the opening statement. Although your general mediation strategy should be to tell the story from your point of view and not worry too much about the other side's "misstatements," you may have important questions. If so, this is the time to ask them.

When both opening statements are complete, most mediators will ask if either party has questions or wants to clarify any point. But because some mediators skip this step, be prepared to speak up if you want to ask questions.

Neighbor Dispute: *Ms. Ferraro: "There's something I don't understand, Mr. Rafferty—when I called your home to complain about the noise, why didn't you show me the courtesy of taking the call yourself and talking with me about the problem of a few out-of-control guests? Instead, you let one of your guests handle it. If you didn't want me to call the police, I don't see why you did this.*

During this give and take, listen carefully to the other party. Just as you did during the opening statement, try to discern from the discussion what her real needs are and what she is seeking from mediation.

3. Calling Witnesses

In most mediations, there is no need for witnesses. The facts may be in dispute, but proving who's right and who's wrong is not what mediation is about. However, there are some situations in which a witness's attendance will be helpful, such as when the other party denies crucial facts and the mediation isn't likely to progress until they are established. For example, you may need to establish the cause of an electrical fire in your home (witness: consulting electrician) or the seriousness of injuries you received in an automobile accident (witness: physician). As noted in Chapter 5, Section C, you do not always need to bring a "live" witness; sometimes, a letter, memo, or report from the person will do the job. If you have any of these documents, you should present them as you tell your story in your opening statement.

Many mediators ask the witnesses to wait outside the room during opening statements. During the discussion stage, the mediator will call them back in and, in the presence of both parties, invite them to tell what they know about the dispute. As the disputants were allowed to make their opening statements without interruption, so the witnesses will be given a chance to say what they came to say:

Neighbor Dispute: *Mr. Rafferty's Witness: "I was at the party in July where Mr. Rafferty's neighbor says she called to complain about the noise and that people were rude to her. But you should have heard how nasty she was when she called and some of the language she used. I'm not going to repeat it here. If she'd asked us nicely to turn down the music we would have. But when someone starts off by calling you a bleep, well, forget it. The point is that most of the folks at the party—we all work together—are not the kind of people who would purposely disturb someone. She's got the wrong idea about us."*

If you have any questions of the witnesses, you can usually ask them directly. The mediator may ask a few questions, too. After that, the mediator will probably tell the witnesses that they can go home. Unlike witnesses in court, who are sometimes asked to wait around just in case someone wants to recall them to the stand, witnesses in mediation are allowed to leave. The rest of the session focuses exclusively on the disputants and possible solutions to their problem, not on rehashing the facts underlying the dispute.

D. Stage Four: The Caucus

At this point in the session, most mediators take advantage of one of mediation's truly distinctive features: the private caucus. During the private caucus, the mediator will ask questions, share impressions of the strengths and weaknesses of both sides' arguments, and kick around settlement ideas, all with an eye towards bringing the parties closer to a compromise.

1. Purpose and Procedure

The caucus is a private meeting between you and the mediator, during which the mediator can talk with you more informally and candidly than if the other side were present. Some mediators consider it "the guts" of the mediation process, because they use it to do most of the business of working out a settlement. During the caucus with each side, the mediator may discuss the strengths and weaknesses of your position and the other party's position, and float new ideas for settlement. The mediator may caucus with each of the parties just once, or several times back and forth.

As discussed earlier, most mediators and mediation services use caucuses, but there are notable exceptions. These are principally in divorce and some community mediations, on the theory that the disputants are likely to be so distrustful of each other that it is better to keep them together so they always know what each is saying to the mediator. Some mediators don't use caucuses to mediate any dispute in which the parties will have an ongoing relationship; they believe that staying in joint session provides opportunities to improve communication, which will prove valuable long after the mediation ends.

To begin caucusing, the mediator will ask one party to leave the room and wait in the reception area while the mediator meets alone with the other party. Or, the mediator may ask one party to move into a second conference room, and the mediator will shuttle back and forth from one room to the other, meeting separately with each side.

During the caucus, your mediator may assume a more relaxed posture—and may step over the line of strict impartiality just a little, to convey concern about your situation and hope that a solution can be found. By openly empathizing with the parties, the mediator continues to win their trust and maintain control over the mediation.

Neighbor Dispute: *Mediator to Ms. Ferraro: "Well, I can see you've been under tremendous stress because of this situation. I really hope we can find a positive way to solve this problem so that you can get some sleep."*

2. Confidentiality

Generally, most mediators will not repeat anything you say in caucus to the other side unless you expressly okay it. For example, if the mediator is using the caucus to try to help you craft a compromise offer, the background chat won't be communicated to the other side, but—with your permission—the offer will be. If the mediator has not made this policy clear in the opening statement or when the first caucus begins, ask what the policy will be so you are clear about it before the caucus begins. (Some mediators take the opposite approach—they assume that they can share anything you say with the other side, unless you expressly request confidentiality—so be sure to check on your mediator's policy.)

Typically, the mediator will caucus with each side several times during the course of mediation. In a relatively simple two-party mediation—for example, involving an auto accident or dispute between two business people—it would be typical for a mediator to caucus two or three times with each side during a half-day mediation. A mediation that lasts a full day may involve three to five caucuses with each side. But there is no rule on this. The frequency of caucusing depends entirely on the mediator's style and assessment of whether the caucusing process is moving the parties closer to settlement.

3. The Mediator's Strategy

During the caucus, the mediator will probably challenge your attitudes and positions, probe to find additional facts, and seek out your underlying interests and your bottom line. The mediator may even point out some weaknesses in your case in order to create some doubt in your mind and help you bring your expectations in line with reality. However, the mediator should not ridicule you or find fault with your past behavior.

The mediator will also try to translate what the other side is trying to tell you into language you can more easily understand. For example, if the other party spoke mostly in jargon or euphemisms, the mediator during caucus may tell you in plain words what the person seems to be saying.

Business Ownership Dispute: *Mediator, in caucus, to Ted: "Ted, I think what I've heard Mike say this morning is that he doesn't think it's possible for him to remain in business with you any longer, but he is willing to sell his share in the business, or buy yours, for a reasonable price."*

Here are some of the strategies mediators commonly use to move the parties closer to a settlement.

a. Challenging Your Position

To help you arrive at a solution to your dispute, your mediator has to get both parties to change their positions (or simply to see that their positions don't really conflict). One way to do this is to question the correctness or wisdom of the position you expressed in your opening statement. The mediator's questions will be designed to make you wonder if you are being realistic about your case. For example:

- "Do you think someone who didn't know you would think that you were entirely without fault in this dispute?"

- "If this case went to trial, is it realistic to think a jury would find the other side 100% at fault?"

- (To Ms. Ferraro in the neighbor dispute): "I know Mr. Rafferty was not living behind you when you bought your house, but did you know the house behind you had an outdoor pool fairly near your house?"

- (To Mr. Nehru in the lease dispute): "According to the strict wording of the lease you signed for this office space, doesn't the landlord get to decide how much of the security deposit should be returned?"

- (To Mike in the business ownership dispute): "I know you feel Ted's involvement has prevented the pizza restaurant from being successful. Have you ever run a business successfully on your own?"

Don't get too upset if the mediator challenges your version of events or your position. The other party is surely getting the same treatment in the conference room next door. And the answers you and the other party give to the mediator's questions may help you to evaluate your case more realistically—and move toward settlement.

b. Giving You a Reality Check

Your mediator may also play the "agent of reality." In this role, the mediator will point out the likely consequences of holding firm to your present position. Mediators usually do this by asking questions rather than making statements. Expect to hear questions like these:

- "If the other side were to agree to your last proposal, how workable do you think that plan would be in the long run?"

- "How much time and money are you likely to spend in this dispute if you can't settle it in mediation?"

- (To Mr. Nehru in the lease dispute): "What happens when customers, job applicants, and others go to your former office address and can't find you?"

- (To Ms. Ferraro in the neighbor dispute): "If Mr. Rafferty sold his house tomorrow, do you think the new owners might use their pool on warm evenings?"

Again, one possible response to your mediator's efforts to give a reality check is to get angry. After all, the mediator is asking you questions you don't want to answer or giving you feedback you don't want to hear. A more positive response is to accept and take advantage of your mediator's role. After all, the mediator has loads more experience in settling disputes than you do, and this feedback, whether in the form of questions or advice, is likely to be sensible.

One good approach is to come right out and ask your mediator for a reality check: "Am I on solid ground here? Is there some aspect of this problem I'm not seeing clearly?"

c. Creating Settlement Options

An important part of the mediator's job is to help you think of new ways to resolve your dispute. People caught up in a conflict often get stuck seeing it from only one perspective. Ask your mediator, "Are there possible ways of solving this mess that I'm not thinking of?" To help you move off the dime, your mediator might ask you questions like these:

- "How would you really like to see this dispute resolved, from a practical perspective?"

- "If you were in the other person's shoes, what sort of solution would you propose?"

- "What are some ways of settling this dispute that would be fair to you and to the other side?"

- "Can you think of a solution to which you and the other side might agree?"

- [To Ted in the business ownership dispute] "As an exercise, let's see how many different ways of dividing or breaking up this business we can think of. Can you help me come up with a list of ten different ways?"

Good mediators are skilled at creating new options. Here are some techniques your mediator may use to bring you closer to a resolution.

- **Compromise.** It's a simple and obvious approach, but a mediator who has won the trust of both parties may be able to settle a dispute merely by encouraging each to move a little toward the middle.

Neighbor Dispute: *Mediator to Ms. Ferraro: "Closing up his pool at 10 p.m. is a little early for Mr. Rafferty, and keeping it open on weeknights until midnight is clearly too late for you. Could we compromise and say on weeknights the pool will close at 11 p.m.?"*

- **What If.** Closely related to the compromise approach, a mediator might ask you if you would agree to a particular resolution if the other side would agree.

Lease Dispute: *Mediator: "Mr. Nehru, what if Ms. Sherman were to give you a check today for half of the security deposit? Would you be willing to walk away from this whole dispute and call it even?"*

- **Apology.** The mediator might persuade one party to provide a verbal or written apology to the other for past conduct. This is most often effective in disputes involving an interpersonal relationship, particularly where there was a power imbalance between the parties, such as between a large corporation and an individual employee. It also can be effective in a dispute between neighbors.

Neighbor Dispute: *Mediator to Mr. Rafferty: "Ms. Ferraro might be more willing to agree to a reasonable compromise if you would offer her a sincere apology for the some of the things your friends said to her when she called your house."*

- **Make an Exception.** One party agrees to make an exception to its normal policy, with the understanding that it will not apply to other people who were not involved in the mediation and that the terms of the settlement will be kept confidential. This can work well where one party is willing to bend the rules in order to get a settlement but does not want to face similar actions from other potential disputants. For example, a utility company facing a complaint from a homeowner over location of its poles and wires might be willing to move the poles to settle this case, as long as other homeowners are not told about it.

• **Go Beyond the Contract.** In order to create a "win-win" solution for both sides, the parties might agree to create additional benefits for each other—or "expand the pie"—by doing things that were never planned in their original contract. This technique can also be applied to situations where there is no formal contract. In our neighborhood dispute case, for example, Mr. Rafferty might be able to "expand the pie" by occasionally inviting Ms. Ferraro and her boyfriend to use his pool.

EXPANDING THE PIE: AN EXAMPLE

A small company was hired by a large defense contractor to make parts for a new armored vehicle. The small company made the parts, but the big company rejected them, saying they did not conform to the contract. Executives of the small company thought the parts were just fine, and were angry. Not only had they spent a lot of money to make the parts, but now they were losing a major customer. Feeling cheated, the small company sued the big company for $6 million. After many months, the two firms agreed to mediate.

After several sessions over a two-week period, the two companies got within $200,000 of settling the case, but just couldn't close the gap. Then the mediator proposed a solution: the big company would give the small company a new contract to make a different type of part. If the parts were made correctly, the profit for the small company would exceed $200,000. Executives of both firms wrote thank you notes to the mediator, who effectively had helped them "expand the pie."

• **Staged Agreement.** A settlement made up of a series of small steps can create a sense of security among parties who initially do not trust each other. For example, "Mr. Rafferty will begin immediately to close his pool each weekday by 11 p.m. If, for a period of 30 days starting today, Ms. Ferraro is not disturbed after 11 p.m. on weeknights by noise from Ms. Rafferty's pool, Ms. Ferraro will not call police in the event she is again disturbed by noise, but instead will first call Mr. Rafferty directly to inform him of the problem. Mr. Rafferty will come to the phone himself if Ms. Ferraro calls."

- **Interim Agreement.** The parties agree to try something for a few weeks or months and to meet again at a future date to evaluate the results. For example, a divorcing couple who cannot agree on a visitation schedule for the noncustodial parent may agree to try a plan for six months, and then meet again with the mediator to evaluate how it is working for each of them and their children.

Neighbor Dispute: *Mediator to Mr. Rafferty: "I don't think Ms. Ferraro is ready yet to give up her right to call the police. She's been too disturbed too often. What we need is to rebuild some trust between you. If we can agree that you will try to control the noise from your pool for, say, three weeks, and then we'll meet again to see how it went, that experience may allow us to move ahead to a permanent agreement. Would you be willing to try it?"*

- **Partial Settlement.** The parties settle what they can and leave the rest for later. Although similar to the interim agreement strategy, here the disputants make a partial settlement and decide to put the rest of their dispute "on hold" for a while. They agree that during the holding period they will not file lawsuits and will treat each other civilly. Later, they will meet with the mediator again to see if circumstances or their positions have changed in a way that might allow them to resolve the rest of the dispute.

Neighbor Dispute: *Mediator to Ms. Ferraro and Mr. Rafferty: "I'm glad we've been able to work out this matter of noise from Mr. Rafferty's pool. Unfortunately, the matter involving Ms. Ferraro's dog raises some issues that are going to take more time to resolve, and we have agreed to meet again in two weeks to discuss them further. In the meantime, Mr. Rafferty, you have agreed not to call Animal Control if you find Ms. Ferraro's dog loose in your yard, and Ms. Ferraro, you have agreed to try to restrain your dog from wandering in the neighborhood."*

4. Let the Mediator Negotiate for You

Mediators are trained to help people settle disputes. When a settlement occurs, the mediator has succeeded. When no solution is arrived at, the mediator has failed. This means that the mediator has a strong personal interest in getting a settlement. Take advantage of this by letting the mediator negotiate for you.

Here's how it can work. Assume you are Mr. Nehru in our lease dispute. You want at least $6,000 of the $7,000 security back from Ms. Sherman, the landlord. During caucus, tell your mediator you want $6,000 and that's it. No ifs, ands, or buts.

Lease Dispute: *Mr. Nehru to Mediator: "Look, I appreciate all your suggestions and will concede my people may have spilled some tea on the carpet. Ms. Sherman can keep $1,000 for damages but I want $6,000 back and I'm not leaving here with less. And I hope you will clearly tell her that!"*

Would you really refuse to accept anything less than $6,000? Maybe yes, maybe no. For the moment, you can keep that to yourself. But for now, $6,000 is the message you want to send to the other side, and if you're wise, you'll let the mediator carry it for you. The mediator will see that, in order to get a settlement, the other side will have to agree to pay you $6,000—or something very close to it. And the mediator will have to persuade the other side to do this.

Lease Dispute: *Mediator to Ms. Sherman: "Well, I've talked with Mr. Nehru and I'm glad to say we've got some movement on the damage issue. Although he's not conceding liability, he is willing to pay up to $1,000 for damages; is that something you can live with?"*

You can also use your mediator to float trial settlement balloons by posing your own "What if…" questions. Although you might not want to propose any settlement ideas directly to the other side (for fear of seeming too eager to settle), you can try the idea out on the mediator during caucus. If the mediator thinks it holds promise, the mediator can then present it to the other side as his or her own idea, not as your settlement proposal.

Lease Dispute: *Mr. Nehru to Mediator: "When you meet with Ms. Sherman again, ask her what she'd think of a package deal like this: She keeps the full damage deposit of $3,500, returns to me the $3,500 security, my people pick up the samples she's got in storage, and she agrees to post our company's new address in her office lobby for the next six months. Don't say directly that I'm proposing this, but just kind of float the idea and see what her reaction is."*

In this way, Mr. Nehru, has just proposed a comprehensive settlement package to Ms. Sherman, but Ms. Sherman may choose to believe it was the mediator's suggestion, not Mr. Nehru's idea. Moreover, the proposal will be presented to her by the mediator—whom she has come to trust, respect, and regard as impartial—thus increasing the chances she will give it favorable consideration.

E. Stage Five: More Joint Negotiations

At any point during the caucus process, your mediator may conclude that it would be more productive to bring the parties back into one room for another round of joint discussions.

1. Purpose and Procedure

If your mediation is making progress, it should begin to show now. After honest exchanges with the mediator during private caucuses, the parties should be focused on a narrower range of forward-looking issues. As you and the other party search for a workable settlement, your relationship may begin to change. For example, you might start working together more collaboratively, rather than seeing each other as adversaries.

Mediators often notice at this stage that the parties start using each other's first names.

If you and the other side are able to conduct your own negotiations, the mediator may decide to be quiet at this point, adding a suggestion or word of caution as necessary. Or, the mediator may be an active orchestrator of your negotiations, proposing new ideas for settlement and using information learned in private caucus to let you know when changes in bargaining positions might be helpful. If necessary, the mediator may call another round of private caucuses, or perhaps caucus with just one of you again.

During this stage, the mediator's goals will be:

- to keep the negotiations focused on the real issues in dispute.

Lease Dispute: *Mediator to Mr. Nehru and Ms. Sherman: "The question you're discussing—how efficient the Postal Service is at forwarding business mail—is interesting, but not within our ability to influence. Let's stay focused on the things we can do something about."*

- to help the parties confront any new issues that must be addressed before a settlement can be reached.

Neighbor Dispute: *Mediator to Mr. Rafferty: "This fence we've been talking about that separates your backyard from Ms. Ferraro's yard—did you just mention something about it protruding onto your property? Is that an issue we need to look at today?"*

- to make sure that the negotiations do not head towards an unworkable settlement (one that is likely to fall apart or be difficult to honor later). A settlement would be unworkable, for example, if requires a party to do something illegal or something that is not within the party's power.

EXAMPLE: *A company and former employee are mediating the employee's wrongful termination claim. The company offers to find the employee a new job at another firm. It's a nice offer, but probably unrealistic. The company owner can certainly try to help the employee find a new job, but can't guarantee success. A more sensible solution might be for the company to offer a letter of reference and outplacement assistance to help the employee find a job.*

DON'T RELY ON THE MEDIATOR TO BLOCK AN UNFAIR SETTLEMENT

Some mediators will try to discourage the parties from settling their dispute on terms that the mediator believes are clearly unfair to one side. In divorce mediation, particularly if one spouse appears to be overpowering the other psychologically or in terms of financial knowledge, many mediators will intervene against what they see as a highly one-sided settlement. (See Chapter 10 for more on divorce mediation.) Most mediators will also intervene against unfair settlements in disputes involving children. Indeed, in California, where the law requires divorcing parents to try to reach agreements about child custody and visitation through mediation, rules require such intervention.

But in disputes that don't involve family relationships, particularly business disputes, most mediators do not see their role as protecting one side or the other. Therefore, you should not rely on the mediator to protect you from making a bad bargain—it's up to you to protect yourself. One way to do this is by having a lawyer or other adviser review any settlement agreement before you sign it (see Chapter 7, Section E, for more on this safeguard).

---

2. Changing Your Negotiating Position

Sometimes, you will learn something during the mediation that makes you want to change your bargaining position. You might fear that you will lose face if you announce a major change in front of the other side. One way to solve this problem is to use the mediator to help you communicate the change. For example, in our neighbor dispute case, Ms. Ferraro had been insisting all along that her neighbor, Mr. Rafferty, adhere to strict "quiet hours" as set down by the Town's noise code. Later in the mediation, she realizes that it may advantageous to be a little more flexible in order to strike a deal with Mr. Rafferty. Because she usually stays at her boyfriend's on weekends, she doesn't really care about noise after the weekend noise curfew, but because she often has to get up early for work, she would love to see things quiet down a bit earlier on weeknights.

Neighbor Dispute: *Ms. Ferraro: "Well, the mediator has convinced me that the 'quiet hours' in the town's noise code that was written 80 years ago are a little unrealistic on Friday and Saturday evenings, so I'm not going to insist that you follow that law to the letter on weekends, but…."*

Make the mediator a scapegoat. Although it may seem unfair, it sometimes works well to blame last-minute changes of position on the mediator. ("The mediator's really pushing me on this and I'm just tired of fighting over it…") The mediator can take it; it's part of the job. A more positive way to achieve the same result is to credit the change in your position to the persuasive powers of the mediator.

3. Consult With Outside Advisers, If Necessary

In some types of disputes, you may want to have a lawyer, law coach, or other adviser on call during your mediation, so you can consult by telephone as needed. If you do have an advisor standing by, this is the time to check in and get some advice. For example, in our business ownership dispute, Ted, who is considering accepting a cash buyout offer for his stock from his partner, Mike, may want to step out of the mediation to call his accountant and find out what the tax consequences of the proposed plan might be.

Business Ownership Dispute: *Mike to mediator: "I need to take a break at this point. You know, I didn't really expect us to be talking today about a cash buyout, and I'd like to run the idea by my accountant before we discuss it further. There may be more or less beneficial ways to structure it from a tax point of view. I think I can probably reach him at his office. Is there a phone available where I can make a private call?"*

In disputes that involve lots of money or important legal rights, the parties should condition their agreement on a more thorough review of the legal, tax, and business consequences by their respective lawyers and other business advisers. But for now, getting at least an initial opinion from his accountant will probably be enough to help Ted decide whether he should continue negotiating a possible cash buyout of his stock. (For more on having your agreement reviewed before you sign, see Chapter 7, Section E.)

F. Stage Six: Closure

The final stage of mediation occurs when the parties reach an agreement that resolves the dispute—or decide, with the help of the mediator, that they are going to end the session without reaching an agreement. If an agreement is reached, the mediator will announce the agreement and review its terms with the parties, then (sometimes) the parties will sign the agreement or a memorandum that sets out the basic terms. If an agreement is not reached, the mediator announces this fact and ends the session. (For useful things you can do if your dispute does not settle in mediation, see Chapter 8.)

1. Reaching an Agreement on Terms

"Closure" in mediation occurs at the moment you and the other side say "yes" to a proposed agreement. Mediation sessions tend to speed up as this point nears. By now, disputants are speaking directly to each other and probably using first names. Everyone is intimately familiar with the issues, so a kind of shorthand language typically develops that helps move the discussion along quickly. The mediator is also more direct in proposing refinements to possible settlement terms.

Your mediator will also be listening carefully to detect the first instance when a package of terms for settlement emerges from your negotiations. When this occurs, the mediator will seize the moment by stopping the discussion and reviewing the tentative terms of settlement.

Neighbor Dispute: *Mediator: "Ms. Ferraro, Mr. Rafferty, if I'm hearing you both correctly, I think you have reached agreement on all the major issues. I've tried to write them down in a very rough format. Let me read them to you and you tell me if I have it straight:*

"On the noise issue, Mr. Rafferty is willing to turn off any amplified sound, including stereos and radios, in his backyard by 10 p.m. on weeknights and by midnight on weekends, and will encourage his guests not to use the pool after 10:45 on weeknights and midnight on weekends. In the rare event this isn't possible, he will insist that they conduct themselves quietly.

"Ms. Ferraro, you will agree to call Mr. Rafferty directly, before calling the police, if you are disturbed again at night.

"On the dog issue, Mr. Rafferty agrees to call Ms. Ferraro directly, before calling police or animal control officers, if he thinks her dog has disturbed his trash barrels, soiled his lawn, or in any other way disturbed his property. For her part, Ms. Ferraro has agreed to buy Mr. Rafferty one dog-proof trash container; if replacement or additional containers are needed, Mr. Rafferty agrees to buy these at his own expense."

Lease Dispute: *Mediator: "I'm pleased to tell you both that in caucus each of you has told me you will agree to the same settlement terms. These include: 1) Ms. Sherman will return to United Tea $4,000, keeping $3,000 to cover damage to the office space, 2) United Tea employees may have access to the building next Thursday and Friday to remove product samples left in storage, 3) Ms. Sherman will post, in the building's lobby, a prominent notice showing United Tea's new address and phone, for a period of six months, and 4) none of the parties nor their employees will discuss with anyone outside their respective companies the nature of this dispute or the terms of its settlement."*

Business Ownership Dispute: *Mediator: "Mike, Ted, I believe we have an agreement here. Ted, you have agreed to sell all of your stock in Big Slice Pizza, Inc., back to the company in exchange for an immediate lump-sum payment of $70,000, plus 8% of company gross revenues in the next fiscal year beginning October 1. Mike, you have agreed to lend the company $50,000 to allow it to make the cash payment to Ted. You have also agreed to prepare a contract to Ted's satisfaction under which Big Slice Pizza will agree, for a period of three years beginning October 1, to buy all its imported cheese at market rates as quoted weekly in the 'Cheese World' price sheet from Pure Cheese, Inc., a company owned by Ted's brother-in-law."*

Although the mediators in these three disputes may be acting as if these are the final agreements, they are actually still testing the terms to make sure that both parties really agree, and that they will be workable in the long run. They are also trying to make sure that there are no underlying issues, not mentioned in their recaps, that could cause the agreement to unravel.

Before the mediation goes further, carefully evaluate how satisfied you would be with the tentative terms of settlement. Just because the terms have been announced, you don't have to accept them. If the mediator didn't get it right, or if you just have second thoughts, say so. One good way to deal with doubts or worries is to request a caucus with the mediator to give yourself a chance to talk over the proposed terms and how they would affect you.

⚠️ **Never agree to things that you can't—or aren't willing to—do.** If the proposed terms don't look right to you, now is the time to say so. Don't wait until the agreement is in writing and everyone is standing around waiting for you to sign your name. At that point, the compulsion to sign may be too great, and you might end up signing an agreement you don't believe in.

If you need a face-saving excuse to change your mind about some of the settlement terms, you can:

- blame it on the mediator ("I didn't understand that this is what the mediator was proposing")

- say you need to review it with your lawyer

- say you need to review it with another adviser, such as an accountant, member of the clergy, or trusted friend.

Once the mediator hears the parties say "okay" to the proposed terms, the deal is set. The mediator will mark the occasion by saying something like "We have an agreement." Congratulations!

2. Ask to Have the Agreement Reviewed Before You Sign

It is always a good idea to put your mediation agreement in writing. And it's absolutely essential if the terms are fairly complicated, as is often the case in business ownership, child custody, and employment disputes. A good written agreement:

- clarifies the decisions, intentions, and future behavior of the parties

- provides a permanent record of your agreement

- exposes issues that might be overlooked if not for the discipline of putting them in writing, and

- encourages compliance with the agreement.

(For more on the importance of written agreements—and tips on writing your own—see Chapter 7.)

In some minor consumer cases or interpersonal disputes, like our neighbor dispute example, your mediator may offer to draft the agreement while you wait, and you and the other party can both sign it before you leave. But in more complicated cases, it will take some time and work by both parties (and possibly their lawyers or advisors) to get the language of an agreement just the way both sides want it. For example, an agreement over who can use a trademark must be prepared in a way that complies with U.S. Patent & Trademark Office rules. And if an agreement between businesses involves potentially serious tax consequences, the parties will want a tax advisor to review it. Similarly, if your dispute involves business contracts, property, or important legal rights, you should probably not sign the agreement until you have it reviewed by a lawyer, law coach, or other business advisor.

Tell the mediator and the other party that you are pleased to have reached an agreement and that it looks fine to you, but you want a couple of days to run it by a lawyer or other adviser. You are entirely within your rights to make this request. The mediator will probably respond by offering to write an outline of the main terms of the agreement, giving each of you a copy and retaining the original. In the next chapter, we will discuss how your mediated agreement should be structured and drafted, how to have it reviewed by an advisor, what to do if you want to change it, and when and where you should sign it. ■

CHAPTER 7

Write an Agreement That Works

When an agreement is finally reached in mediation, it's fairly common for the participants to be worn out and just want to go home. Patience. You have one more major task—you need to put your agreement in writing. Even if your dispute was complicated and advisers will have to work out the details, you should still at least put an outline of it in writing before you leave the mediation table. In this chapter, we will explain how and when the agreement is written, what form it should take, and what it should include.

 If you did not reach a settlement in mediation, skip to Chapter 8, which outlines your options.

A. Why You Need a Written Agreement

A written agreement that spells out the parties' decisions, intentions, and promises for the future serves four important purposes:

- **It creates a permanent record.** A written agreement creates a permanent record, just in case you and the other party remember parts of the agreement differently. Anyone who has ever referred back to a lease, contract, or other written agreement knows just how tricky memory can be. Putting it in writing will guard against future memory lapses, intentional or otherwise.

- **It exposes overlooked issues.** Putting the terms of your agreement in writing may reveal issues or details that you overlooked during the mediation session. For example, if your business partner agrees to buy out your share of the business by making equal monthly payments over 32 months, you may realize only when you're writing the agreement that you haven't discussed how to handle late payments.

- **It encourages compliance.** When settlement terms are put in writing and signed in the presence of a mediator, disputants are far more likely to comply with them than if the agreement is left unwritten. It is customary for the mediator also to sign the agreement, a gesture that further encourages the parties to keep their word.

- **It allows the agreement to be enforced.** Mediation agreements are difficult, and often impossible, to enforce unless they are in writing. After all, if the other side disputes that a certain agreement was reached, how would you prove otherwise? The mediator will probably be prevented from testifying by confidentiality rules, so it will just be your word against the other party's. To make sure that your agreement can be enforced by a court, put it in writing.

DON'T LEAVE THE MEDIATION ROOM WITHOUT SOMETHING IN WRITING

If you've reached a settlement in your mediation, it's a mistake to leave drafting the agreement to another day, unless the settlement terms are so complex that an agreement can't be prepared on the spot. And even if your settlement is complicated, you should prepare an outline of all key points before you call it a day. Delay can be dangerous. Not only does it give the other side time to have second thoughts and possibly even be persuaded by others who were not at the session—such as friends and relatives—that the agreement is not in his or her best interest, but it also allows time for each party's memory to play tricks.

B. Ten Guidelines for Writing an Effective Agreement

Here are ten simple guidelines to keep in mind as you work with the other party and the mediator to draft your settlement agreement. Following these rules will help you produce a document that is understandable, thorough, and forward-looking.

1. Be an Active Participant

Whether your case is large or small, take an active role in helping to write your mediation agreement. You might volunteer to write the first draft of the agreement yourself—this will give you a great opportunity to make sure the agreement reflects your views. Even if you don't get to write the agreement, make sure to offer your two cents on what the agreement should include. It's a lot easier to influence the final agreement if you participate in the drafting than if you sit on the sidelines.

2. Use Plain English

In a mediation agreement, legalese should be kept to a minimum. You simply don't need to use incomprehensible gobbledygook like "the party of the first part stipulates to heretofore abrogate the prior stipulation of the parties annexed hereto as exhibit A." Far better to use plain English, such as this: "John will cancel the agreement that he and Bill signed earlier. A copy of that agreement is attached."

Here are examples of formal or legalistic terms that can easily be replaced by simpler words that are easier to understand.

Instead of	Use
abrogate	cancel
afford an opportunity	allow
apprise	inform
cease	stop
commitment	promise
communicate	write, telephone
demonstrate	show
desire	wish
effectuate	bring about
eliminate	remove, strike out
employment	work
endeavor	try
expiration	ending of
heretofore	earlier
locality, location	place
locate	find
objective	aim, goal
prior to	before
remuneration	pay, wages, salary, fee
reside	live
stipulate	agree
terminate	end
utilize	use

3. Identify People by Full Names

In writing the agreement, always use full names (first and last) rather than using the term "parties" or another legalistic word such as "the Claimant" or "the Respondent." It's true that we have had to violate this rule in this book, by referring to the people who participate in mediation as "the parties," but that's because we have been writing in the abstract, without real people in mind. When you write your settlement agreement, you will know the actual names of the people involved in the case. Use them. Real names, rather than terms like "the parties," make an agreement much easier to read and understand.

WRONG WAY: *The parties to this dispute have reached an agreement...*

RIGHT WAY: *Marla White and Bonnie Silverman agree...*

Similarly, when naming a business corporation, use the business's full name, such as Brannigan's Craft Centers, Inc. If a store has branches, name the specific branch involved in the dispute.

WRONG WAY: *Brannigan's will allow leaflets to be distributed to passersby in front of its main entrance...*

RIGHT WAY: *The Brannigan's Craft Centers store at 1140 Ridgeway Avenue will allow leaflets to be distributed...*

Another advantage to using full names rather than terms like "the parties" or even lots of pronouns like "him," "their," or "its," is that it makes each part of the agreement understandable on its own, if you ever need to discuss a provision separately.

WRONG WAY: *The piano store will let him exchange his piano...*

RIGHT WAY: *The Hilltop Mall branch of Locke's Pianos and Organs, Inc., will allow Richard Goldberg to exchange...*

4. Specify Dates

Be sure your agreement specifies precise dates when things should happen.

WRONG WAY: *The respondent, Mark Rothman, agrees to remove the rusted Chevy from his front lawn as soon as possible.*

RIGHT WAY: *Mark Rothman will remove the rusted Chevy from his front lawn by July 1, 2004.*

WRONG WAY: *The bonus to Susan Marshilock will be paid at the end of Southwest Saving's next fiscal year.*

RIGHT WAY: *The bonus to Susan Marshilock will be paid on or before October 30, 2004.*

5. Explain Who, What, When, Where, and How

To be clear and complete, your mediation agreement must cover every important aspect of your dispute and its resolution, beginning with the most basic issues: Who is involved in this dispute? What is the dispute about? Who is going to do what as part of resolving it? When are they going to do it? How are they going to do it? In short, the agreement (like a good news article) should answer the five key questions of who, what, when, where, and how.

EXAMPLE: *[Who] Locke's Pianos and Organs, Inc., will allow [who] Richard Goldberg to [what] exchange his Yamaha U-131 model console piano for any piano currently in stock of equal or greater value. The value of the Yamaha U-131 piano is $6,300. The exchange can be made [when] during regular business hours until August 4, 2004 [where] at Locke's main showroom, 1330 Washington Street, Heneson, Pennsylvania. [How] Locke's store manager, Suzannah Locke, will make herself available to help in the exchange.*

6. List Each Key Provision Separately

Your agreement will probably require each of you to do certain things. To keep the agreement clear and understandable, it's best to state each significant action in a separate, numbered paragraph. An agreement organized in this bite-sized way is far less likely to be misinterpreted than an agreement that's crammed into several long paragraphs. In addition, using single-subject numbered paragraphs makes it much easier to discuss problems in interpreting or living up to the agreement's provisions.

WRONG WAY: *The Turims agree to keep their dog confined to their house, and the Hershmans agree to instruct their children not to throw things into the dog's enclosed run. The dog will be enrolled in an obedience school and they will keep it confined when they're not home, and their children will not tease the dog.*

RIGHT WAY:

- *Larry and Amy Turim agree to begin immediately keeping their dog, Tammy, confined to the house after 6 p.m. if they are not at home.*
- *Larry and Amy Turim agree to enroll their dog, Tammy, in the Canine Obedience School of the Livingston County Humane Society for the next available program beginning after September 1, 2004 and to take the dog to each class of the program.*
- *Jacob and Marie Hershman agree to immediately instruct their children, Sarah and Valerie, not to tease the Turim's dog, Tammy, and particularly not to throw any items into the dog's enclosed run.*

7. Specify Method and Details of Any Payment

Many mediation agreements call for one person to pay money to the other. When this occurs, follow a simple rule: Spell out every detail.

Your agreement should state exactly who is to pay how much to whom, when, and in what form (check, money order, cash). If more than one payment is involved, the agreement should also say what will happen if a payment is missed. Will there be a late fee and interest on that installment? Will the whole debt become due, allowing the creditor to sue and get a judgment immediately?

> **Don't take a rubber check.** If you are dealing with a person or small business that may have trouble meeting its obligations, insist on payment by money order, certified bank check, or, if you are a business, credit card. This is standard business practice and shouldn't be a problem. On the other hand, if you are confident that the other party will pay, there's no need to insist on a money order or certified check (and it might even insult the other party).

WRONG WAY: *Ralph Edwards agrees to pay Frank Richardson the sum of $845.*

RIGHT WAY: *Ralph Edwards will pay to Frank Richardson the sum of $845 by money order or certified bank check sent by U.S. mail to Frank Richardson at 35 Eulalia Way, Coniston, South Dakota 57453, by February 3, 2005.*

8. Do Not Involve Third Parties in Payments

Some mediation agreements require one party to pay money to someone who wasn't involved in the mediation instead of paying the other party directly. (This type of arrangement is most common among people who don't want to have any personal contact with each other.) Usually, this approach is a mistake. If the money isn't paid, having a third-party payee may make it more difficult to enforce the agreement in court. Avoid complications by making sure your mediation agreement requires the party who owes money to pay it directly to the other by an appropriate means (by mail or in person).

WRONG WAY: *Garden Way Landscape Company agrees to pay $650 to any other landscape company Gerald Secor selects to do the work on his lawn.*

RIGHT WAY: *Garden Way Landscape Company agrees to return to Gerald Secor the sum of $650 by August 15, 2004.*

If you can't pay each other, pay the mediation service. If there is so much animosity between you and the other party that you suspect you might never get paid, the agreement can require the other party to pay the mediation service on your behalf. The mediation service will receive the funds and write a check to you for the same amount. (Of course, you should check with the mediation service to make sure it will agree to act as intermediary before you put this in your agreement.)

EXAMPLE: *Garden Way Landscape Co. agrees to pay Gerald Secor the sum of $650. This provision shall be satisfied by issuance of a corporate check, made payable to The Center for Dispute Settlement, Inc., and sent by U.S. mail to the Center, 87 North Clinton Ave., Rochester, NY 14604, by August 15, 2004.*

9. Omit Any Mention of Blame, Fault, or Guilt

One of the nicest things about settling a dispute via mediation is that, unlike court or arbitration procedures, it does away with any need to officially find fault. To keep this spirit alive, mediation agreements should never include statements that either party is "guilty," "has behaved immorally," or "has violated ethical standards." Not only does this help each party save face, it also makes it easier for the parties to have an ongoing relationship, if necessary. In addition, nonjudgmental wording makes it more likely that both parties will keep their promises going forward.

For example, even if it became clear during the mediation that the landlord let the plumbing break down and refused to fix it, the agreement should not state that the landlord was "lazy," "negligent," or even "wrong." Instead, the agreement should just spell out what the landlord agrees to do in the future.

WRONG WAY: *"Whereas Francis Riley, manager of the Seneca Tower Apartments, failed to keep the piping to the apartment of Mr. and Mrs. Lester Aggazis adequately insulated against freezing temperatures…"*

RIGHT WAY: *"Mr. Francis Riley, manager of the Seneca Tower Apartments, agrees to repair all piping necessary to the proper functioning of the bathtub, shower, sink, and toilet in the master bathroom of Apartment 7-C, occupied by Mr. and Mrs. Lester Aggazis. Mr. Riley agrees to complete these repairs by 5 p.m. on June 3, 2004. If plumbing problems recur in the future, Mr. Riley agrees to arrange for repair within 12 hours of being notified of the problem."*

Apologies are okay. Though words of blame do not belong in the agreement, a written apology for past conduct is often a key part of the settlement. In these cases, the apology must be included. For example, when a respectable middle-aged African-American man was falsely arrested for shoplifting, mediation with the store resulted in a cash settlement and a promise of a written apology from the store manager. Because the man would not have made the agreement without the promise of a written apology, it had to be either included in the agreement or prepared separately and referred to in the agreement.

10.   Guard Against Conflicts in Interpreting Mediation Agreements

Despite everyone's best efforts to draft a clear mediation agreement, it is always possible that a question will arise in the future about who was supposed to do what, or when. Or, the other party may fail to live up to his or her part of the agreement. How will these new disputes be resolved?

As you may have guessed, we think that the best way to handle any problems and avoid future lawsuits is to make the final provision of your agreement a mediation clause, in which everyone agrees to return to mediation if problems or new issues arise. It should clearly detail who will provide the mediation, the timing of the process, and how fees will be shared. Usually, it's most efficient to simply name the same mediator or mediation service that handled the original dispute; it will be easier for them to reopen the file than it would be for another mediator to start from scratch.

SAMPLE MEDIATION CLAUSE: *If any dispute arises out of, or relates to, this agreement or its performance, that Charles Washington and Everett Boyd cannot resolve through negotiation, Mr. Washington and Mr. Boyd agree to try to settle the dispute by mediation through the Minneapolis Mediation Network, Inc., before resorting to arbitration, litigation, or any other legal remedy. The costs of the mediation will be shared equally by Mr. Washington and Mr. Boyd.*

You may want to take the additional step of referring disputes that can't be settled through mediation to binding arbitration. This is done through a clause requiring mediation and arbitration as a two-step process. Agreeing to binding arbitration assures that the dispute will be resolved reasonably quickly and privately, one way or the other. However, arbitration is usually a win-lose proposition and you can never be absolutely sure if you will prevail.

SAMPLE MEDIATION CLAUSE:

[Step One: Mediation] *If a dispute arises out of, or relates to, this agreement or its performance, that Irina Sungren and Susan London cannot resolve through negotiation, Ms. Sungren and Ms. London agree to try to settle it by mediation at the Minneapolis Mediation Network, Inc., before resorting to arbitration, litigation, or any other legal remedy.*

[Step Two: Arbitration] *If the dispute is not resolved in mediation within 90 days of its referral to the Minneapolis Mediation Network, Inc., Ms. Sungren and Ms. London agree to submit it to binding arbitration by the American Arbitration Association, Inc., and agree that judgment upon the award made by the arbitrator may be entered in any court having jurisdiction.*

Fees for mediation and arbitration will be shared equally by Ms. Sungren and Ms. London.

C. Sample Agreements

On the following pages you'll find three agreements reached at actual mediations, with the disputants' names and other identifying information deleted or changed. These documents were selected both to show what an agreement might look like and to illustrate the broad range of disputes that can be mediated successfully.

1. Landlord/Tenant Dispute

In this case, the landlord of a residential apartment building threatened to sue a former tenant over property that was missing from the apartment after the tenant moved out. The missing items included doorknobs, curtains, and lamps. In mediation, the parties agreed on a list of items that the tenant would either return or pay for by a set date. For his part, the landlord agreed to return the tenant's collection of tapes, records, and CDs that the tenant had inadvertently left in the basement. The agreement was drafted with reciprocal promises to give it the effect of a legal contract. (For information on how to make a contract legally enforceable, see Section D, below.)

In the Matter of Mediation Between:

Judith Stevens

and   SETTLEMENT AGREEMENT

Seymour Wilson (Wilson Prop. Mangmt, Inc.)

Case Number: C-111-94

Under the Rules and Procedures of The Center for Dispute Settlement, Inc., Judith Stevens and Seymour Wilson (for Wilson Property Management, Inc.) agree that the following provisions fully resolve all the claims they submitted to mediation on July 3, 2004.

1. Ms. Judith Stevens, formerly a tenant at Bedford Street Apartments, owned by Wilson Property Management, Inc., will return no later than July 22, 2004 to Mr. Seymour Wilson of Wilson Property Management, Inc., the following articles: two doorknobs, door plate, kitchen curtains and rod, bath and back bedroom rods, four draw drape rods, one extension cord, and two ice trays. Ms. Stevens will telephone Mr. Wilson at 555-3321 to arrange a convenient time and place for delivery.

2. Ms. Stevens will pay a total of $174 to Wilson Property Management, Inc., for the following items that were broken or are missing from the apartment:

$26.00	Security lock
43.00	Kitchen light fixture
24.00	Bedroom light fixture
66.00	Miniblinds from study
15.00	Smoke alarm
$174.00	Total to be paid

Ms. Stevens will pay the $174 as follows: $40 per month beginning August, 2004 by money order mailed by the 10th of the month to: Mr. Wilson, 280 South Hollywood Drive, Apt. 1, Rochester, NY 14620. The fourth and final monthly payment will be for the amount of $54.00.

3. Mr. Wilson will consider that all possible legal claims that he might have against Ms. Stevens concerning her being a tenant at the Bedford Street Apartments have been settled if she delivers to him as promised all the items in paragraph 1 and also pays him the amounts in paragraph 2.

4. Upon satisfactory return of all items named above and payment of all amounts due, Mr. Wilson will release the tape, record, and CD collection belonging to Ms. Stevens, and arrange with her a date and time when she can collect these items from the offices of Wilson Property Management, Inc.

If any dispute arises out of this agreement or its performance that Ms. Stevens or Mr. Wilson cannot resolve themselves, they will try to settle the dispute by mediation through the Center for Dispute Settlement, Inc.

Judith Stevens

Judith Stevens

Seymour Wilson

Seymour Wilson

Eva Marie Peterson

Mediator

2. Neighborhood Dispute

The next dispute concerns two families, the Bertlesons and the McKays, who are next-door neighbors. Each family has small children. At one time the families were quite friendly, but during the course of one summer tension developed between them. Helen and Arthur McKay complained that Melinda Bertleson's three children (she is a single mother) often came into their yard uninvited to use their play equipment, and left clothes, food wrappers, toys, and other items in the yard, and also that the cars of Ms. Bertleson's house guests often blocked their driveway. For her part, Ms. Bertleson complained that the McKays had made verbal threats against her and her visitors. When the McKays finally called the police to have parked cars removed from the end of their driveway, the responding officer encouraged both sides to consider mediation at the local community mediation center. They agreed, and in one afternoon worked out the following settlement. The agreement was drafted by the McKays and Ms. Bertleson with the help of the mediator, and they signed it before leaving the mediation center.

In the Matter of Mediation Between:

Melinda Bertleson

and   SETTLEMENT AGREEMENT

Helen and Arthur McKay

Case Number: C-352-94

Under the Rules and Procedures of The Center for Dispute Settlement, Inc., Melinda Bertleson and Helen and Arthur McKay agree that the following provisions constitute full satisfaction of all claims submitted to Mediation on July 3, 2004.

1. Helen and Arthur McKay agree that Ms. Bertleson's children and their friends can play on the swing set and other play equipment in the McKays' backyard at any time they wish as long as they are supervised by an adult.

2. Melinda Bertleson agrees that her children and their friends will clean up after themselves when they play in the McKays' yard, and that she will be responsible for seeing that they do.

3. Ms. Bertleson further agrees to tell her visitors not to park in or block the McKays' driveway, and that she will be responsible for seeing that they do not block the driveway.

4. Mr. and Mrs. McKay agree not to make any verbal threats to Ms. Bertleson or her visitors and to contact her directly in person or by phone if they have any complaints about the conduct of guests at her home.

5. Ms. Bertleson and Mr. and Mrs. McKay also agree that if future disputes arise between them they will try to resolve them by talking together, but if they are unable to do so they will return to mediation at the Center for Dispute Settlement, Inc.

Melinda Bertleson
_____

Melinda Bertleson

Helen McKay
_____

Helen McKay

Arthur McKay
_____

Arthur McKay

Signature of Mediator
_____

Mediator

3. Contract Dispute

This next dispute arose when a large manufacturing company, Unity Corp., claimed that machine parts made for it by a smaller firm, JHL, Inc., were defective and refused further delivery of parts halfway through the contract. JHL, Inc., on the other hand, claimed the parts conformed perfectly to the specifications in the purchase order, and threatened to sue Unity for $2 million ($1.8 million for the actual cost to JHL of making the rejected parts, plus $200,000 in anticipated profits if JHL had been allowed to complete the contract). But JHL was reluctant to file the lawsuit because Unity was a major customer; winning the lawsuit while losing Unity's business would not be in JHL's long-term interest. The two companies agreed to mediate.

The mediation took about four days over a period of three weeks. Although Unity still would not agree to accept the disputed parts, it did agree to pay two-thirds of what it cost JHL to manufacture them (about $1.2 million). Half of this amount would be in a lump sum payment and the balance would be in the form of a purchase by Unity of some excess equipment owned by JHL (but virtually worthless to JHL), which Unity could use at one of its own manufacturing sites. In addition, the two companies agreed to try to continue doing business together. Specifically, Unity agreed to give JHL a contract to do additional work; if the new work was done successfully, the profit on it would about equal the $200,000 that JHL had anticipated but not realized on the original job.

A brief outline of the agreement's main points was drafted by the principals of each company and the mediator before the last mediation session concluded; the final version was signed a few weeks later, after attorneys for both sides reviewed it and worked out the details.

A noteworthy aspect of this agreement is the total absence of fault-finding in the contract that gave rise to their dispute. The agreement is entirely forward-looking and is designed to preserve the both companies' business relationship to their mutual advantage.

In the Matter of Mediation Between:

Unity Corp.

and   SETTLEMENT AGREEMENT

JHL, Inc.

Case Number: 12345-05

1. The Unity Corp. agrees to award to JHL, Inc., within six months from the signing of a final mediation agreement, a contract or contracts for the manufacture of unspecified machine parts with a net profit margin to JHL upon successful completion of not less than $200,000. Counsel for the parties will draft a document further describing the parties' rights and obligations concerning this agreement for future manufacturing work.

2. Unity will pay to JHL, Inc., not later than 30 days from the signing of a final mediation agreement, the amount of $600,000 to offset part of the costs incurred by JHL, Inc., to manufacture machine parts under the disputed contract that was the subject of this mediation. Full or partial payments of this amount made after the 30-day period will include interest at the rate of 9% per year.

3. As further offset against JHL's manufacturing costs, Unity will purchase from JHL three Model X7 Impurities Testers for a total price of $600,000. Delivery will be made FOB Unity's East Ridge facility within 60 days after a final mediation agreement is signed. Unity will pay JHL in full for this equipment within 30 days of satisfactory delivery.

4. JHL agrees that when the steps outlined above in items 1-3 are completed, it will consider all issues concerning the disputed contract to have been settled, and will not in the future bring any legal actions against Unity concerning that contract.

5. The parties will prepare and exchange papers releasing each other from all present legal claims when the steps outlined above in items 1-3 are completed.

JHL, INC.

By: _Vic Lentz_

UNITY CORP.

By: _Hank Smith_

Missy Longstockings
Mediator

D. Make Your Agreement Legally Enforceable

Experience shows that most mediation agreements are voluntarily followed by the parties who sign them. Indeed, studies show that people are even more likely to live up to the terms of a mediation agreement than they are to abide by a court order. The reason is as simple as it is logical: People who help craft the solution to their own dispute and sign an agreement to abide by it are more likely to comply than people who are ordered to do something that they don't want to do by a judge.

However, it makes sense to protect yourself against the chance that the other party will buck this trend and refuse to honor the agreement. The best way to do this is to prepare your agreement as a legally binding contract. If the other side breaks the agreement, you will have the option of going to court to enforce it or seek compensation (unless you have opted for binding arbitration).

Don't bother writing a legally binding contract if enforcement isn't an issue.
There's no point taking the time to draft a legal contract if you aren't going to enforce the agreement—for example, if you would not want to enforce the agreement even if you could (such as in disputes

between friends involving personal issues), or if so little money is involved that it wouldn't be worth fighting over, even in small claims court.

There are a couple of different ways to make an agreement legally enforceable:

- write the agreement as a legal contract, or

- if a lawsuit is already pending, request a "consent judgment"—a court order that includes the terms of your agreement.

Agreements to take actions that are not legally required pose special enforcement problems. A court isn't likely to order the other party to take an action (other than paying money), even if you both agreed to it in mediation. For example, if your neighbor promises to trim a tree in her backyard twice a year to keep it from blocking your view, a judge isn't likely to order her to do it unless the tree is legally encroaching on your property. One way to deal with this potential problem is to include a monetary fallback if the other side doesn't live up to the agreement. In our tree example, the agreement could say that if your neighbor didn't trim her tree as promised, you would be entitled to hire a tree service and she would have to pay the fee. Keep this kind of provision in mind if your dispute concerns an interpersonal or neighborhood problem.

Now let's look at the two ways to make a mediated agreement legally enforceable.

1. Write the Agreement as a Legal Contract

To make sure that you'll be able to enforce your agreement, you will want to write it in the form of a binding contract. To accomplish this, the agreement must meet a handful of contract law requirements. Though the technicalities of contract law are beyond the scope of this book, here are the basic requirements your agreement will have to meet in order to be enforceable as a contract:

- **The parties have the legal ability to make a contract.** This is an easy requirement to meet, as long as both parties are adults. All mentally competent adults have the power ("capacity," in legalese) to make a contract. Unless the other party is a minor or has a serious mental impairment, you have no problem.

- **The agreement doesn't call for illegal actions.** The terms of your contract must not call for an illegal act, such as gambling, prostitution, or (more commonly) a loan of money requiring a person to pay interest above the legal rate—somewhere between 10% and 12% in many states.

- **The terms of the agreement must be clear.** If your agreement is so vague that a reasonable person might have difficulty understanding it or carrying it out, it does not qualify as a contract. To guard against this, each provision should state clearly who does or pays what to whom, when, and how. (See Section B4, above.) For example, if you want the roof of your house ripped off and replaced with a new asphalt roof that has a 20-year guarantee, your agreement should say exactly that. By contrast, an agreement that says only that the other party will "fix the roof" may be too vague to be enforced as a contract.

- **There must be an exchange.** To have a contract, both parties must do, or promise to do, something of value. (Lawyers refer to this action or promise as "consideration.") As long as your agreement reflects either an exchange of services for money ("Rowan will pay Martin $200 dollars; Martin will reseal the driveway") or reciprocal promises ("Smith will keep his dog indoors after 9 p.m.; Jones will call Smith before calling the police"), it will meet this requirement. Similarly, a promise not to file a lawsuit or badmouth someone is also valid legal consideration. It's really not all that complicated—an agreement that lacks consideration because only one person has promised to do something (as in: "Betty will turn her pool lights off before 10 p.m.") can easily be fixed by adding some reciprocal promise or act ("and Andy will stop calling the City to complain").

- **Everyone must agree to the contract terms.** There must be evidence that both parties understand and agree to the terms of the agreement. The signatures of both parties at the bottom of the agreement will normally satisfy this requirement. But in a few states, agreements must explicitly state, in writing, that the parties intend them to be binding. Although not technically required in most states, including this type of statement is always a good practice. If your agreement is written or typed onto a printed form provided by the mediator or mediation service, look to see whether it contains a printed statement that the agreement is intended to be legally binding. It probably will. But if it does not, ask the mediator to insert a statement at the end of the agreement. The following statement should do the job:

The parties understand and accept the terms stated above and intend this agreement to be a legal contract, binding upon them and enforceable by a court of law.

⚠ Get help if your agreement may be tough to enforce. If your dispute involved substantial amounts of money or important legal rights, you should consult with a lawyer who is familiar with contract law and local court rules for help in drafting your agreement.

2. Request a Consent Judgment

A lawsuit may be pending when you reach a mediated settlement. This is common if a judge referred the dispute to mediation in the first place. But it also can occur if one party suggests putting the court action on hold while you try mediation. Either way, you will probably have two options when writing up your agreement:

- ask the judge to dismiss the lawsuit and then write your settlement agreement in the form of a legally binding contract (see Section 1, above), or

- ask the court to approve the agreement and issue a consent judgment (sometimes called a consent decree) turning your mediated settlement into an official court judgment. If the other side violates the judgment, you can enforce it as a court order. By contrast, to enforce a settlement agreement or contract that is not made into a court order, you have to file a new lawsuit and get a judgment based on breach of contract.

If you are concerned that the other side may not honor the agreement, you will probably want to get a consent judgment. If you do not anticipate a compliance problem, however, you can skip the consent judgment—and avoid some added legal fees, court costs, and delay—and rely on the settlement agreement as a legally binding contract. (Some mediation agreements, such as those concerning child custody and visitation, will not be enforceable under federal and state laws unless they are approved by a judge and issued as a court order. For more on this, see Chapter 10.)

3. Remedies for Breach of a Mediated Agreement

Courts usually enforce mediated agreements. But how a particular court will enforce a particular mediation agreement depends on various factors, including how well the agreement was drafted, the type of actions called for under the agreement, the facts of the case, and the state law the court is applying. Generally, agreements that call for the payment of money are much more likely to be enforced as contracts than are agreements that call for something more intangible (such as a promise to treat each other civilly, weed someone's garden, or not call the police). It's best to write these agreements to include a monetary fallback if someone doesn't do a promised act. For example, if the private mechanic doesn't fix your car as agreed, you can get the job done at another shop and make the first mechanic pay the bill.

Here are the legal remedies that are generally available for breach of binding mediation agreements:

- **Damages:** The court can award you financial compensation for losses you suffered as a result of the other party's breach. This is the most common way for a court to enforce an agreement.

- **Rescission:** If the other party fails to perform as promised but still expects you to live up to your side of the bargain, you can ask a judge to void the agreement and release both of you from your obligations.

- **Specific performance:** The court can order the other party to live up to the agreement—for example, for a bank to give you a mortgage or another person to sell you a piece of land. Courts generally will not order specific performance of contracts involving personal labor, such as requiring someone to paint your house or fix your car.

If your agreement contains an arbitration clause, you can get most of the same remedies at arbitration with less expense and delay than would be involved in a lawsuit. However, enforcing the arbitrator's award would still require a court proceeding.

E. Providing for a Lawyer's or Other Adviser's Review

If your dispute involves significant amounts of money or property, or may limit important legal or financial rights (for example, your right to a job, a patent, or a big tax refund), you should consult a lawyer or another professional before signing the agreement. In some situations, it may make sense to have a piece of property that's central to the dispute (for example, land, a painting, or a business) appraised before signing off. You don't want to pay $100,000 to buy your partner's half of a business that you think is worth $200,000, only to later discover that its value is much lower. Similarly, if property is to be exchanged under your agreement, particularly if it has gone up in value, you may need to consider tax issues. If you need any kind of expert help, ask the mediator to insert a clause in the agreement making your signature conditional on review by a lawyer or other expert or adviser. The clause could read as follows:

The terms of this agreement will go into effect five business days after the parties sign, unless the attorney (or CPA, appraiser, or other adviser) for either party notifies the [mediation service] in writing of objections.

The "adviser's review" clause can also provide a longer period for review or state that the agreement will not become effective until co-signed by the adviser. Bear in mind, though, that the longer you delay making the agreement effective, the greater chance there is that the other party will experience buyer's remorse and decide to back out of the deal.

F. Signing the Agreement

When you and the other party have read and agreed to each provision of your agreement (and, if necessary, your advisers have reviewed and approved it), you are then ready for the last act of the mediation session: the signing.

If you sign at the mediation service, the mediator will likely hand you and the other disputant a typed copy of the agreement, then read it aloud to make sure that no further changes are needed. If the agreement is written in the form of a contract, the mediator may remind you that it is legally binding and potentially enforceable in court, and that the mediation service will be available to help if you need to revise the agreement. (See Chapter 9, Section A, for information on handling modifications.) The mediator may also remind you that you agreed to keep everything said or revealed during the session confidential.

The mediator will then ask each of you to sign the agreement. The mediator, too, will probably sign. Sometimes, signatures will be notarized by a notary on staff. Having a signature notarized is a good idea if you anticipate any need to prove, to a court or arbitrator, that the signature on the agreement is genuine. Be sure to get a copy of the agreement for yourself before you leave the mediation.

If you signed an outline or preliminary draft of the agreement in the mediator's presence and saved the details to be negotiated later, then the signing of the final mediation agreement will most likely be done by phone or fax.

SHAKE ON IT?

Exactly what do people who have been engaged in a bitter dispute do when they sign their names to a paper ending the matter?

Some mediators have handled cases, such as those involving estranged relatives or friends, where the parties reconciled through mediation and concluded the session with an embrace. At nonprofit community mediation centers, disputants are sometimes so grateful for the center's help that before they leave they offer a financial contribution, even though none is required.

Typically, though, the mediator will end the session simply by shaking hands with each of the parties and congratulating them on the successful result of their hard work. With a nod to one or both of the parties, the mediator may encourage them to shake hands. Some disputants feel enough relief and understanding of each other's positions to take the cue and end the session with a handshake. Others prefer to simply take their copy of the agreement and go home. ■

CHAPTER 8

If You Don't Reach an Agreement

In the film "Little Big Man," the Native American grandfather decides it is time to die. He climbs a nearby mountain, wraps himself in a blanket, and lies down to wait for the Great Spirit to take him away. When it begins to rain a little while later, he realizes he is still alive. "Sometimes the magic works, and sometimes it doesn't," he says.

The same is true of mediation. The fact that it works far more often than not is probably small solace to those who find themselves in the unfortunate minority. But even if your mediation didn't end in a settlement, there is still hope that your dispute can be resolved without a painful court fight. This chapter examines the range of options that may be available to you.

A. Get Help From the Mediator

There are three ways that you can continue to make use of the mediator's services, even if your mediation did not lead to a settlement. You can ask the mediator to:

- adjourn and reconvene your mediation

- make a written recommendation, or

- return your dispute to the judge, prosecutor, or agency that originally referred it to mediation.

1. Reconvene the Mediation

If your session ended without agreement, you can ask the mediator and the other party to try again later. You could propose, for example, that another session be scheduled in three months. By that time, the parties' positions or circumstances may have changed in such a way that settlement is more likely. If you and the other side are willing to give it another try, the mediator will probably be happy to schedule another session.

Set a date right away. If you believe that another mediation session might produce a settlement, you should schedule the next meeting while everyone is still together at the first mediation. If you leave the date to be worked out later, the other party may lose interest—or decide to take some other action, such as going to court—and be unwilling to reconvene.

2. Ask for a Written Recommendation

If you and the other party respect and trust the mediator, you can ask the mediator to make a written recommendation as to how the dispute should be resolved. After all, if the mediation involved private caucuses, the mediator probably knows more about the dispute than either party does. And you really have nothing to lose—the mediator's recommendation will not be binding. If you and the other side are both willing to accept the recommendation, you have a settlement. If either of you says no, you're right back where you started.

The main disadvantage of having the mediator recommend a settlement is that it probably forecloses the possibility of using that mediator again in the same dispute. A mediator who has given an opinion as to how the case should be resolved can no longer be considered neutral. So before you ask your mediator to recommend a settlement, be sure you will not want to reconvene your mediation later before that same mediator.

Encouraging the reluctant mediator. Some mediators may hesitate to give a written recommendation to the parties because they see it as violating their pledge of neutrality. It may help to remind the mediator that a recommendation is not a legally binding decision. You and the other party will be free to decide for yourselves whether you want to follow it. You can also suggest that the mediator formally close the mediation session before making a recommendation, to avoid violating ethical standards that require the mediator to be impartial during the proceedings.

If the mediator agrees to make a recommendation, make sure that the document will not reveal anything said in confidence during private caucuses. Also, the recommendation should not contain any statements finding fault or blame with either of the parties. It should simply state the mediator's opinion as to what steps both sides should take to create a fair and workable settlement of the dispute. Because the parties will be expected to pay the mediator for the extra time spent preparing the recommendation, you should agree on a fee in advance.

Because it is based on information obtained during the mediation, the mediator's recommendation should be considered confidential under most mediation rules. This means that neither the mediator nor the parties would be allowed to introduce it as evidence in a later arbitration or court proceeding. Nevertheless, because you and the other party probably weren't contemplating a written recommendation when you signed the agreement to mediate, it is a good idea to sign a separate agreement making it absolutely clear that the recommendation will be kept confidential. Ask the mediator to draft a brief confidentiality agreement to cover the recommendation, and try to get everyone to sign it before they leave the session. Here is a sample:

Confidentiality Agreement

The undersigned parties have requested _____*name of mediator*_____,
who acted as mediator on ____*date*____ in regard to their dispute concerning
____*describe nature of dispute*____, to make a written recommendation to them
about how their dispute might be resolved. The parties and the mediator agree to
maintain the confidentiality of the recommendation and will not rely on it, or seek to
introduce it as evidence, in any arbitration or judicial or other proceeding, nor disclose
it to any regulatory agency, prosecutorial authority, or other governmental agency.

A mediator's recommendations are typically made in writing and
mailed to each of the parties within a couple of weeks after the close of
the mediation session. The parties are then free to accept the proposals
contained in the recommendation or to use them as a basis for further
negotiations.

3. Return Your Dispute to the Judge, Prosecutor, or Other Referring Agency

If your dispute was referred to mediation by a judge or other law enforcement agency, one option (and sometimes a legal requirement) is to
return the case to the person or organization that referred it to mediation
in the first place. The mediator or mediation service can do this for you
by sending a letter to the judge or other referral source, noting that
mediation was tried but didn't result in an agreement.

EXAMPLE: *When Pam's ex-boyfriend Bruce moved out of Pam's home, he took
with him several items of her personal property, including a television set and
some valuable photography equipment. He refused to return them. Pam called
the police and asked that Bruce be arrested.*

*When Pam talked to the assistant district attorney who approves the issuance
of arrest warrants, he referred her to the community mediation center. Bruce
showed up for mediation, but the session did not result in an agreement to
return Pam's property.*

Either as part of their regular procedures or at Pam's specific request, the mediation center will send a letter to the assistant district attorney, explaining that Pam attempted mediation and still wants to press charges. Now, the attorney will consider whether the facts support issuing a warrant for Bruce's arrest.

A judge, police officer, or prosecutor who sees that you have made a good-faith attempt to work out a dispute through mediation may be more inclined to grant you the legal action you originally requested. In a sense, you may be rewarded for having tried mediation as a first option.

B. Small Claims Court

If your dispute involves a relatively small amount of money, you can bring a lawsuit in small claims court, where it is easy to represent yourself. Small claims court judges resolve disputes involving modest dollar amounts. You can present your case in small claims court without a lawyer—the rules encourage a minimum of legal and procedural formality. Once the case is presented, the judge will issue a decision fairly quickly.

The type and value of cases you can bring in small claims court is limited. In most states, the dollar limit for small claims court is between $2,500 and $10,000. And most states will not allow you to bring lawsuits that request something other than money (such as a lawsuit to get your neighbor to stop cutting down trees on your boundary line). You cannot use small claims court for divorce, either.

To find out the rules for small claims court in your area, simply contact the court. Or, you can go to Nolo's Legal Research Center at www.nolo.com/lawcenter/statute/index.cfm, and click on "Small Claims Courts," then select your state—you'll find a variety of self-help materials for small claims litigants. For help in preparing your case for small claims court, check out *Everybody's Guide to Small Claims Court* (California and National editions), by Ralph Warner (Nolo).

⚠ **Things you learned in mediation probably can't be used in court.** If you file a lawsuit in a case that you've already tried to mediate, the confidentiality rules of mediation prohibit you from using in court much of the information disclosed by the other party during mediation. State law determines how broad this prohibition will be, but it nearly always prevents you from using the other party's statements to show the validity or value of a claim being advanced in the court. If you learn the same information outside of the mediation, however, then you can use it in court. If you are unsure whether a particular statement you heard in mediation can be raised in court, consult with a lawyer or law coach before going to your court hearing.

C. Arbitration

If you've tried mediation and "the magic didn't work," arbitration might be a good option. At the very least, it will assure you and the other party of a fast, private, and—at least as compared to court—reasonably-priced way to resolve your dispute.

In binding arbitration, a neutral third party (called the arbitrator or sometimes the arbiter) conducts a hearing between the disputants and then makes a final and legally binding decision (called an award). The arbitrator's award is almost always enforceable in court just like a judge's order. Unlike mediation, arbitration requires you to give up control of your dispute to the arbitrator, who takes the place of judge and jury. If you go to binding arbitration, your hearing is, in effect, your "day in court"; you will not get another. For more on the differences between mediation and arbitration, see Chapter 1, Section D.

Except in highly unusual circumstances, an arbitrator's decision will not be overturned in court. Most state laws allow a court to overturn an arbitrator's decision only if there was fraud involved in the hearing, the arbitrator was biased against one of the parties, or important procedures were not properly followed. A judge almost never overturns an arbitrator's award just because the arbitrator made a bad decision or misapplied the law. These very restricted appeal rules make sense, because the whole point of arbitrating is to let disputants resolve a case once and for all without a court fight.

A full discussion of how to prepare for and present a case in arbitration is beyond the scope of this book. However, to familiarize you with the process, here is a brief overview of arbitration.

1. Which Cases Are Suitable to Arbitrate

Arbitration tends to work best in cases that have a "dollars-and-cents" solution, such as insurance claims, consumer complaints, and contract disputes. Cases involving interpersonal disputes often are not well-suited to arbitration, because problems with the relationship probably will not be discussed or decided. Also, because one side may win everything and the other lose everything, the result is unlikely to repair an ailing relationship.

Similarly, cases involving relatively small amounts of money—less than a few thousand dollars—are often too small to arbitrate, because the arbitration fees will be too high compared to the amount you hope to gain. (However, this isn't always true, as some community mediation centers do offer free or low-cost arbitration.)

2. Arbitration Through "Med/Arb"

When you first submitted your dispute to mediation, some mediation services may have offered an option known as "med/arb" (pronounced "meed-arb"). In med/arb, the disputants consent to mediation, with the added provision that if mediation does not produce a settlement, then the mediator (or another neutral party) can act as arbitrator and make a binding decision. Med/arb assures that, one way or the other, the dispute will be resolved: Either an agreement will be reached or a decision will be handed down.

Most mediation services that offer med/arb use a system in which the decision-making arbitrator is someone other than the person who acted as mediator. In the jargon of the dispute resolution field, this system is often called by the horrendous title "sequential med/arb." First there is a mediation. Then, if that fails, an arbitration session is scheduled before a different neutral. Separating the two eliminates the problem of a mediator-turned-arbitrator rendering a decision based, in part, on information provided in confidence during the caucus stage of mediation.

If you submitted your case to med/arb, then at some point in the mediation—after caucuses and negotiation—the mediator might indicate that it's just about time to move to arbitration.

EXAMPLE: *Mediator to Disputants: "I have to tell you candidly that I'm not seeing a lot of progress here. You've been over the issues thoroughly several times, both in joint session and in caucus. Some promising settlement options have been put on the table, but I don't see much movement. Let's give it a little longer, but if nothing develops, say in another hour, I will consider declaring the mediation closed and asking that an arbitrator be assigned to conduct a hearing and make an award."*

If you did not submit your case to med/arb and your mediation effort was unsuccessful, you can still ask the mediator to arbitrate a decision. (Also see Section A2, above, for a discussion of asking the mediator for a nonbinding recommendation instead .) Of course, the other side will have to agree to this plan, the mediator will have to be willing to arbitrate, and the proper agreements and disclosures will have to be signed by the parties.

But again, having your mediator become an arbitrator can raise a problem if, during mediation, either party disclosed information to the mediator that was not also shared with the other side. This would happen, for example, if the parties prepared pre-mediation memoranda for the mediator (see Chapter 5, Section D) but did not exchange them with each other, or if private caucuses were held with the mediator. In either case, you can't be sure that the mediator-turned-arbitrator will disregard this information when making the arbitrator's award.

If you and the other party did not sign up for med/arb but now agree that you both want the mediator to arbitrate a decision, you will have to sign an agreement to arbitrate.

 For information on the various types of arbitration, see Chapter 1, Section D.

3. Where to Go for Arbitration

If you used (and were satisfied with) a mediation service that also offers arbitration, you and the other party may be able to sign an agreement to arbitrate before you leave the mediation session. But if the mediation service does not offer arbitration (many community mediation centers do not), ask the mediator or a staff member to refer you to an organization that does.

Most private dispute resolution companies that provide services to business clients also offer arbitration. For a list of some national and regional private firms, see Appendix C. Private firms offering arbitration in your community may also be listed in your local telephone directory under "arbitration" or "legal services."

⚠ **The problem with some independent arbitrators.** Lawyers, retired judges, and others sometimes promote themselves as independent arbitrators who hear cases on their own, outside of an arbitration service. This is often less expensive than using a service, but there are some disadvantages as well:

- Without an administrative agency, there is no independent source of information about the background, skill level, and achievement record of the arbitrator.

- There is no buffer between the parties and the arbitrator; the parties must contact the arbitrator directly, which creates the potential for communications in which one side may improperly influence the arbitrator—even inadvertently.

- If any problems arise with the arbitration—for example, one side believes incorrect procedures were followed—there is no one to evaluate or help remedy the problem.

4. Initiating Arbitration

If you and the other party are still at the mediation session when you agree to arbitrate and the mediation service also handles arbitrations, then you can both just sign an "agreement to arbitrate" form supplied by the service. If, however, you have already left the mediation session or the mediation service can't help you with arbitration, then one of you will need to begin the arbitration process much as you did mediation, by going to an arbitration service and completing an intake form, usually called either a "submission to arbitration" or, if your dispute is covered by a contract that includes an arbitration clause, a "demand for arbitration." Arbitration clauses are often found in contracts involving the construction industry, professional sports, sales of stocks and bonds, and employment.

No matter which form you use, it will ask you to describe the nature of your claim and the remedy you seek, including the amount of money (if any) at stake.

All arbitration services conduct their hearings in accordance with a set of rules that spell out in detail such things as the duties of the arbitrator, use of evidence, confidentiality, fees and expenses, and appeals. Study these rules and ask questions about any provisions you don't understand.

5. Choosing an Arbitrator

Most arbitration services maintain rosters or "panels" of arbitrators who have expertise in fields like business contracts, construction, personal injuries, and employment. Staff members of the arbitration service or panel members with more general backgrounds may also be available. When you are ready to choose an arbitrator for your case, the service will send you a list with the names of half a dozen or more arbitrators, sometimes with a brief biographical sketch of each. From this list, you will usually be asked either to cross off the names of anyone you do not want to hear your case, or to rank in order of preference the names of arbitrators you would like to hear your case.

The procedures and strategies for investigating and choosing arbitrators from a panel are the same as for choosing a mediator. (See Chapter 3.) These include reading the material sent by the arbitration firm, looking for someone who is knowledgeable about the subject area of the dispute, and getting referrals from friends, businesses, community leaders, lawyers, and others.

Although most arbitrations are conducted before one arbitrator, a panel of three arbitrators is sometimes used, either because an arbitration clause in a contract requires it or because the parties agree to this procedure. For example, some auto insurance policies require three arbitrators to decide a case when a claim is made under the policy.

Although cases heard by three arbitrators will obviously be more expensive than those heard by a single arbitrator, there are reasons why you may want to consider using a panel. For example, if a very large monetary award is possible in your case, and you are the party who will be paying out the money, you may prefer the "averaging" effect of having multiple arbitrators, which eliminates the possibility of a single arbitrator rendering too large an award. Similarly, if your dispute is very complex and has many facts and witnesses, multiple arbitrators may be better able to remember and apply all the evidence in the case.

6. Do You Need a Lawyer?

In mediation, you generally don't need a lawyer, unless lots of money or property is at stake, or the underlying legal issues are complex. By comparison, it's often wise to have a lawyer represent you in arbitration.

When you agree to participate in arbitration, you are giving up your right to go to court on this particular dispute, and the decision of the arbitrator will be binding and final, just like a decision by a judge. If you have a significant amount of money or property in dispute, or you would be severely affected by losing the case, then hiring a lawyer or a background law coach to help you prepare for arbitration (and possibly go with you to the hearing) makes more sense. Because most arbitration hearings last a day or less, your legal fees won't be too overwhelming.

7. The Arbitration Award

Many arbitration services require the arbitrator to issue an award within 30 days after the hearing, unless additional information has to be submitted. The arbitrator has broad authority to make any award that she "deems just and equitable and within the scope of the arbitration agreement made by the parties." Nevertheless, a typical arbitration award simply orders one party to pay money to another.

D. Start a Lawsuit

If mediation fails, you still have the right to file a lawsuit (unless you have already signed a contract to proceed to binding arbitration). To do this, you can bring an action in civil trial court, either by hiring a lawyer to represent you or by representing yourself.

Even if you end up having to file a lawsuit, don't feel that the time you spent trying to mediate was wasted. At least one study has shown that those who tried to mediate their cases are more likely to pay a judgment than those who never tried mediation.

If you decide to represent yourself, pick up a copy of *Represent Yourself in Court*, by Paul Bergman & Sara Berman-Barrett (Nolo), an excellent resource that will help you prepare and try your own case. If you will be working with a lawyer, *The Lawsuit Survival Guide*, by Joseph Matthews (Nolo), explains every step in the litigation process. ■

CHAPTER 9

If Your Mediation Agreement Doesn't Work

Your long-term satisfaction with mediation will largely depend on whether your agreement solves your problem once and for all:

- Does the contractor who agrees to repaint the hallway do a good job?

- Does your former business partner make all payments as promised to buy out your share of the business?

- Does your neighbor stop harassing your kids?

Sometimes, however, despite everyone's best efforts, your mediated agreement just won't work. This may occur because circumstances have changed since the agreement was made, one party has failed to honor the agreement, or the agreement proved to be unworkable in the real world. This chapter explains your options in these circumstances.

A. Changing Your Agreement

Even the most thoughtful and well-drafted mediation agreements may need to be modified if later events make the terms irrelevant or impossible to perform. As a general rule, the more an agreement depends on things that haven't happened yet, the more likely it is to unravel. This might occur, for example, if an unforeseen event makes the agreement ineffective, the agreement turns out to be unworkable, or one party is unable to meet its obligations. Consider these examples:

EXAMPLE: *Marcia was fired from her job as restaurant manager at a hotel. Believing she had been dismissed for inappropriate reasons, she filed a wrongful termination lawsuit against the hotel. To avoid a full-scale court battle, the hotel's lawyer and Marcia and her lawyer agreed to try to mediate a solution. Following a full day of mediation, they reached an agreement to rehire Marcia at her former position for a trial period of six months, after which she would be evaluated and considered for permanent reinstatement. Marcia's lawsuit would remain inactive pending completion of the six-month period.*

Three weeks after the agreement is made, Marcia's husband learns that he will be transferred to a new job out of state, which makes Marcia's agreement with the hotel unworkable. Though the hotel might have taken the position that it had complied with its end of the agreement and would do no more, it decided instead (for the practical reason of avoiding a likely lawsuit from Marcia) to attend another mediation session. The result was a new agreement in which the hotel agreed to pay Marcia a sum of money to cover most of the time she missed from work, and to give her a favorable letter of recommendation.

EXAMPLE: *Two teenage boys were arrested and charged with breaking antennas and hood ornaments off cars at an auto dealer's lot. As part of a mediated agreement, the dealer agreed to drop charges if the boys would perform 40 hours of work without pay at his dealership on weekends. The boys agreed and the mediation was closed.*

Soon after, however, the owner learned that his insurance coverage prevents anyone under the age of 18 from working on the lot. He informed the mediation center and suggested, as an alternative, that the teens could perform 40 hours of community service at a local camp for disabled children. The boys agreed to the change. The center staff circulated a memo to both sides, got their signatures, and the agreement was officially amended.

EXAMPLE: *A general contractor caught a subcontractor stealing lumber. In a mediated agreement, the subcontractor agreed to pay back $2,500, in two monthly payments of $1,250 each. The subcontractor made the first payment on time, but then received a notice from the Internal Revenue Service demanding immediate payment of a substantial amount of back taxes. If the money wasn't immediately forthcoming, the IRS threatened to padlock the business, which would probably force the subcontractor into bankruptcy. The subcontractor told the mediator that he could not make the second payment on time. After conferring with both sides and obtaining a mutual agreement to an extension of time to pay, the mediator circulated a modified agreement for signature.*

1. Get Help From the Mediation Service or Mediator

If your agreement needs to be modified, the easiest way to do it is to negotiate the change yourself and put it in writing. But if you want the mediator's help, don't hesitate to call. While most mediation rules do not require mediators to provide follow-up assistance after a case is closed, in practice, most will be glad to help. (There may be state laws that govern modifications to child custody and visitation agreements— see Chapter 10).

a. Major Problems

If you notify your mediation service or independent mediator that you believe a major issue needs to be renegotiated in a face-to-face mediation session, they will usually contact the other party to get consent to reopen the mediation. For instance, consider the dispute in the first example, above, in which the hotel was going to rehire the restaurant manager, who then learned that her husband was being transferred to another state. This is the kind of major issue that almost surely requires another face-to-face mediation session. Typically, the case manager at the mediation service, once alerted to the problem, will contact all the parties to arrange another session with the original mediator. The session may not take long—everyone will be familiar with the facts of the dispute and can begin working right away on alternative plans for a settlement.

b. Minor Problems

The best way to fix minor problems with your mediated agreement is to negotiate them directly with the other side. Even if you need help from the mediator or mediation service, they can often get involved without convening another formal mediation session. Instead, the mediator or staff will conduct "telephone shuttle diplomacy" between you and the other side to work out the needed modification, then circulate an amendment to the original agreement for both of you to sign. For instance, in the second example above (concerning the teenage boys who vandalized cars), the parties had agreed that the boys would perform 40 hours of unpaid service at the dealership. When this became impossible, the dealer himself suggested the boys do community service at a camp for disabled children. To agree on this new plan, the parties didn't need another mediation session—the principle of having the boys perform unpaid labor to compensate for past behavior remained the same. Working out the details of where and when the work would now be performed was a relatively minor issue that the center staff could handle by phone and mail.

2. Fees for Changing an Agreement

Whether you will be charged an additional fee for help changing your agreement will depend on the rules of the mediator or mediation service you used and on how much they do to help you. If the problem requires a new mediation session, you probably will be charged for the mediator's additional time but will likely not need to pay another administrative fee. If the problem doesn't require a new session, you will probably be charged for the mediator's telephone time (unless it is just a few minutes), but may not be charged if the change is negotiated by a staff person.

KEEPING THE CUSTOMER SATISFIED

Why should a mediation service help you modify an agreement? For starters, most people who work in the mediation field genuinely care about providing good quality service. But beyond that, private dispute resolution companies, especially, recognize that their business's ability to attract new clients depends on their reputation for helping foster agreements that work. Mediation is a business in which providers prosper only by generating positive word of mouth.

Nonprofit community mediation centers also have a stake in your long-term satisfaction. Their ability to attract state, local, and foundation funds depends, in part, on the success or failure rate of their operations as measured by client satisfaction. Some community mediation centers even monitor closed cases to see whether agreements are working well.

The staff at court-connected mediation programs should also be willing to help you modify your agreement. Because many of these programs are pilot projects, the state agencies that fund them keep track of user satisfaction.

B. If the Other Party Reneges

Although parties tend to comply with mediated agreements—even more so than with court orders—this will be cold comfort if your case is one of those in which the other party reneges.

If the other party fails to send you a check when due, fails to fix your water heater, continues to call you at home late at night after agreeing not to do so, or otherwise doesn't keep a promise, what action can you take? Step one is to call the person and try to work it out directly. If that fails or is impractical under the circumstances, consider these other possible remedies.

1. Involve the Mediation Service

The mediator or mediation service will probably be willing to lend a hand if the other side fails to carry out the agreement. For example, assume that you used a private dispute resolution company to mediate a dispute over ownership of a small business. Under the agreement, your former partner was to pay you monthly installments to purchase your shares in the company. But your former partner has stopped making payments, claiming that the deal is too favorable to you and refusing to fork over another dime. What can you do?

Because it appears that further negotiations with your ex-partner would be useless, your next step is to tell the case manager at the mediation company about the problem. Although case managers have no obligation to get involved, most will be willing to step in and try to solve the problem.

Case Manager to Reneging Party: *"Stan, Joe told me that there's some problem with the agreement you both reached in mediation last summer. Can you tell me about it?" (The case manager begins simply by offering to listen. He wants to remain neutral until information from both sides convinces him there really is a compliance problem.)*

(Later in conversation): *"From what you're telling me, it sounds as if you've just decided not to honor the agreement. If you and Joe both want, I can see about reopening the mediation. But I have to remind you that you both agreed to have the settlement written as a legal contract. By making the agreement a contract, you both intended that if one of you broke it, the other could sue for breach of contract. If Joe did that and won, you might be looking at liability not only for what you still owe him, but also interest, damages, court costs, and Joe's legal fees, as well as your own. You'd risk having a judgment issued against you that would be a matter of public record and available to banks. Unless you paid it promptly, that could make it difficult for you to get a line of credit for the business. Are you sure it wouldn't be in your best interest just to finish up the payments as you agreed?"*

Community mediation centers also have some persuasive authority. In cities and towns where mediation centers are well established and strongly supported by local government and business, centers are often perceived as representing the "the community." After all, they receive public funds, and prominent judges and community leaders sit on their boards of directors. The staff will try to convey to a reneging party that the community at large—as represented by the center—expects both parties to live up to the agreement.

In cases originally referred from the police or a judge, the center will use a more direct approach to encourage compliance, often threatening to send the case back for further legal action. For example, assume that criminal harassment charges were brought against a man for harassing his former girlfriend. The city court judge referred the exes to mediation, where they worked out an agreement. A few months after the mediation, however, the man starts calling and following his ex again. As a first step, the woman calls the mediation center to alert them to the problem. Someone from the staff then contacts the man to discuss the situation, and to remind him of his obligations under the agreement:

EXAMPLE: *"Hello, Mr. Winters, this is Nancy Hoyer from the Center for Dispute Resolution. I'm calling in regard to your case with Amy Present. Ms. Present tells me there's a problem with the way your agreement is being followed. Is there a problem?" (Discussion follows confirming that there is a compliance problem.)*
"I notice from the file in your case that this case was referred to us by Judge Venditto in City Court. He was willing to adjourn the case for six months if it could be settled through mediation. I need to tell you that if you don't comply with the agreement, the Center will send the case back to Judge Venditto with a recommendation that the original charges be reinstated."

2. Ask the Mediator to Intervene

You can also ask the mediator who handled your original case—as opposed to a mediation center's case manager—to call the other party directly. If you used a mediation center, contact the mediator through them. If you used an independent mediator, call the mediator yourself.

If the other party still trusts and respects the mediator, the mediator may be able to put the agreement back together. Many mediators will be willing to help out in this way, although some may decline to do so on the ground that involving themselves in matters of compliance is inconsistent with a mediator's neutral role. Mediators who work with private dispute resolution companies tend to be more inclined to help out as a matter of customer service; mediators at public centers are more likely to decline on ethical grounds.

IF YOU WANT TO RENEGE

If you are the party who does not want to honor the mediation agreement, what can you do? If your agreement was written in the form of a binding contract, you don't have the legal right to change it by yourself. Unless you want to just ignore the agreement and hope the other side will give up, you have to convince the other side to change the original agreement. Here are a few arguments that might work:

- It's in his best interest to do so. Try to persuade the other side that the agreement made in mediation is not maximally beneficial to either of you, and that changing it will benefit you both.
- It's the only way to avoid more problems. Tell the other side that the agreement failed to address important issues (or that new ones have arisen since the agreement was made). Explain that you will not comply with the agreement unless the mediation is reopened to deal with these matters.
- It's better than going to court. If you can convince the other party that you are not going to abide by the agreement, you might persuade him to return to mediation and work out a new arrangement, simply to avoid the hassle of a lawsuit.

3. Sue to Enforce the Agreement

Going to court to enforce a mediation agreement is a last resort. Unless you can make use of small claims court, you will endure at least some of the costs and delays that you tried to avoid by going to mediation in the first place. Nevertheless, if the other party reneges on the agreement and ignores all the persuasive efforts of the mediation service or mediator, then court might be where you have to go.

Fortunately, with a well-drafted, binding mediation agreement in hand, your job (or your lawyer's job) in court will be much easier than it would have been otherwise. When you come into court with a mediation agreement, the only question for the judge is: "Is this a valid and enforceable contract?" If it is, the judge can enforce it by entering a judgment in your favor. Had you gone to court without mediating, the judge would have had to figure out the underlying dispute, including what the facts are, who is right and who is wrong, and what should be done about it. And of course, there is no assurance that you would have come out of court with anything resembling what you wanted.

Having a contract should also help speed you through the court process. You may even be eligible for what is called a "summary judgment"—an accelerated process available when the facts supporting one party's case are so clear that the judge decides in that party's favor without a trial.

In some states, mediation agreements reached under state-sponsored mediation programs are assumed by law to be enforceable in court. Otherwise, you will need to convince a judge that your agreement satisfies the requirements of a legally binding contract. (For information on these requirements, see Chapter 7.)

If your agreement requires the other party to pay you an amount of money that falls within the small claims court limit in your state, you will probably want to represent yourself in small claims court. If so, be prepared to show the judge that a contract exists and to explain the process that led to its creation. Be sure to present a copy of the contract to the judge. Also bring a copy of the mediation service's rules, or even a descriptive brochure explaining how mediation is conducted. The judge may be looking for assurance that your session was conducted fairly, that the other party was not coerced into making the agreement, and that both of you intended the agreement to be binding. If you take your case to a regular trial court, you or your lawyer will need to offer the same types of proof.

4. Enforce the Mediation Award

If a judge finds that your agreement was a contract and that the other party breached it, the judge can issue a judgment in your favor for the full amount due, plus court costs and interest from the date the money was supposed to have been paid. If you have suffered damages because of the other side's failure to live up to the agreement, the judge might award you some money for that, too.

Unfortunately, winning in court does not necessarily resolve your dispute. The same party who reneged on the mediation agreement may balk at paying a court judgment. You may be facing years of collection proceedings before a wage garnishment or seizure of assets yields the money due you. The unfortunate truth is that a party who doesn't honor a mediated agreement is equally unlikely to honor a court judgment.

Collecting judgments in California. *How to Collect When You Win a Lawsuit in California*, by Robin Leonard (Nolo), gives California readers the practical tips, step-by-step instructions, and forms they need to locate difficult debtors, find debtors' assets, and get the money they're owed. ■

CHAPTER 10

Divorce Mediation

An increasing number of divorcing couples are going to mediation. Some go to mandatory court-sponsored programs, because they live in states that require mediation of child custody and visitation issues. Others voluntarily seek out private divorce mediators because they understand mediation to be a more civilized and less expensive alternative to the traditional two-lawyer, adversarial divorce.

This chapter covers both court-sponsored and private divorce mediation, so you can mediate effectively in either setting.

This chapter applies to both married and unmarried couples. Tens of thousands of couples in the United States, straight and gay, never marry. When their relationships end, unmarried partners often face many of the same issues as married couples when they separate and divorce, including division of commonly owned assets and debts and the custody, visitation, and support of children they have coparented. Fortunately, unmarried couples can mediate their breakups. For example, though courts usually won't order mediation for unmarried couples, court-sponsored mediation programs often are available to help unmarried parents mediate parenting plans for their children, and private mediators are always available to work with unmarried couples. Although the examples in this chapter are written as though a legal marriage had taken place (and the terms "separation" and "divorce" are used), unmarried readers may assume the terms and examples in this chapter also apply to them.

A. What Is Divorce Mediation?

Divorce mediation is a process that can help a couple find a fair and practical way to end their marriage, divide their property, and, if minor children are involved, work out parenting issues.

1. Types of Issues That May Be Mediated

In divorce mediation, a mediator works with a couple to help them reach their own agreement on the issues related to the end of their marriage. As in other types of mediation, the mediator has no authority to impose a decision.

A couple in mediation will likely try to work out the same issues that lawyers would help a divorcing couple negotiate or fight out in court in an adversarial divorce:

- **Division of property (assets and debts).** How should jointly owned or marital property (which may include real estate, small business ownership, stocks, automobiles, and household and personal items) be divided? Similarly, how should marital debts such as college loans, mortgages, and outstanding credit card debt, be divided?

- **Spousal maintenance (alimony).** How much money, if any, will one spouse regularly pay to help cover the other's living expenses, and for how long?

- **Child custody and visitation.** Will only one parent have custody of the children, or will custody be shared? How often, for how long, and under what circumstances will the children spend time with each parent? How will the parents resolve major issues like education, medical treatment, and discipline?

- **Child support.** How much money will one parent regularly pay the other to help cover the cost of raising the children?

2. Types of Divorce Mediation

There are two basic—and very different—types of divorce mediation offered throughout the country today: court-sponsored mediation and private mediation.

a. Court-Sponsored Mediation

Court-sponsored mediation occurs in those states where courts can require couples to mediate issues of child custody, visitation, and sometimes child support. In some of these states, all couples with child-related issues are routinely ordered to mediation. In others, judges have the power to order mediation on a case-by-case basis. (The frequency with which judges actually order spouses to mediation varies greatly from one court district to another.)

Court-sponsored mediation generally doesn't last long: just one or two sessions is typical. This is due, in part, to the high volume of cases passing through the mediator's office, and to the limited scope of most court-sponsored mediation—couples usually mediate only issues relating to their children, not disputes over property.

Court-sponsored mediation is usually free or provided at nominal cost. Mediators in these programs are often full-time court employees.

b. Private Mediation

In private mediation, couples voluntarily retain the services of a mediator of their own choosing. The couple can choose to mediate all or most of the issues in their divorce, or to tackle only a few issues. A half dozen or more lengthy sessions may be required, depending on the number and complexity of issues being addressed.

Fees vary widely, from about $100 to $300/hour per couple, with $150 per hour being typical in a mid-size city. The mediators tend to be solo or small group practitioners who specialize in divorce and family mediation.

Court-Sponsored vs. Private Divorce Mediation

How cases get to mediation	Parents are ordered to mediate by the court	Couples agree voluntarily to hire private mediator
Cost	Usually free (but there may be cancellation fees)	Ranges widely from $100 to $300 an hour per couple, depending on geographical area and other factors; lower fees available at some community dispute centers
Issues addressed	Usually limited to parenting arrangements (custody and economic) support and property issues in some states	Couple can mediate all issues (custody and visitation); may include child or just a few, as they choose
Confidentiality	Process is confidential, unless mediator has the power to make a recommendation to the court, or child abuse is revealed	Process is confidential, unless child abuse is revealed
Length of time	Often just one or two sessions of an hour or two each; some programs offer more sessions	Typically, four to eight sessions of a couple of hours each, spread over a few months; length depends on whether the couple has minor children or complicated finances to work out
Involvement of lawyers	Lawyers may, but need not, attend sessions; spouses can consult a lawyer other adviser if they wish	Lawyers may, but need not, attend sessions; spouses can consult a lawyer or other adviser if they wish

3. Advantages of a Mediated Divorce

Divorce mediation offers a number of benefits as compared to a litigated divorce. These include:

- **Cost savings.** Divorce mediation almost always costs less than a two-lawyer adversarial divorce. Even including the cost of consulting lawyers for each spouse, mediation still costs a fraction (perhaps one-third or less) of what it costs to fight out a divorce in court. Mediation greatly reduces the amount of time lawyers need to spend on a case (and therefore, the legal fees each spouse will have to pay).

- **Time savings.** In private divorce mediation, a couple could reasonably expect to work out an agreement on all major issues—children and economics—in half a dozen sessions of one to two hours each, over a period of three to four months. A couple with no minor children (or no major disputes over custody and visitation) and garden-variety, middle-class property issues might finish in half that time. By comparison, two lawyers negotiating the same range of contested issues on behalf of their clients, while at the same time preparing for a contested court action in case negotiations fail, would probably spend a lot more time—running up hundreds of billable hours in the process—to reach a comprehensive settlement.

- **Success and satisfaction rates.** Couples who mediate—whether in court-sponsored programs or privately—more often than not reach agreement on at least some of the issues addressed. Regardless of whether couples reach an agreement, they report a high level of satisfaction with the process, often because it gave them a chance to discuss their concerns with someone who was willing to listen.

- **Post-divorce relationship.** Studies have shown that couples who mediate have more stable agreements (that is, they don't need to modify them as often), more generous visitation plans for the noncustodial parent, fewer missed payments of child support, and a more cordial relationship with each other, than couples who go through an adversarial divorce.

4. Conditions for Successful Mediation

Successful divorce mediation requires that both spouses be able to participate effectively. If either spouse is so impaired psychologically that sustained, rational discussion is impossible, mediation will not work. (A good mediator will usually be able to tell during the first session if a spouse won't be able to mediate effectively. If so, the mediator will terminate the session and refer the couple to a social service agency or another professional who can help, such as a therapist.)

On the other hand, mediation does not require you and your spouse to like each other, or even to be on speaking terms outside the mediation room. It is simply not true, as some divorce lawyers tell their clients, that mediation works only for the relatively small number of couples who remain friendly while they are splitting up. Even couples who are dissatisfied with their marriages and angry at each other can mediate successfully.

5. The Mediation Agreement

When mediation is successful, the mediator will write up an agreement detailing, in plain language, the terms of the settlement. This can be a brief document that covers just the basics—dividing a moderate amount of property and describing the basic child custody and visitation arrangements—or a lengthy agreement that specifies exactly how the couple will divide a long and complicated list of property and how they will handle a number of parenting issues that are likely to arise.

In any type of divorce mediation, the agreement must ultimately be submitted to a judge for approval as part of a legal divorce decree.

B. Issues Common to Court-Sponsored and Private Mediation

Court-sponsored and private mediation are similar in many ways, but there are also significant differences. This section covers issues that are common to both types of divorce mediation. In the two sections following, you will find information specific to each type of divorce mediation:

Section C covers court-sponsored mediation, and Section D covers private mediation (read both if you are not yet sure which type you will use). As you work through the specialized information in Sections C and D, refer back to the general material in this section to fill in the gaps.

> ⚠ **You can't have it both ways.** In theory, you could mediate custody issues in a court-sponsored program and economic issues with a private mediator, but splitting up the issues this way will probably make it difficult to work out an agreement that recognizes the close relationship between custody and economics. For example, in a comprehensive mediation, you could agree that the parent who will have custody of the children most of the time will receive the family home in the property division. If you want to mediate both types of issues, it's best to address them together at one mediation. Because most court-sponsored programs do not handle economic issues, this means that you will probably have to use private mediation.

1. The Role of the Mediator

The goal of any divorce mediator is to help a couple reach a fair and workable agreement on the various issues involved in ending their marriage, including a plan to care for the couple's minor children, if any. The mediator does not function as a lawyer-advocate or a therapist (even if the mediator has a professional background in law or counseling), and usually has no authority to impose a decision.

> ⚠ **In a few states, a mediator can recommend a solution to the judge.** Although mediators have no power to impose a decision, some states allow a mediator to influence a judge's decision in a divorce case. In these states, if the couple does not reach an agreement, the mediator may recommend to the judge how the issues should be decided. For more on mediator recommendations, see Section C, below.

Divorce mediators do not try to help a couple reconcile. Helping a couple deal with hurt or anger, and hashing out problems in the marriage, are relevant to divorce mediation only to the extent that they help the couple deal with current and future issues. Indeed, mediators generally will not consider a couple ready for mediation unless both spouses have accepted that the marriage is really over. (Despite this strong bias against acting as a marriage counselor, mediators report that some mediating couples reconcile, perhaps because mediation helps them communicate in a nonadversarial manner—and drives home the consequences (economic and otherwise) of divorce.)

2. Role of Lawyers

Although the mediator may inform you about the law, you should not rely on the mediator to evaluate the legal consequences of a particular approach to settlement or to recommend a decision or course of action for you. If you need that kind of advice, you should do your own research or get help from a lawyer. (See Chapter 13 for more information on both.)

As a practical matter, not everyone will want, or even need, to retain a consulting lawyer. For example, if you and your spouse have no minor children and no significant property to divide up, or if your income is such that child support will be at the minimum level required by state law and there will be no spousal support, it doesn't make sense to pay a hefty hourly fee for a lawyer's advice during the mediation. On the other hand, if you own a thriving business, have major stock and real estate assets, and are looking at a potentially big claim for spousal support from your stay-at-home spouse, you really should get good legal advice. (The lawyer should be advising or representing just you—not both of you—because you and your spouse will not have the same legal interests or rights.)

If you decide to pay for legal advice, here are some suggestions on working with a lawyer during each phase of the mediation process:

- **Before mediation:** Consult with a lawyer or law coach to:

  ✓ learn about your legal rights—or be referred to good self-help resources

  ✓ learn how a judge might decide your case, and

  ✓ plan your negotiation strategy.

- **During mediation:** If you already understand the legal rules that apply to your dispute, you probably won't need a lawyer present at your mediation. But you may want to consult with your lawyer between sessions to review developments and get advice. If your mediation may last only one session (as in many court-sponsored mediation programs), try to arrange for your lawyer to be available by phone during the session so you can consult right away, if necessary.

  There may be some situations when you do want your lawyer to accompany you to a mediation session. For example, you may expect that a legal issue you don't fully understand will arise during the session and, under the court-sponsored program, a second session will not be available. Or, you may be intimidated by your spouse and want your lawyer there to bolster your confidence and to speak for you.

- **After mediation:** Have your lawyer review the agreement before you sign it to be sure that your legal rights are protected.

3. Preparing for Divorce Mediation

The issues you discuss and the agreement you reach (if any) in divorce mediation will have an important effect on you and your family for many years. It's worth taking the time necessary to prepare yourself. Also, if you carefully consider the range of realistic options available for the major issues involved in your case and what you want a final plan to look like, you will be have an easier time negotiating with your spouse.

In some ways, preparing for divorce mediation is just like preparing for any other mediation. You should:

- **Carefully read the mediation rules and any other materials about the mediation program.** Look for information about the expected length of the session(s), what to bring with you, what issues you will be allowed to discuss, and what will happen if you don't reach a settlement.

- **Research the law.** Because the state bears some responsibility for the welfare of children, the law plays a greater role in custody and visitation cases than in mediation generally. The more you know about your state's rules, the better you will be at negotiating an agreement that meets your needs *and* complies with applicable legal rules.

- **Gather evidence.** If you have documents that show the value of various items of marital property or pertain to the care of your children, bring them to the mediation.

NOLO RESOURCES ON FAMILY LAW

Nolo publishes several books on custody, divorce, and other family law topics. These books will give you a great starting point for your legal research—and for your mediation planning.

- *Using Divorce Mediation*, by Katherine E. Stoner. This book offers readers a step-by-step guide to divorce mediation, including many helpful tips and strategies for a successful mediation.
- *Divorce & Money*, by Violet Woodhouse with Dale Fetherling. Figure out how to assess your goals, divide property and debts, and negotiate a fair settlement, with the help of this book.
- *Child Custody: Building Parenting Agreements That Work*, by Mimi Lyster. This book shows separating parents how to build a comprehensive custody agreement that will stand the test of time.
- *Living Together: A Legal Guide for Unmarried Couples*, by Toni Ihara, Ralph Warner, & Frederick Hertz. Provides information on the legal rights of unmarried couples.
- *A Legal Guide for Lesbian & Gay Couples*, by Hayden Curry, Denis Clifford, & Frederick Hertz. Provides information on the legal rights of same-sex couples.

In addition to this general preparation, you'll need to identify your mediation goals.

a. Identify Your Personal Goals

What do you want to do with the next five or ten years of your life? Keep your current job, find a new one in the same field, go back to school, or begin a new career? What are your goals in terms of your relationship with your children? Spend more day-to-day time with them? Or spend more time with them on weekends and vacations?

Consider how your goals for the foreseeable future might be supported by various possible outcomes in mediation. You might, for instance, want to concentrate on getting higher spousal support payments while going to school, in exchange for being more flexible in other areas. Or, if you're planning to retire and move to another state in a few years, you may be willing to let your spouse keep the family home in exchange for a greater share of other marital property.

b. Identify Your Children's Needs

If you have minor children, the court is obligated to make sure that your custody and visitation decisions are in the best interests of your children. So, to prepare for your mediation, it's a good idea to try sincerely to identify your children's best interests. You'll know you're on the right track if you can acknowledge that your best interests and those of your children may sometimes differ. Start by thinking about what your children most need now. Consider financial support, parental supervision, opportunities for study, recreation, access to siblings and friends, and relationships with other adults such as teachers, grandparents, other relatives, and family friends.

c. Assess Your Financial Needs

In order to negotiate effectively in mediation, you will need to understand what your financial needs will be after the divorce. For example, how much will it cost you each month both to pursue your own goals and to support your children? Do you and your ex-spouse earn or own enough to make these goals realistic?

A good way to begin thinking about financial issues is to try to list all post-divorce living expenses you can reasonably anticipate. Major categories of monthly expenses are likely to include:

- residence payments (rent or mortgage, taxes, insurance, and maintenance)

- groceries and household supplies

- utilities

- telephone

- laundry and cleaning

- clothing

- medical and dental costs (insurance and out-of-pocket payments)

- other insurance (life, disability, and long-term care)

- child care

- education

- entertainment (including restaurants, movies, and so on)

- transportation and auto expenses (lease payments, insurance, gas, repairs, and maintenance)

- installment payments (credit cards and loans), and

- incidentals.

If your mediation will cover financial issues like child support and/or spousal support, bring this financial information to the mediation. If you are going to a private mediator and you will be discussing financial issues, your mediator will probably ask you and your spouse to prepare detailed financial disclosure forms (usually as "homework" in advance of the second or third mediation session). If you suspect your spouse may be inclined to overlook or conceal assets, try quietly, before your mediation begins, to make a list of what you know to be your own and your spouse's assets.

WILL SPOUSAL SUPPORT BE AWARDED?

In most states, a court decides whether to award spousal support based on factors such as each spouse's needs and earning capabilities, the age, health, and standard of living of each spouse, and the length of the marriage. For example, if a couple was in a very short marriage and both have decent jobs with similar earnings, a court probably will award little or no support to either spouse. But if the marriage has lasted 15 years and one spouse has been out of the job market for a decade or more while raising the children, a court is more likely to award spousal support.

Make sure you are informed. If you have reason to believe your spouse is hiding a pile of assets (stocks, bonds, cash, gold, ownership of real estate), you may want to take some legal action that will allow you to subpoena financial records (from banks and stock brokerages, for example) and question your spouse under oath. Talk to a lawyer if you find yourself in this situation.

d. Focus on the Future

Mediation is not about which spouse was right or wrong in a particular dispute or who said what to whom and who was hurt the most. Instead, it's about creating a plan that will allow you and your spouse to dissolve your marriage and, if applicable, continue to parent your children together effectively.

To get the most out of mediation, you need to prepare yourself to use it as a problem-solving process, not as a place to fight old battles. If you can approach mediation looking toward the future, then you will be well prepared to get the most out of the process.

EIGHT TIPS FOR CONDUCTING YOURSELF IN MEDIATION

Mediators are human beings and may be influenced in their work by the impressions they get of you and your spouse. For example, if the mediator comes to see one spouse as more reasonable and reliable than the other, she may try to move the other spouse's position in that direction. Given the choice, you want to be the one the mediator sees as more reasonable. If you are mediating in a court-sponsored program and the mediator has power to make a recommendation regarding child custody and visitation, this becomes all the more important.

Here are some tips that will help you stay on the right track:

1. Remember that your mediator is not a judge. Expecting your mediator to function as a judge, therapist, lawyer, or marriage counselor just wastes time. The mediator's only job is to help you and your spouse reach an agreement.

2. Don't demonize your spouse. Don't try to prove what a bad person your spouse is and what a great person you are. Deciding who is good and who is bad is not the mediator's job.

3. Don't play the victim. Showing how poorly you have been treated, even if it's true, may appear self-serving and the mediator may not take you seriously. In any case, it's usually not relevant to what will happen in the future.

4. Focus on the future. If your spouse persists in bringing up his or her version of the past, simply say that while you don't necessarily agree, you want to focus on the future and look for a solution that will be good for your children and acceptable to both you and your spouse.

5. Keep in mind the best interests of your children. The law says decisions about custody are to be based on the best interests of the child. Develop your arguments around this standard and the mediator will be more likely to help you achieve your goals.

6. Show how you relate to your children. Show what your relationship has been with the child in the past with clear examples (projects, homework, trips, meals, hobbies you share, bedtime rituals, regular time together).

7. Show you can be a good coparent. Emphasize that you understand that a child needs the support and love of both parents (even imperfect ones) and that you can cooperate with your spouse in coparenting your child.

8. Raise whatever forward-looking issues are important to you. Raise important issues—even if they are not legal ones—involving children, your extended family, and future relations with your spouse, while you have the opportunity.

Keep your head while all about you are losing theirs. It can be tough to keep your cool in divorce mediation, especially if your spouse is speaking in anger. Your best approach in this situation is to stay calm. Just politely repeat that you are there to work out what's best for your children in the future. You can count on the mediator's support in helping to calm down your spouse.

4. Who May Attend Mediation?

Usually, just the spouses attend mediation sessions, but you and your spouse can invite others to participate if you both believe that their presence would be helpful (and the mediator agrees). For example, when you are negotiating visitation plans, you may want to include one or more of the children's grandparents or other relatives. You can also invite people who have been involved in an important way in your marriage and family life, such as relatives or friends living in your home. (Your new partner may be welcomed, but not if his or her presence would make it more difficult for your spouse to participate effectively in the mediation.)

Or you may simply want to bring someone with you for emotional support, to assist in describing your family situation, or to help you consider settlement options as they arise during the session. (This would be more typical in court-sponsored mediation, when you may have only one session to get everything on the table and decided.) You also have the right to bring a lawyer to mediation.

Some mediators like to devote part of a session to meeting with children (usually only those who are at least eight or nine years old). This occurs after the parents have completed negotiating their parenting plan. The mediator, meeting alone with the children, will review the plan, ask for the children's reaction, and assure them their parents love them and have worked hard to create a good plan for the future. If the children have questions or problems with the plan, the mediator will review these with the parents. Other mediators prefer not to involve children. Whether your children will be able to participate will depend in part on their ages and on the rules followed by the particular court-sponsored program or private mediator.

If you have children, relatives, or other friends whom you would like to bring to the mediation, check the mediation brochure, or printed rules, or call the mediation office or private mediator to see if this will be allowed.

5. Confidentiality

As a general rule, your mediator will be required by law and/or court rules to keep confidential everything that is said during mediation. This means that if you do not reach a settlement and your case ends up in court, you cannot call the mediator as a witness to tell the judge what your spouse said during mediation. There are some important exceptions to this general rule, however:

- In many states, mediators are required to report reasonable suspicions of child neglect or abuse. This means, for example, that if you tell the mediator—even in private caucus—that you or your spouse has physically abused your children, the mediator may be required by law to report it to a social service agency for investigation.

- Mediators may have a duty to report anyone who, in the mediator's opinion, makes a specific and believable threat against another person. For example, you might say to the mediator in caucus, "I don't care what happens at this mediation, because next Saturday night I'm going to deal with this problem once and for all." If the mediator concludes that this is a threat, he may be legally required to report it to the police or other authority.

⚠ **Don't make threats—even in jest.** Every year, people who work in areas relating to child custody and support, including judges, lawyers, social workers, and occasionally even mediators, are attacked and sometimes killed. As a result, everyone in this field is extremely sensitive to threatening behavior. Just as you wouldn't tell a joke about bombing an airplane while walking through an airport metal detector, you shouldn't make remarks as part of your mediation session that could possibly be interpreted as threats to the mediator, your spouse, or anyone else.

C. Court-Sponsored Divorce Mediation

There are several types of court-sponsored divorce mediation programs. In some states, a court can order a couple to mediate certain issues (usually disputes over child custody and visitation). Some states make mediation available to divorcing couples on a voluntary basis. And in some states that have court-sponsored programs, the mediator has the authority to make a recommendation to the judge as to how the dispute should be resolved, if the parties can't hash things out on their own.

📖 **To find out whether your state requires or makes available court-sponsored divorce mediation, ask the court clerk.** Or, go to Nolo's Legal Research Center, at www.nolo.com/lawcenter/statute/other_courts.cfm, and click on your state. There, you'll find a listing of state court websites. Go to the website of the court where your divorce is pending to look for mediation information.

Most court-sponsored mediation programs have these three things in common:

- they are usually free (if they charge a fee, it is often calculated on a sliding scale)

- the discussions are often limited to parenting issues, such as child custody and visitation, and

- the process usually lasts only one or two sessions.

However, the rules and procedures for mediation will vary from state to state, and from court to court. Ask the court clerk for materials on your state's divorce mediation program.

1. How Court-Sponsored Mediation Works

Every state's court-sponsored mediation program works a bit differently. However, these programs generally have the same broad outlines.

a. Getting Started

When parents with minor children file a divorce action in court, they will automatically be kicked into a state's mandatory mediation program (or given information on any available voluntary program). Unmarried couples might get into a court-sponsored program whenever one parent files a legal action concerning the other's parental rights and responsibilities. Typically, you will receive a written notice from the court that you are required or invited to participate in the mediation program, if you are unable to settle matters among yourselves.

The written notice may tell you the date and time when you should report for mediation, or may instruct you to contact the office to schedule a time. Some states and courts hold mandatory orientation sessions, explaining the mediation program. You may also be required to fill out some paperwork, such as a questionnaire about your dispute.

b. The Mediator

Many court mediators are full-time employees of the court system; others are in private practice and work for the court part time. Most court mediators must meet strict training and educational requirements, although this wasn't always the case. Today, you have a pretty good chance of being assigned a skilled and experienced mediator through a court-sponsored program.

In many court-sponsored programs, you will be assigned a mediator at random, from a pool of available mediators. Sometimes, a particular mediator will be assigned based on the facts of your case (for example, if your child is physically disabled and has special needs, you might be assigned a mediator who has experience with these issues).

Make your needs known if your mediation involves special issues. If you think your case requires a mediator with special training, education, or language ability, make this request to the staff. They will probably accommodate you if they are able.

Once a mediator is assigned to your case, do some checking to make sure that the mediator doesn't have a conflict of interest. (See Chapter 3, Section C, for more on conflicts of interest.)

c. Inside the Mediation Session

Mediation sessions might take place in a conference room in the courthouse or another government building. If you are referred to a private mediator, the mediation might be held at the mediator's private office. In either case, flip charts, blackboards, and tissue boxes often adorn the room.

Some programs and mediators use private caucuses; others do not. If you want the chance to speak privately with the mediator, ask for a caucus; if it is not prohibited under the rules of the program, the mediator probably will agree unless your spouse strongly objects.

d. If You Reach an Agreement

If you are able to come to an agreement in mediation, the mediator will probably draft a document setting out the terms of your agreement on custody, visitation, and any other issues you covered. Once you sign the agreement, it will be sent to the court for approval.

If your agreement involves important legal rights, consider having a lawyer or law coach review it before you sign. Some mediators will give you a draft of the agreement with instructions to take it to your lawyers to review within a set number of days. If no objections are raised, they will then forward it to the court. If the mediator does not make this proposal, you can make it yourself and offer the following "lawyer review" provision:

PROCEDURE FOR LAWYER REVIEW

The above-stated terms may be deemed to reflect the agreement of the parties unless the attorney for either party notifies the [mediation program] in writing of objections within five business days.

You may also want your agreement to include a dispute resolution clause, indicating that you and your spouse will return to mediation if you can't work out any future problems living up to the agreement. After all, your children will grow up, and your parenting arrangements may require some changes. If you wish to include a dispute resolution clause, ask the mediator to add one to the agreement. Here is some sample language you can present to the mediator.

PROCEDURE FOR RESOLVING FUTURE DISPUTES

The parties agree to return to [Name of Court-sponsored Mediation Program] if they are unable to resolve any proposed changes, disputes, or alleged breaches relating to this agreement.

Of course, if mediation is mandatory in disputes over child support or visitation, you won't need a provision like this.

e. If You Don't Reach an Agreement

The rules of your court-sponsored program will determine what happens if you can't reach a settlement. Some programs will offer you additional sessions if the mediator believes you could reach an agreement given more time, but other programs limit each case to a single session.

If you cannot reach an agreement in the time your program allots to you, you can:

- continue negotiating with your spouse on your own

- hire a private mediator and try again

- ask the court to appoint an independent evaluator to make a recommendation (available in some communities)

- submit the case to arbitration. Arbitration is most appropriate when a couple is unable to agree on some critical point, such as the amount of spousal support (alimony). Some states prohibit arbitration of child custody and support, although the trend seems to favor increased use of arbitration.

- litigate the issues in court.

2. Mandatory Mediation

Generally, you don't have to do much to comply with a mandatory mediation requirement. Most programs require only that you show up for at least one session—you don't have to agree to anything.

Despite these minimal requirements, there may be good reasons why you do not want to mediate (or you don't want to mediate in the court-sponsored program). If you believe that it would not be a good idea to attend mandatory mediation, you may be able to avoid it. Typical reasons that would convince a court to let you out of the program include:

- **Reaching an agreement before mediation.** If you and your spouse can come to an agreement on parenting issues, you won't have to use the court's program

- **Choosing a private mediator.** If you would like to try mediation but are leery of the court's program, you may be able to opt out of the court program by using a private mediator or community mediation center. You will have to pay for the mediation if you go this route, but it will give you an opportunity to reach a comprehensive agreement, choose your own mediator, and spend more time negotiating. It will also allow you to avoid a mediator's recommendation.

- **Domestic violence.** Some states will excuse you from mandatory mediation if you can show that you have been a victim of violence or abuse in your marriage. Other states will require you to mediate, but will allow you to meet with the mediator separately, rather than in joint sessions.

- **Substance abuse.** Some programs will excuse you from mediating if your spouse has problems with alcohol or drug abuse.

- **Child abuse.** If the court determines, through past convictions or evidence presented, that one parent engaged in child abuse, the court may let the other parent opt out of a mandatory mediation program and go directly to a judge. In these cases, courts have a greater interest in supervising the disposition of parenting issues, to make sure children are protected.

3. If the Mediator Will Make a Recommendation

As noted earlier, mediators in some states have authority to recommend how your case should be decided if you and your spouse cannot reach an agreement. Even in these states, however, not all local courts give mediators the power to recommend.

When you are first referred to a court-sponsored mediation program, find out whether the mediator has the authority to make a recommendation. If the mediator has this power, you will be under more pressure to settle and therefore not risk a negative recommendation, and you should plan your mediation strategy accordingly. You will also want to avoid any conduct that could turn the mediator against you.

a. Mediation Strategies

Here are some tips for dealing with a mediator who has the power to make a recommendation:

- Know—and address—applicable legal standards. If you and your spouse are not able to reach an agreement, the mediator will have to make a recommendation based on specific legal standards. If you can base your presentation on those standards, it will make it easier for the mediator to recommend in your favor. In most states, the standard for determining custody is "the best interests of the child," which includes such factors as:

  ✓ the child's health, safety, and welfare

  ✓ any history of abuse against the child, and

  ✓ the nature and quality of contact between the parents (that is, each spouse's willingness to be a coparent with the other spouse).

- **Show that you can get along with your spouse.** The mediator will be impressed by your ability to act civilly toward your spouse. It suggests maturity, emotional stability, and reliability—all traits a mediator would want to see in someone asking for custody or liberal visitation. On the other hand, if you cannot control yourself in the presence of your spouse, it may discourage the mediator (and therefore, the judge) from wanting to see you have custody of your kids.

- **Mind your manners.** Mediators—especially those who are full-time employees of the court-sponsored program—are trusted coworkers of the family court judges. If you act disrespectfully to your mediator or otherwise make a poor impression, the judge will often find out about it, and may hold it against you in making a custody award.

b. Challenging the Recommendation

If you do not agree with a judge's decision that is based on the mediator's recommendation, some states give you the right to challenge the decision in court. Typically, you would cross-examine the mediator to show some important fact was omitted, misstated, or misinterpreted in the recommendation the mediator prepared for the judge. You might show, for example, that the recommendation failed to mention that your spouse was, until recently, a heavy cocaine user. You should know, however, that these challenges don't succeed very often.

Get help if you plan to challenge a mediator's recommendation. It's a tough job to overcome a mediator's recommendation. If you plan to try, consult with an experienced family lawyer or law coach—and consider having the lawyer represent you at the court hearing.

D. Private Divorce Mediation

Private divorce mediation has grown in popularity since it first became widely available in the 1970s. Today, it is used by many couples who understand that a good divorce is almost as valuable as a good marriage.

This section covers some issues specific to private divorce mediation.

1. Getting Started

To get your case into divorce mediation, you'll have to convince your spouse to give it a try.

a. When Should You Propose Mediation?

The best time to propose mediati V to your spouse is after both of you have accepted that your marriage is over (until then mediation will not be productive) but before either of you has filed for divorce. Once you file court papers and get lawyers involved, it can be much more difficult to reach an agreement to mediate. However, you do not need to be living apart in order to mediate; many divorcing couples, for example, start mediation while still living together but planning to separate (perhaps because they are waiting for their house to sell).

If divorce papers have already been filed in your case, you can still propose mediation. In the early stages of a contested divorce proceeding, positions have usually not hardened, as often occurs later when the very nature of the adversary process propels at least one side to go for the jugular (and by so doing, convinces the other to respond in kind).

You can even try mediation if you and your spouse have not decided to divorce, but only to separate temporarily. You could, for example, agree to a trial separation and mediate how to divide household bills and parenting responsibilities during the period you are living apart.

b. Proposing Mediation to Your Spouse

Rather than trying to "sell" your spouse on mediation, it's usually best to just provide some information about the process and the advantages of mediation, and suggest that you both consider it as an option. If you are on speaking terms, you can raise the idea during a regular conversation and offer to send some literature. If you are not speaking, you can do the same in a brief letter. Whether in person or by letter, here are some points to make:

- "We can both save money on legal fees and avoid a possibly nasty public court fight."

- "Mediation offers us a cooperative, nonadversarial approach to problem-solving—if we both agree to a settlement, nothing can be imposed on us."

- "In mediation we can both think through what we really want rather than engaging in a legal tug of war."

- "Mediation will benefit our children by reducing conflict between us now and in the future."

- "Our discussions will be confidential, so we can avoid public disclosure of our personal problems."

- "In mediation, we can complete our agreements more quickly, so we can move ahead with our lives."

- "Neither of us will be risking anything legally because we can each have our own lawyers review the agreement before we sign anything."

- "If we don't go to private mediation we'll be required to go to the court-sponsored program anyway [if you and your spouse have minor children and if your state has a mandatory court-sponsored program], so we might as well go private and take advantage of choosing our own mediator, discussing all issues, scheduling the sessions at our convenience, etc."

You can also offer to call several divorce mediators in your area and have them send printed material to you and your spouse, then get back in touch later to see if you can both agree on a mediator.

DEALING WITH A RELUCTANT SPOUSE

If you have proposed mediation but your spouse is reluctant to participate, try the following:

- Have materials sent about mediation. If you have not already done so, have a local divorce mediator or mediation service send printed materials to your spouse. Some state and national organizations that promote use of mediation also will send materials upon request.

- Have your spouse talk to a mediator. Suggest that your spouse have a private phone conversation with one of the mediators you would be willing to use. Most mediators would be willing to accept a call from your spouse to answer questions about mediation.

- Offer to pay for the first session. Many mediators will offer an initial session of one-half to one hour during which the mediator can assess whether mediation is appropriate for a couple and the couple can consider whether they want to go ahead with the mediation. To encourage your spouse to participate, you can offer to pay the full fee for this session.

---

2. Choosing a Mediator

There are many thousands of mediators in the United States today who specialize in divorce and family cases. The majority are in solo practice; most of the rest work at community mediation centers or in small group practices. The easiest way to find a list of divorce mediators is to look in the telephone directory under "mediation" or "divorce." Other resources in your community who may be able to give you the names of divorce mediators include:

- the staff of your community mediation center

- matrimonial lawyers

- the staff at a family services office (some are connected to a local court; others are independent, nonprofit agencies)

- clergy

- therapists

- employee assistance personnel at large corporations

- friends and relatives who have used a mediator.

Once you get a list of possible names, you should check the person out. The mediator you select should not only be professionally competent, but should also have a style and approach to mediation that is broadly compatible with your own. For example, if you are a practical, down-to-earth person, you probably don't want a mediator who speaks what you see as New Age psychobabble. On the other hand, if you feel that your inability to maximize your potential as human beings is precisely what has been wrong with your marriage, you may find that a mediator who focuses only on practical issues to be jarring.

THE MEDIATION CONTRACT

Your mediator will probably require you and your spouse each to sign a contract for mediation services. The purposes of the contract are to clarify in writing the procedures that will be followed in the mediation, and to make sure that the mediator gets paid.

The contract will probably set out the mediator's fees and schedule of payments, and recite the goals of mediation, your right to have an attorney, rules of confidentiality, disclosure of financial information, and rules about participation by third parties. It will express the willingness of both spouses to make a good faith effort to work toward a settlement, and may commit you not to pursue litigation, arbitration, or other remedies during the course of the mediation.

If the mediator sends you a contract that obligates you to more than one session of mediation, call the mediator and explain that, while you are willing to pay for the first session up front, you prefer to wait until its conclusion before making a longer-term commitment. This will give you time during the first session to decide if you really want to use this mediator.

When you find a mediator you think you would like to work with, there are a number of ways to evaluate his or her suitability for your case. For example, ask for names of lawyers who have reviewed agreements the mediator has drafted for other couples; the lawyers can give you an opinion on the mediator's technical competence. You can also ask the mediator for references from former clients. The mediator will not give you another client's name, but may be willing to take your name and have a former client call you.

QUESTIONS FOR A PROSPECTIVE DIVORCE MEDIATOR

Here are some topics you will probably want to discuss with a mediator you are considering:

- fees
- training and accreditation
- experience
- willingness to intervene to protect a weaker party or block an unfair agreement
- willingness to provide referrals to lawyers and other professionals
- use of private caucuses (some divorce mediators use private caucuses; others don't)
- desire or willingness to meet with your children
- form of the final agreement (some mediators prepare a memorandum detailing your agreement, which must then be translated into a legal agreement by one of your lawyers; other mediators will draft a final, legally binding agreement).

3. Inside the Mediation Session

Private divorce mediation tends to be much slower than court-sponsored mediation and cover more issues. Indeed, it's different enough from court-sponsored mediation and from mediation generally, that it's worth going through the process step by step.

- **STAGE ONE: Intake and Commitment.** The mediator will start the first session by reviewing the procedures, rules, and goals of mediation. This is the time to ask questions, and to decide whether you can trust and feel comfortable with this mediator. If you and your spouse have not previously signed a contract with the mediator, you will likely be asked to sign it now. If you want, you can have your lawyer or law coach review it and then bring it to the next session either signed or with specific questions for the mediator.

- **STAGE TWO: Financial Disclosure and Fact-Finding.** At the end of your first session, the mediator may give you financial worksheets asking you to list your assets, such as bank accounts, stocks, bonds, real estate, partnerships, pension funds, and business interests. (If your mediation is limited to parenting issues, you may not have to make such detailed financial disclosures.) In some states, the information requested on the forms is dictated by state law, and each spouse will later need to affirm to the court that complete disclosure of assets was made. You may also be asked to turn over to each other payroll records, checkbooks, pension plan summaries, and three years' worth of past federal and state tax returns. You will probably spend the second session (and perhaps longer) analyzing these records together.

If substantial assets are involved, you may want to have a lawyer or an accountant review your spouse's financial records to interpret financial data and be sure everything has been disclosed. If you believe your spouse is hiding assets, a lawyer can issue a subpoena for additional records. But consult with the mediator before asking a lawyer to do this; the mediator will want to know about any actions that are likely to make the process more adversarial.

- **STAGE THREE: Identifying the Issues.** After the financial cards have been laid on the table, the mediator will invite discussion of the issues. This will likely occur late in the second or early in the third session. On some issues—who will have primary custody of the children, for example—you may already be in agreement. But as to others—for example, the details of visitation and amount of child support—you may be far apart. Some property issues may also emerge that are going to need a lot of negotiation: Should the cost of one spouse's professional degree be considered marital property, some of which is owed to the nonprofessional spouse? Who should get the home computer? Once all the issues are identified, the mediator may help the couple decide the order in which they should be discussed.

- **STAGE FOUR: Negotiations.** For the next several sessions, you and your spouse will address—in order—the issues you've identified. As you cover each issue, the mediator will help you think of ways to resolve it that you may not have thought of on your own. Often, due to anger and emotional fatigue, couples are unable to see options for settling disputes beyond a few obvious choices. The mediator will help you take a fresh look at the issues in order to think of all options for settlement. If your mediator uses caucusing, you are most likely to caucus during the negotiation stage.

- **STAGE FIVE: Agreement, Drafting the Memo, Lawyer Review, Closing.** When negotiations have concluded because an agreement has been reached, the mediator will draft the proposed agreement, often referred to as a "memorandum of understanding." The mediator will review each part with you in session to make sure the wording accurately reflects your agreement. At this point, mediators who include children in the process may invite you to have your older children come in for part of a session so the mediator can explain the process you have gone through and the decisions that have been made.

You and your spouse will each receive a copy of the draft memorandum for your lawyers or other advisers to review, if you wish. Most mediators will hold one session in reserve in case you need to come back to discuss questions raised during this review. Typically, one or both parties will take the final memorandum to a lawyer to be drafted into appropriate legal form (sometimes called a "separation agreement" or "marital settlement agreement") and presented to the court for approval and issuance of a legal divorce decree. In some cases, the mediator will draft the court papers for you directly. ■

CHAPTER 11

Mediating Business Disputes

Owners and managers of large businesses are extremely sensitive to the high costs of litigation—not only in money paid for legal fees, but also in executive time, damage to customer relationships, and potential harm to their public image. This is why many large companies are turning to mediation to resolve disputes.

Smaller businesses have been somewhat slower to embrace mediation, but this seems to be a result of lack of awareness of the potential advantages of mediation rather than a deliberate business strategy. Indeed, because small businesses often have less comprehensive insurance coverage and are therefore at risk of being wiped out by an outsized court judgment or arbitration award, they can realize huge benefits through mediation.

Unlike mediating a simple neighborhood squabble or a straightforward damage claim against an insurance company, mediating a business dispute usually takes considerable time and energy. For example, a mediation between two partners about the division of a $3 million business might take a week of daily sessions. The partners might need to invite financial experts to help create and refine various buyout scenarios. And even when everything is supposedly settled, the final agreement will have to be drafted painstakingly, to account for all of the important details.

Here are some of the advantages mediation offers to the business owner:

- **Control of the outcome.** The terms of settlement, if any, will be decided by the parties, not imposed by a judge, jury, or arbitrator. This greatly reduces anxiety, especially when the dispute is large enough to threaten the solvency of the business or its owners.

- **Control of the process.** The parties will select the mediator and decide which issues will be addressed, when sessions will be scheduled, and how fees will be apportioned. In short, the process of mediation is far more defined and predictable than the free-for-all of court proceedings.

- **Ability to accommodate multiple parties.** Business disputes often involve three, four, or even more parties. For example, even a relatively simple mediation over the construction of a small retail store might involve not only the store owner and general contractor, but also an architect, a soils engineer, and several subcontractors. Mediation is the one forum where everyone involved in a dispute can come together to try to hammer out a settlement.

- **Savings on legal fees.** In mediation, lawyers are usually used only in a consultative role, with executives normally participating directly in the mediation. In a lawsuit, lawyers take over all of the important decisions—and run up tremendous legal fees in the process.

- **Savings on expert fees.** Instead of paying a high-priced expert to explain technical issues to the judge and jury, the knowledgeable parties can handle those discussions in mediation. Using a mediator who has expertise in the technical subject matter can be a big benefit, too.

- **Time savings.** Mediation can be scheduled and likely concluded as quickly as the parties need.

- **No unwanted publicity.** Mediation avoids public exposure of business mistakes, internal problems, and trade secrets. This is no small matter. For all sorts of sensitive issues, a prominent local or national company has a huge interest in preserving its reputation and goodwill, and not becoming media fodder.

- **Preserving important relationships.** Nonadversarial mediation can allow the relationship between disputing businesses to outlast the dispute. The very process of arriving at a consensus decision can be the foundation for the parties to continue to do business together. By contrast, going to court destroys relationships almost every time. Many businesses are also realizing the value of using mediation as part of an overall strategy to build and keep good customer relationships.

Against this positive background, this chapter is designed to help business owners and managers successfully mediate disputes that arise out of the ownership and operation of their businesses. In so doing, it deals with several important considerations not generally a part of other types of mediation, such as:

- where to look for and how to find a business mediator

- which types of business disputes are typically mediated, and

- how to get the other company to agree to mediate.

Read this chapter along with the rest of the book. This chapter does not repeat the essential information covered in Chapters 1 through 9. Instead, it covers only the special issues that are most likely to come up in mediating small business disputes. To get the full picture, read the first nine chapters of the book before you get into this material.

A. Selecting a Business Mediator

In selecting a mediator for your business dispute, you should consider a few special factors regarding the skills and style of the mediator you choose. This section briefly examines these factors, as well as where to find mediators who can handle business disputes.

1. Mediator Skills

As discussed in Chapter 3, mediators bring to their work a combination of process skills (knowledge of how to conduct a mediation) and subject-matter skills (understanding of the subject area in dispute). Mediators with good process skills can handle a wide array of cases, even if they start with very limited knowledge of the dispute's subject matter.

a. Choosing a Mediator With Subject-Matter Skills

In some business mediations, having a mediator with subject-matter knowledge can be especially useful. Some business disputes (partners breaking up, for example) cry out for a mediator with financial savvy. Although the parties are the ones who have to agree, a mediator who knows how to structure a sensible buyout plan that includes safeguards to be sure installment payments are made and anticipates likely tax consequences would probably be more helpful than a mediator from a community mediation center who has trouble balancing a checkbook. Similarly, if your business dispute involves technical issues—such as manufacturing processes, patents, or construction law—it makes sense to use a mediator who understands these issues.

A mediator with subject-matter expertise can help you in two ways: you won't have to spend time at the beginning of the mediation educating the mediator about the issues, and the mediator may be better able to generate creative settlement proposals that involve the technical aspects of the dispute.

b. Choosing a Mediation Team

An alternative is to use co-mediators. Often, a mediation team consists of a skilled general mediator paired with a second person who serves as a technical adviser. The advisor might be another mediator who doesn't feel up to handling the case alone, or simply a technical expert from outside the mediation field. If you want to use a co-mediation team, you will probably want to go through a private dispute resolution company. The case manager should be able to put together a team that will meet your needs.

c. Choosing a Facilitative or Evaluative Mediator

You will also have to decide whether you want someone whose style is facilitative or evaluative. (See Chapter 3 for a discussion of these different styles.) The facilitative mediator sees his or her role primarily as a neutral listener, helper, and message carrier. The evaluative mediator is more inclined, after listening to everyone's point of view, to help the parties develop a concrete settlement proposal. Many business people prefer evaluative mediators because their input tends to speed up the process. This approach also puts executives in the familiar role of weighing options rather than having to start from scratch and work cooperatively with an opponent to create a solution to the problem.

2. Finding a Business Mediator

Private dispute resolution companies will have on their panels a number of capable mediators for business disputes. You can also use an independent mediator who specializes in business cases. To find a mediator for your business dispute, try the following:

- Ask a local lawyer who specializes in that subject area—for example, patent law, securities, or construction—to recommend a good mediator.

- Call the national office of a professional association involved in the subject area.

- Contact a mediator association, such as the Association for Conflict Resolution (www.acrnet.org) or Mediate.com (www.mediate.com). These organizations offer referral services on their websites.

Community mediation centers generally do not take on cases between businesses. If your business is small and your dispute reasonably straightforward, however, your local community mediation center may be able to handle it. If so, this would be the least expensive place to take your case. And even if they can't help you, they may be able to suggest a good local mediator who can.

3. Fees

Fees will depend on the number of parties involved, how long the mediation lasts, whether the mediation service or independent mediator operates nationally, regionally, or locally, and the particular mediator you select. Typically, fees will be quoted as a combination of administrative charges plus an hourly or daily rate based on the mediator's time. In general, for a relatively straightforward two-party mediation lasting one full day, using a mediator from a national firm, the cost per party will be in the range of $1,500 to $2,500. If the mediator is provided by a regional or local company, the daily cost per party would probably be more like $1,200–$1,500.

Business mediations may take anywhere from a day to a week of a mediator's time. The mediator will spend at least several hours of that time reviewing documents submitted by the parties; the rest will be spent in actual mediation sessions.

B. Business Disputes That Can Be Mediated

Many disputes typically faced by businesses are good candidates for mediation. Some examples are discussed below.

1. Disputes With Another Business

Many business disputes involve contracts between two or more businesses—written or oral agreements you have with your suppliers, vendors, or customers, for example. Typically, contract disputes are about the quality of goods or services, responsibilities of the parties, late delivery, or payments due.

But business disputes can go well beyond contracts. Any issue that a business might work with another business on—or sue another business over—could turn into a dispute. These issues include intellectual property (trademarks, copyright, and patents), leases, advertising, customer sharing, and much more.

EXAMPLE: *The owner of a pizza franchise rented space in a shopping plaza for a new restaurant. Unfortunately, asbestos was discovered in the ceiling, and the space was unusable for a year while the asbestos was removed. The restaurant owner demanded $70,000 in damages from the plaza, based on his estimates of lost profits. The plaza manager refused, saying the space had been rented "as is," and that, in any case, it was unlikely that a new restaurant would have cleared a $70,000 profit. As a complicating factor, the restaurant owner also had a contract with the franchiser, which required the restaurant to be open by a certain date and charged the restaurant owner a monthly fee regardless of income.*

After weeks of acrimonious negotiation, the restaurant owner suggested that they try mediation as an alternative to his filing a lawsuit. Both the plaza owner and the franchiser agreed to participate.

The mediation lasted two full days. On the afternoon of the second day, during private caucuses between the mediator and each party, the general outline of a three-way agreement took shape. Under this plan, the plaza agreed to pay the restaurant $20,000 for lost profits and to pay the franchiser one-third of the restaurant's franchise fee for the months during which opening was delayed.

The franchiser agreed to forego one-third of the fee, and to look to the restaurant owner for the balance. But instead of paying this in cash, the restaurant owner agreed to reduce the size of his exclusive franchise territory, which would allow the franchiser to make up the lost income by selling another franchise in a nearby town. In addition, once the restaurant finally opened, the restaurant owner agreed to give the plaza manager $10,000 in gift certificates, which the manager could distribute to other tenants and their customers to build good will and help ensure the restaurant would succeed.

2. Customer Complaints

Some of the most expensive and publicly embarrassing lawsuits a business faces are those brought by irate customers. These can include allegations of defective products or substandard services, misleading advertising, and/or illegal collection practices. Some grievances are relatively small, while others are much more serious, as might be the case if an organized group of customers claims your advertising has intentionally misled or defrauded them. Either way, mediation gives your customers a confidential way to vent their anger and lets your company settle privately without risking an adverse court decision that might encourage similar claims. Hopefully, it also results in a happier customer—who won't badmouth your business until the end of time.

EXAMPLE: *A couple who had requested a smoke-free hotel room complained that the room they were given was instead contaminated by chemical cleaning agents. They demanded their money back, plus an unspecified amount for what they claimed was false advertising (the hotel emphasized "clean, smoke-*

free air"), and unspecified damages for inhalation of the chemicals. When they threatened to get a lawyer and bring a class action on behalf of themselves and other former hotel guests who had experienced the same problem, the hotel invited them to mediate, offering to pay all fees.

In mediation, the health risks claimed by the couple were discussed at length in the presence of both parties and in private caucuses between the couple and the mediator. Although the couple continued to claim that they had both gotten headaches and felt nauseated during their stay, they reluctantly concluded that they probably wouldn't be able to prove significant long-term injuries from inhaling the cleaning agents. The hotel manager also explained that the hotel had some unusual difficulties on the day in question, because the assistant manager abruptly quit, and a small business meeting had suddenly demanded 20 additional rooms. The couple eventually settled with the hotel for an apology, a cash payment equal to three times what they paid for their room, and free passes to several restaurants and movie theaters owned by the hotel's parent corporation. In addition, the couple agreed in writing not to bring any lawsuit on their own behalf or on behalf of other former hotel guests.

3. Construction Disputes

Construction disputes are particularly well-suited to mediation. Not only do they often involve many parties (owner-developer, architect, engineer, primary contractor, and subcontractors), but they also tend to involve technical issues that might be costly and difficult to explain to a judge or jury. In addition, because construction often halts while a dispute is being resolved, time may be a critical factor. In fact, the cost of having a job shut down sometimes eclipses the value of the underlying dispute.

EXAMPLE: *The construction of a retail store was interrupted when cracks appeared in the concrete slab floor. The owner, who had to pay to have the floor ripped out and redone, sued seven parties for a total of $2 million in money damages on claims of breach of contract, negligence, and breach of warranty. The defendants included the architecture firm that designed the building, the engineering firm that supervised construction, the primary contractor, the concrete manufacturer, the subcontractor who mixed and poured the concrete, and the subcontractor who finished the concrete floor. After initial depositions in the case were completed, the owner contacted a private dispute resolution company for help convincing the other parties to mediate. Everyone agreed to participate. The mediation service arranged for a co-mediation team consisting of an attorney-mediator who had experience as both a construction litigator and a mediator of multiparty disputes, and a second mediator with a background in civil engineering and a specialty in soils, foundations, and concrete technology. During the first full day of mediation, much of the discussion concerned proper and improper ways to pour concrete. Once this issue was hashed out (about halfway through the second day), the defendants met privately among themselves and proposed to pay the owner $1.2 million, to be split among them according to a formula they themselves had worked out. By the end of the day, the owner accepted the offer and the case settled.*

4. Ownership Disputes

Disputes among business owners—partners, stockholders, or members—can destroy a business and, in the case of family-owned businesses, sometimes tear a family apart. For these disputes, mediation offers a protected forum where the parties can safely work out a private settlement.

EXAMPLE: *The widows of two brothers who together had founded a large chain of auto service centers, were shocked when a nephew revealed that one of the brothers had used corporate funds to develop a private real estate business on the side. This disclosure, coupled with a demand that the money be repaid to the company immediately, threatened to tear apart the extended family of siblings and cousins, all of whom owned shares in the auto business. To avoid a wrenching, public battle, the two women retained a private dispute resolution firm. After several months of mediation, the family agreed on a restructuring plan. The children of the brother who had set up the real estate venture agreed to pay the other brother's children the present value of the approximate amount their father had siphoned from the company. Everyone agreed that these payments could be made over ten years. This solution kept the real estate business on one side of the family, while at the same time dealing with the improper diversion of cash from the business.*

C. Getting Your Case to the Table

Overcoming the other party's reluctance to mediate can be a problem in business disputes (as in other types of disputes). Here are some techniques to consider in getting your business case into mediation.

1. Contract Provision

If your dispute arises out of a contract that requires the parties to mediate, you shouldn't have a problem. Your first step in a contract dispute is to check the contract for a mediation clause. These clauses usually appear near the end of the contract, under a heading such as "Mediation," "Dispute Resolution," or sometimes, mistakenly, "Arbitration." Even if the contract calls for arbitration rather than mediation, you can propose to the other party that you mediate first to see if you can mutually arrive at a solution, thus avoiding the risk that an arbitrator will impose a result one or both of you doesn't like.

SAMPLE MEDIATION CONTRACT CLAUSE

For those in a position to think ahead, the best way to get your business's disputes to mediation is by adding a contract clause requiring the parties to mediate before going to court. Below is a sample mediation clause:

If a dispute arises out of or relates to this contract, and if the dispute cannot be settled through direct negotiation, the parties agree to try in good faith to settle the dispute by mediation before resorting to arbitration or litigation.

You can make your mediation clause more detailed by specifying which mediation service the parties must use, the minimum amount of time the parties must spend in mediation, and how fees will be apportioned. Use this kind of clause only if you have a strong preference for a particular mediation service. For example:

If a dispute arises out of or relates to this contract, and if the dispute cannot be settled through direct negotiation, the parties agree to try in good faith to settle the dispute by mediation before resorting to arbitration or litigation. To fulfill the requirements of this provision, the parties agree to participate in at least four hours of mediation provided by the ABC Mediation Co., Inc., of Grand Rapids, Michigan, and to split the mediation fees equally between them.

2. Invoke the Other Party's ADR Pledge or Policy

Hundreds of major American companies (and thousands of their subsidiaries) have pledged in writing to try mediation as a first resort when disputes arise. This pledge, called the Corporate Policy Statement on Alternatives to Litigation, is circulated by a nonprofit group called CPR Institute for Dispute Resolution. It reads, in part:

We recognize that for many disputes there is a less expensive, more effective method of resolution than the traditional lawsuit. . . . In the event of a business dispute between our company and another company which has made or will then make a similar statement, we are prepared to explore with that other party resolution of the dispute through negotiation or ADR techniques before pursuing full-scale litigation.

If another party in your dispute has signed this pledge, you can remind them of this, and tell them that you expect them to honor their pledge and give mediation a try.

EXAMPLE: *A small machine tool company and a major copier manufacturer had a contract dispute that looked like it was headed for court. The president of the tool company suggested that they try mediation. At first, the copier manufacturer said no. But when the tool company's lawyer discovered that the copier company had signed an ADR pledge and pointed this out to its general counsel, the copier maker agreed to mediate.*

To find out whether a company involved in your dispute has signed the pledge, ask the person you are dealing with or the head of the company's law department. If you can't reach anyone who knows the answer (or if you don't trust the answer they give you), go to the website of the CPR Institute for Dispute Resolution, at www.cpradr.org. Click "ADR Pledges" to see the text of the pledge, plus a list of signatories.

In a few places, business have developed their own ADR pledges, sometimes at the urging of a local chamber of commerce or another business organization. For example, nearly 1,000 businesses have signed "The Colorado Pledge" committing themselves to explore mediation. To find out if a party to your dispute has signed a similar local or statewide pledge, try contacting the chamber of commerce or the bar association where the other party has its principal place of business. To find local chambers of commerce, go to the chamber's national website, at www.uschamber.com.

IF YOU DON'T WANT TO MEDIATE

What if the other party demands that you mediate based on a mediation clause in a contract you have signed? Do you have to go to mediation? The answer is yes, but that's not a major commitment. Most mediation clauses commit the parties only to make a "good faith" effort to mediate. In real life, this means only that you must agree to go to the mediation, behave pleasantly, and at least go through the motions of giving it a fair try. It does not obligate you to agree to pay for the most expensive mediator, prepare an exhaustive premediation memorandum, confide to the mediator all your hidden agendas and business secrets, or help the mediator come up with settlement proposals. However, we urge you to keep an open mind about the process—you might find that it's more useful than you expected.

3. Invoke the Other Party's Attorney's Pledge

Not to be outdone by their business clients, more than 1,500 of the nation's law firms have pledged to discuss with their clients the availability of mediation and other forms of dispute resolution. Called the "Law Firm Policy Statement on Alternatives to Litigation," the pledge is circulated by the CPR Institute for Dispute Resolution (see above). It states, in part:

(W)here appropriate, the responsible attorney will discuss with the client the availability of ADR procedures so the client can make an informed choice concerning resolution of the dispute.

If you are unable to get the other party to even consider mediation, ask your lawyer to find out if the other party's law firm has signed this pledge. If so, your attorney can remind the opposing lawyer of the firm's pledge to at least consider the use of mediation. To find out if the other party's law firm has signed the pledge, check the CPR Institute's website, at www.cpradr.org.

4. Invoke Government Policy Favoring Mediation

If your dispute is over a contract to supply goods or services to the federal government, you can encourage a federal agency to mediate by invoking government-wide policies favoring alternative dispute resolution. Under the Alternative Dispute Resolution Act, federal agencies must appoint a "dispute resolution specialist" to develop policies for the use of mediation and other dispute resolution methods. Many agencies, including all branches of the military, have gone further and signed a government "ADR Pledge." The Pledge says the agencies will use mediation and related techniques to try to prevent and resolve disputes arising from outside procurement contracts.

D. Preparing for Your Business Mediation

Chapter 5 covers preparing for your mediation. As you read Chapter 5, note especially Section E, which explains how expert consultants can help you prepare for mediation. If you are involved in the breakup of a small business, for example, consulting with an accountant, business broker, or business valuation expert can help you define your goals and consider various options—including some you may not have considered—for carving up or selling the business, or for buying out your partner's share.

E. Inside the Mediation Session

Business mediation sessions will generally follow the six-stage process described in Chapter 6. Pay particular attention to Section E, which explains the value of consulting with expert advisers during the mediation.

As your mediation moves toward a conclusion, proposals and counterproposals are likely to fly back and forth fairly quickly. This is when consultation with the right experts can be vitally important. Unfortunately, this will be difficult or impossible unless you have had the foresight to line up your experts in advance. For example, suppose your case involves a business breakup, and you propose to buy all of your partner's shares for cash. Your partner counters by saying that she wants to retain all of the company's patents and copyrights, and will pay for them in a complicated formula of a down payment and a percentage of profits over five years, with various additions and subtractions depending on market conditions. In this situation, you will want someone on your side of the table to crunch the numbers and consider the tax consequences of various scenarios. If you want this information available at the mediation, you'll need to have skilled help at the ready.

Typically, both parties will want to consult privately with their own experts and use that information to develop their own negotiating positions. But sometimes this approach will lead to an impasse, especially when one or both side's experts stake out a position that is too extreme. For example, your accountant may say your partner's shares are worth $50,000, but your partner's accountant may insist they are worth $500,000. These expert opinions won't advance your negotiations very far, even though both sides are paying dearly for them.

In certain circumstances, you can avoid or break this expensive stalemate by agreeing to abide by the opinion of just one expert. Because no one is bound to make a settlement based on the single expert's opinion, this is less radical than it might at first seem. But how will you choose the expert? One approach is to ask the mediator to select someone. Mediators who handle a lot of business breakups, for example, probably can locate a good business valuation expert on short notice. Or, you could ask your accountant and the other party's accountant to get together and select a third accountant.

F. Writing the Agreement

Because business issues tend to be complicated, and business people are prone to rely on the literal language of contracts in a later dispute, it's especially important that your agreement be clear and complete.

Typically, you will reach a settlement after a long day of mediation, and you will leave the room with only an outline or rough draft of the agreement, initialed by both parties and the mediator. If your mediation ends like this, be ready for days or possibly weeks of phone calls, faxes, and email messages back and forth as lawyers or other advisers for both sides help work out the final language. You may even need to reconvene the mediation for a follow-up session to get the mediator's help in ironing out the final wording. As the saying goes, "The devil is in the details."

It is also fairly common for an agreement to start to unravel during the final drafting stage, as one or both parties is influenced by others who were not at the mediation, or simply has legitimate second thoughts about some aspect of the pending settlement. Don't despair. This kind of "backsliding" is fairly typical and does not mean all your hard work has been for naught. Go back and mediate some more. After all, fighting over details may even be a good thing if it forces both parties to get the final settlement agreement exactly right.

G. Other Dispute Resolution Procedures for Business Cases

If you don't think mediation is right for your case, or if your mediation doesn't result in a settlement, you might want to consider one of these alternative procedures.

1. Mediation With Settlement Proposal

If your case does not settle during the mediation, but you believe the mediator is fair and has a good understanding of the dispute, you can ask the mediator to prepare a settlement proposal (also referred to as a "written recommendation") for the parties to consider. For more on this, including tips on encouraging a reluctant mediator to do it, see Chapter 8.

Timing is key. You shouldn't raise the possibility of the mediator making a settlement proposal before or during the mediation itself, because this will probably result in both parties trying to curry favor with the mediator. It's better to wait until the mediator declares the mediation effort ended before raising the possibility of asking the mediator for a settlement proposal.

2. Mini-Trials

Despite its name, a mini-trial is not a court trial at all. It's an innovative dispute resolution technique that allows top managers from disputing companies to quickly hear the gist of each other's positions, then try to resolve the dispute. Mini-trials have been used successfully by major corporations and government agencies.

Mini-trials are usually arranged through a private dispute resolution company. Participants include a top official from each side who has authority to settle, each side's lawyers, and a neutral advisor supplied by the dispute resolution company. The neutral advisor—companies often like to use retired judges—should be someone who is extremely knowledgeable in both the subject matter and legal issues in dispute. For the process to work, both sides must respect this person.

As the mini-trial opens, lawyers for each side have a chance (within strict time limits—usually half a day) to present their best arguments to executives from both companies and the neutral advisor. This is a unique opportunity for the executives to hear—unfiltered by their own legal staffs—the other side's best legal arguments. The advisor then tells the executives what she believes are the strengths and weaknesses of each side's case and gives her opinion as to how a judge might decide it. The executives then meet in private, away from their lawyers, to try to negotiate a settlement.

The best type of dispute for a mini-trial is one that concerns a factual, not a legal, matter. If the law is fairly clear and only the facts are in dispute, then it is easier for the neutral advisor and executives to make an educated guess as to how a real court might decide the case.

Mini-trials typically cost more than mediation or arbitration. Lawyers for both sides must prepare for and make formal presentations, and the fee for the neutral advisor is likely to be higher than you would pay for a typical mediator. Still, even if the cost for a one- or two-day mini-trial is as high as $10,000 per side, that is still a bargain compared with the cost of conducting a full-blown trial in a complicated business dispute.

If you want to set up a mini-trial to resolve a dispute involving your company, ask one of the national or regional dispute resolution firms listed in Appendix C to send you information about how they would conduct this type of proceeding. ■

CHAPTER 12

Mediating Employment Disputes

As polls, statistics, and the nightly news tell us, we are spending more and more of our waking hours at work. This isn't always a bad thing—the workplace can be a source of pride, accomplishment, and teamwork. However, it can also be a source of disputes and tension—and lawsuits. So it's no surprise that workplace disputes—between employers and employees, workers and managers, or coworkers—make up an ever-growing percentage of the caseloads of state and federal courts.

The good news is that more and more employers and employees are turning to mediation to resolve—and even prevent—workplace problems. And with good reason—the process is well-equipped to handle the special issues and concerns that often accompany employment disputes. Here are some of the benefits mediation offers for dealing with workplace problems:

- **Relationship building.** Particularly if the parties will continue to work together as coworkers or as supervisor and employee, mediation offers a valuable opportunity to air problems, work together towards a solution, and figure out how to deal with each other in the future. Even if no future relationship is in the cards (for example, an employee has quit or been fired and will not return to work), mediation allows the parties to make some sense of what happened—and to move forward with some peace of mind.

- **Confidentiality.** Employment lawsuits can get pretty nasty—the employee wants to show that the company is truly awful and should have to pay for it, while the company wants to show that the employee is a bad egg who deserved to be fired. Mediation allows the parties to keep these kinds of accusations out of the public eye. It can also help protect a company from unwanted publicity and allow for the confidentiality of trade secrets.

EXAMPLE: *John is fired from his job as a chef for a catering company. He believes that he was fired because he complained to his boss about unsanitary food preparation conditions, and the company was afraid he would make a report to the health department. The company says it fired him because his skills were mediocre and he couldn't meet deadlines. If John and the company fight this one out in court, the public record will be full of allegations about the company's unsafe practices and John's poor performance. This is not going to help the company get more customers or help John get another job.*

- **Low cost.** Mediation is always going to cost less than full-scale litigation, but this is particularly true in employment disputes. Experts estimate that employers pay tens of thousands of dollars to defend against a typical employee lawsuit—and that's just on legal fees. Employees pay a high price as well. Although they don't have to pay a lawyer by the hour, they can expect to fork over to their lawyer a large percentage (between 25% and 40%) of any money they recover. Mediation is a much cheaper alternative. In fact, it's often free if the parties mediate through a court-required program or a program sponsored by a government agency (such as the Equal Employment Opportunity Commission), and it may be free to the employee(s) if the employer offers an in-house mediation program.

- **Speed.** Because of the significant role work plays in our lives—and because of the nature of the work relationship—employment disputes are often quite urgent. An employee who feels she is being sexually harassed doesn't want to keep coming into work to confront her harasser day after day, month after month, until her lawsuit is heard—she wants the problem taken care of right away. Similarly, an employee who has been fired often can't afford to wait a couple of years for a jury to award damages. Because mediation can be scheduled right away, it offers a much quicker resolution.

- **Creative solutions.** Mediation offers the parties a chance to work out a settlement that deals with everyone's actual needs, not just the rights and remedies recognized by the legal system. It is a great way to work out nonlegal disputes—for example, coworkers who just can't seem to get along, or a manager whose style grates on her reports. Mediation can also help the parties come up with a resolution that goes beyond dollars and cents to get to the real needs of both sides.

EXAMPLE: *Sheila worked for many years as a secretary in a large company. As the company became more dependent on computers, Sheila's performance started to falter. Finally, the company decided to replace her. Sheila claims that the company fired her because of her age; the company claims that she was fired because she couldn't handle the job's technological requirements.*

In a lawsuit, the jury would have to decide whether Sheila was discriminated against based on her age. If the jury found that she was fired for discriminatory reasons, it could make the company pay her a sum of money. If the jury found that the company had legitimate reasons to fire her, it could give Sheila nothing—and the judge could even make her pay the company's legal fees, if her lawsuit was found to be frivolous.

Instead, Sheila and the company decided to mediate. During the mediation, both sides agreed that Sheila had done excellent work in the past, and that they wanted to reach a solution that worked for everyone. As the mediation progressed, it became clear that Sheila didn't really want her job back. Her main concerns were maintaining her health insurance coverage and getting a new job that didn't require as much computer work. The two parties worked out a deal whereby the company would pay Sheila's insurance premiums for six months, write an honest letter of recommendation, and give Sheila the equivalent of a few months of pay while she searched for a new job.

This chapter explains the special issues that tend to arise in employment mediation, for employers and employees. It will help you figure out:

- whether you should mediate

- how to find a mediator or mediation program

- how to prepare for the mediation, and

- how to come up with a workable agreement.

A. Deciding Whether to Mediate

Not all workplace disputes are amenable to mediation (although most are). This section will help you figure out whether mediation is right for your situation.

1. Factors Favoring Mediation

Consider mediation when some or all of the following are true:

- **Time is of the essence.** As we've said in earlier chapters, if you need to resolve your dispute quickly, mediation is probably the way to go. For example, if your company is planning an initial public offering and an employee is threatening to file a lawsuit, you probably want to get the dispute cleared up right away. Similarly, if you have been fired or are facing mistreatment (such as harassment or bullying) at work, mediation will help you deal with the problem quickly.

- **You have a dispute with a coworker.** If you are having problems with a coworker, the law may not offer you much help. Although coworker disputes can be mightily unpleasant, they often don't constitute legal violations (unless sexual harassment or an assault is involved). Even if you could make a legal claim against a coworker, there probably isn't much to be gained by filing a lawsuit. Unless your coworker is independently wealthy, you aren't likely to win a significant damages award—and even if you do, you may not be able to collect.

Mediation, on the other hand, may offer you the best chance of figuring out how to work together more successfully—and how to avoid problems in the future.

- **There is an ongoing employment relationship between the parties.** Mediation can be especially helpful if your dispute involves a current employee. Unlike litigation, which encourages the parties to take extreme positions and go all out to win, mediation encourages collaboration and emphasizes how the parties will get along in the future. This makes it a perfect way to resolve disputes among people who will have to continue working together.

- **You can mediate through a free or low-cost program.** Many larger private companies have in-house dispute resolution programs. Some government agencies—including the Equal Employment Opportunity Commission (EEOC), which enforces federal antidiscrimination laws—have their own mediation programs as well. These programs offer free or low-cost mediation services for employment disputes. If a program like this is available to you, it makes sense to give it a try.

- **Confidentiality is important.** As noted above, confidentiality is often a significant concern in employment disputes. The company may have trade secrets, business practices, or plain old dirty laundry that it doesn't want to air in public. Employees may not want their every workplace lapse discussed and debated in open court. Mediation offers everyone a way to keep these issues confidential.

2. Factors Opposing Mediation

Although mediation offers some significant benefits, it isn't right in every situation. If any of the following are true, mediation might not be your best bet.

- **You need immediate legal action.** In some cases, an employer or employee might need an immediate court order to prevent serious harm. For example, if an employee has stolen your trade secrets and is in the process of giving them to competitors, you don't have time to mediate a compromise—you need action right away. Or, if a coworker is threatening you with violence, you will want a court's immediate protection, not a negotiation session. These orders—called "injunctions" or "restraining orders"—are available only through the legal system.

- **Violence has occurred or been threatened.** If you have been a victim of physical violence—as might be the case in a sexual harassment case or a workplace bullying situation—you may not want to sit down at a negotiating table with your tormentor. Although some people can mediate successfully in these circumstances, others prefer the built-in protections the legal system offers.

- **You want to set a precedent.** If your dispute involves an important legal principle, you may be more interested in creating a legal precedent than in simply resolving the problem. Mediation may help you work out your immediate dispute, but it won't generate a legally binding court opinion.

EXAMPLE: *Mark is a construction worker in North Carolina. He believes that he was fired because he is gay, but North Carolina law doesn't prohibit discrimination on the basis of sexual orientation. Mark contacts a lawyer at a national gay rights organization, who tells Mark that the organization would be interested in taking his case in order to try to make new law. If Mark mediates the case, he won't have this opportunity—and others who are fired because of their sexual orientation won't have the benefit of his efforts.*

- **You're an employee with a slam-dunk case.** Employers are almost always defending against employment lawsuits, which means the only real variable for them is how much money they're going to have to spend. That's why mediation is generally the right call for employers. Employees, on the other hand, often stand to win quite a bit of money. If you have a very strong case and you're willing to throw the dice in court, a lawsuit may be your best bet.

- **Your problem is just the tip of the iceberg.** Workplace problems that are widespread and affect many employees are not always amenable to resolution through mediation. For example, if an employee claims that the company's promotion procedures are discriminatory, the dispute could potentially involve many employees. Unless the company is willing to consider changing its policies or practices, a solution that resolves just one employee's problem is not going to put the problem to rest—for the company or the workers.

EXAMPLE: *Johanna works for a grocery store chain. Although her job title is "Assistant Manager," she spends most of her working hours doing basic tasks like restocking the shelves and taking inventory—as do the 30 other Assistant Managers who work for the chain. Johanna routinely works 50 to 60 hours a week, but doesn't get paid for any overtime. Johanna believes that she should be earning overtime, and that the company's policy of not paying overtime to Assistant Managers is illegal.*

Should Johanna mediate her claim through the company's in-house dispute resolution program? If she does, there will be 30 "ghosts" at the negotiating table—the other Assistant Managers, whose legal rights are also at stake. If the company and Johanna simply agree that Johanna will start earning overtime and the company will pay her a sum of money to compensate for the overtime she should have earned in the past, that will solve Johanna's problem. But it won't address all of the other employees who are in the same position. Similarly, if the company agrees to change its policy, that change will affect everyone, even though they didn't have an opportunity to give any input. In this case, it might make sense for Johanna—and any other interested Assistant Managers—to talk to a lawyer before proceeding.

B. Choosing a Mediator

Once you've decided to give mediation a try, you'll have to find a mediator. Sometimes, this is an easy call—if your company offers an in-house dispute resolution program, you can mediate there, at little or no cost. And some government agencies and courts offer free or low-cost mediation services for particular types of disputes. If neither of these options are available to you, you can find your own private mediator.

1. Mediation Programs

There are several types of employment mediation programs that might be available for your dispute.

a. In-House Mediation Programs

Some companies—particularly those with large numbers of employees—have set up in-house dispute resolution programs to resolve conflicts between employees and their coworkers or managers. Sometimes, these programs use trained staff members (usually a mix of employees and managers) as mediators. Some companies use outside mediators rather than employees.

When employment disputes arise, the parties are invited (or sometime required) to mediate. The company can establish whatever rules and procedures it wants for how the program will work—including how long mediations will last, when and where they will be held, who may attend, and what evidence (if any) may be presented.

These programs are usually free or low-cost for the participants. For employees, particularly those with interpersonal disputes—trouble working with a particular manager or communication problems with a coworker, for example—these programs can be very helpful. Mediating can help get things back on track quickly, and help employees learn to work together.

However, these programs can have some drawbacks as well. If the mediators are chosen from company staff, the participants may reasonably question the mediator's impartiality. An employee who has a serious dispute with the company—as opposed to a personal conflict with another employee—may find this type of program especially dissatisfying. After all, it's hard to believe that mediators who work for the company are going to be truly willing (or even able) to persuade the company to strike a compromise.

If the mediation program is part of a mandatory dispute resolution policy, that also raises some red flags for employees. Many companies that offer mediation require employees to go through a multistage dispute resolution process, often ending in arbitration. Some of these programs also require employees to give up the right to file a lawsuit. In other words, the employee must use the employer's program—and only that program—to deal with workplace problems. Experts and judges disagree as to the legality and wisdom of these programs, and the law in this area is in flux. If you are an employee in this situation, you may want to talk to a lawyer to find out what your options are.

b. Agency Programs

Many state and federal agencies make mediation available for employment disputes. Some agencies—such as the U.S. Postal Service—have programs that allow their own employees to mediate workplace problems. These programs cover only public employees, however.

Some public agencies make mediation available to private employees who file a complaint with the agency. For example, the Equal Employment Opportunity Commission (EEOC), the federal agency that takes complaints of employment discrimination and enforces antidiscrimination laws, has a voluntary mediation program for employees who file charges of discrimination. If the EEOC believes that mediation may be helpful, and the employer and employee both agree, the EEOC will

provide free mediation services. Those who have used the EEOC program give it pretty high marks: one survey showed that more than 90%
of participants would use the service again. Some state agencies also
offer mediation for complainants.

 To learn more about the EEOC's mediation program, visit the agency's
website at www.eeoc.gov.

c. Court-Sponsored Programs

As explained earlier, some courts require the parties to try mediation or
some other form of dispute resolution before they can proceed with a
lawsuit. If you or your opponent has filed a lawsuit in one of these
courts, you will have the opportunity to mediate free or at a reduced
cost, using a court-appointed or staff mediator. You also have the option
of hiring (and paying for) a private mediator to meet this requirement.

2. Choosing a Mediator

If you are using an in-house or agency mediation program, you may not
have much say in choosing your mediator. However, if you have a
strong concern about the person chosen (for example, the agency
mediator is a lawyer who has sued your company before, or the in-house
mediator is good friends with your opponent in the dispute), you should
speak up. There should be some process for selecting a new mediator if
there is a conflict of interest.

If you are not mediating through a program, you will have to find
your own mediator. The best place to find a mediator for most employment disputes is through a private dispute resolution company. If the
other party has already agreed to mediate and you don't anticipate
significant scheduling or other administrative issues, a mediator in private
practice might be a good bet. (For information on choosing between an
independent mediator and a mediation company, see Chapter 3.)

a. Mediator Skills

In many employment disputes, the parties will want a mediator who
understands employment law and small business issues. A mediator with
an employment law background can help the parties assess the strengths
and weaknesses of their positions and offer some possible solutions based
on what courts have ordered in other cases. Small business experience
can be especially valuable in disputes involving current employees or
changes to company rules and practices. A mediator who has some
knowledge of how businesses really operate can help the parties come up
with solutions that will be workable in the real world.

b. Mediator Style

The facts and personalities involved in your dispute will dictate what
type of mediator will be best equipped to help you resolve it. For a
dispute involving current employees or interpersonal relations, a facilitative mediator—who acts primarily as a neutral listener—is usually the
best choice. For disputes that have already progressed to lawsuits or
agency complaints, or disputes with former employees, an evaluative
mediator—who helps the parties assess their arguments and come up
with a settlement proposal—might be a better option.

In some situations, you might want to choose the mediator who
seems best able to reach the parties, given their current emotional states
and bargaining positions. For example, if you are suing your former
employer, and the company president is a hard-nosed businessperson
who has refused to negotiate with you, you might look for a mediator
whose words will carry special weight with your opponent. A high-
powered lawyer or businessperson or a retired judge might be your best
bet in this type of case, particularly if the mediator is willing to evaluate
the merits of the case. On the other hand, if you are a small business
owner involved in a highly emotional dispute with a long-term employee, a mediator who starts talking numbers during the opening

statement might shut down the whole process. In this situation, you would be better off finding a mediator who will help both sides express their feelings and explore what's really at stake for them in the dispute.

c. Fees

How much you pay in mediation fees will depend on how many parties are involved in the dispute, which mediator you select, where you mediate, and how long your mediation lasts. In generally, you can expect to pay anywhere from $1,500 to $5,000 in total fees for a full day of mediation.

Often, the fees are split between or among the parties. However, in some mediations between employers and employees, the employer will agree to shoulder a larger part of the fee burden, particularly if the employee doesn't have much money. It's quite common for the parties to agree on a different fee payment as part of the mediation settlement— for example, they might agree that the employer will pay all of the mediation fees, generally by reimbursing the employee for fees laid out up front.

C. Preparing for the Mediation

Once you have chosen a mediator, it's time to get ready for the mediation itself. The general tips and information in Chapter 5 will help you identify your goals, consider your settlement options, and prepare your opening statement. This section covers preparation issues that are particularly important in employment disputes.

a. Who Should Attend the Mediation

Everyone who played an important role in the dispute—or will play an important role in resolving it—should come to the mediation session.

For example, if an employee is threatening to sue a company because she believes a particular manager has discriminated against her, then the employee, the manager, and a company representative should all attend the mediation. Similarly, if two coworkers are trying to mediate their problems, it might be wise for their supervisor to attend the mediation as well—after all, the supervisor will probably have to be part of any resolution that changes the way the parties work together.

Anyone who must authorize or approve a settlement should also be at the mediation, or at least be immediately available by phone. Sometimes, this means that a high-ranking company official must either attend the mediation or arrange to be on call during the session. If the employer has employment practices liability insurance or some other type of policy that applies to the dispute, a claims representative from the insurance company (with full settlement authority) should also attend.

DO YOU NEED A LAWYER?

Many employment mediations take place without lawyers. For example, it's somewhat rare to find a lawyer in an in-house mediation session, and agency mediations are often lawyer-free. Particularly if you are mediating an interpersonal dispute, there's no need to rush out and find counsel.

However, there are times when it makes sense to at least consult with a lawyer before the mediation, or even to bring a lawyer along to the session. If your dispute may be worth a lot of money—for example, you have suffered serious injury or a number of your employees have alleged wrongdoing—it makes sense to talk to a lawyer ahead of time. The same is true if important legal rights are at stake. For example, if you believe your employer has discriminated against you, or your employee has complained that one of your policies is illegal, you should get some legal advice.

b. Evidence

At the mediation, you'll want to have any documents or other evidence that can shed some light on the dispute. Chapter 5, Section C, explains evidence in detail, including suggestions on how to gather and present your evidence. Here are some types of evidence that may be especially helpful in an employment dispute:

- offer or hiring letter

- performance evaluations

- records of discipline, warnings, or suspension

- commendations and awards

- termination letter

- employee handbook or other written policies

- written communications, including memos, email messages, letters, and notes

- copies of relevant employment laws

- items posted on company bulletin boards

- work samples

- documents signed by the employee(s)

- customer complaints or comments, and

- attendance records.

c. Legal Research

Whether or not you decide to consult a lawyer, it's a good idea to find out something about your legal rights and obligations *before* you get to the mediation room. Knowing what a court might do with your dispute can help you refine your own goals for the mediation. Employees will want to know what their rights are, whether their employer has violated any laws, and what kinds of damages might be available in a lawsuit. Employers will want to know what their legal duties are, whether they have violated any employee rights, and what kinds of penalties they might face at trial.

Nolo publishes several books about employment law, all of which explain your rights and obligations in plain English. Employees should check out *Your Rights in the Workplace*, by Barbara Kate Repa. For employers, *The Employer's Legal Handbook*, by Fred Steingold, *Everyday Employment Law*, by Lisa Guerin and Amy DelPo, and *Federal Employment Laws*, by Amy DelPo and Lisa Guerin, can help get you started.

There are also many fine websites on workplace issues. Nolo's own website, at www.nolo.com, has a free legal encyclopedia with lots of articles on employment law, written for both employers and employees. Several government sites provide information for employees and employers—these sites include www.eeoc.gov (for discrimination issues) and www.dol.gov (for wage and hour issues, including overtime, compensation, time off, and family leave).

Employees should check out www.workplacefairness.org, a site with plenty of fact sheets and resources on employment laws. Employees in California can use the legal information available on the website of the Employment Law Center, a project of the Legal Aid Society of San Francisco, at www.las-elc.org. Employers can find lots of helpful information at www.toolkit.cch.com and at www.findlaw.com (under the "Legal Professionals" heading, click "Legal Subjects," then "Labor & Employment Law").

D. Settlement Options

One of the great benefits of mediation is that it offers the parties a chance to be creative in coming up with ways to resolve their dispute. In an employment lawsuit, often the only question is whether or not one party will have to pay money to the other. But in mediation, there are lots of non-monetary settlement options—as well as a variety of ways to structure a monetary settlement.

1. Non-Monetary Settlement Terms

Often, a fired or unhappy employee has concerns other than money. For example, the employee may want to find another job, maintain health insurance coverage, switch to a different position in the company, or simply receive an apology. And coworkers who have a problem might simply want a reasonable system for communicating with each other and preventing future disputes. While a court would never order any of these options, you can agree to them in mediation.

Here are some settlement ideas that don't involve money changing hands:

- continued employment

- a different reporting relationship—for example, that the employee will work for a different supervisor or that the employee and supervisor will work together differently

- a consulting relationship between the employee and the company

- letter of reference

- active assistance with the employee's job search—for example, the employee's supervisor might agree to follow up with colleagues at other companies who may have suitable positions open

- mutually acceptable explanation of why the employee left the company

- agreement by the employee to drop a pending agency charge or lawsuit

- agreement by the company to remove items from the employee's personnel file, such as a poor performance review or written warning

- outplacement services

- continued payment of insurance premiums for health insurance, life insurance, and so on

- nondisparagement agreement—that is, an agreement that the parties will not bad mouth each other

- apology

- an agreement not to contest a former employee's claim for unemployment compensation, or

- transfer or continued use of company property—for example, that a former employee can keep or use a company computer, cell phone, tools, or vehicle.

2. Monetary Settlement Terms

Even if your dispute is likely to boil down to dollars and cents, there are some creative ways to structure a monetary settlement in mediation. Generally, the purpose of these alternative arrangements is to make the settlement more valuable—either by making it possible for the employer to pay more or by making the payment itself more beneficial to the employee. Here are some examples:

- Installment payments may make it possible for an employer to afford a larger settlement—and save an employee from the huge tax bill that would result from getting all of the money at once.

- The employer can purchase an annuity from a life insurance company, which then makes periodic payments to the employee over time. The employee doesn't pay tax until the money is received; this can lower the employee's income tax liability considerably.

- Other forms of compensation—such as stock or stock options, increased contributions to a pension or other retirement plan, or continued provision of benefits—might be easier for the employer to provide, and very valuable to the employee.

- Employer and employee can agree on a period of continued work, either as an employee or as a consultant. Often, an employee is not asked to do any real work during this period; instead, the arrangement allows the employee to keep receiving a paycheck and tell prospective employers that he or she is still employed with the company (which makes it a lot easier to find a new job).

- The parties can agree to characterize the payment in a manner that is most likely to result in tax savings to the employee. For example, most severance packages and settlement amounts are fully taxable to the employee when the money is received. However, there is an exception for settlements of bodily injury claims—this money is not taxable. If the employee made a claim for physical injuries (some sexual harassment claims and claims for extreme emotional distress resulting in physical symptoms fall into this category), the parties can agree that at least some of the settlement money is attributable to those claims. Of course, the IRS will make its own determinations about what is taxable and what is not, but characterizing claims in this way in the settlement agreement can only help the employee's cause.

If you're seriously considering putting together a creative monetary settlement, be sure to talk to a tax adviser, CPA, or other financial expert. These professionals can help you figure out which arrangements will be most beneficial in the long run—and make sure that your agreement will hold up under legal or IRS scrutiny. ■

CHAPTER 13

Lawyers and Legal Research

This book provides enough information to help most readers prepare for and bring their dispute to mediation by themselves. But depending on the nature of your case, you may need more advice or information about the law or the probable result of taking a dispute to court. If you are preparing to mediate a case involving complex legal issues or substantial amounts of money or property, you may want to consult with a lawyer before mediation, between mediation sessions, or after mediation to review the settlement agreement before you sign it.

Although you shouldn't expect to settle for exactly what you think you would get in court, it can still be a good idea to consider the likely range of legal outcomes as you consider your mediation goals. For example, if you are mediating with an insurance company about how much they should pay you for a broken leg, knowing what juries in your area have been awarding lately for similar injuries will help you evaluate offers made in mediation by the insurance company.

If your case is relatively simple and you aren't sure who is legally in the right, you might want to do some legal research on your own instead of, or in addition to, consulting a lawyer. A little research—online or in a law library—will help you figure out what the law requires and how it applies to your dispute.

This chapter provides information that will help you find a lawyer or law coach, or do some legal research on your own.

A. Using a Lawyer in Mediation

Whether you should retain a lawyer or law coach to help with your case will depend on the nature of your dispute, your own time and ability to research the law on your own, and the availability of other advisers, such as accountants, business valuation experts, and so on. You'll also have to consider whether the value of your dispute merits paying for a lawyer. If your case concerns a multimillion dollar contract dispute that could put your manufacturing company out of business, hiring one or more lawyers to provide you with information and advice on contract law, taxes, patents, and trademarks probably would be advisable—and the cost would be reasonable, considering what you have at stake. On the other hand, if your case concerns a dispute over a few hundred dollars with your contractor, you probably won't want to pay a lawyer $150 an hour to help you prepare for mediation.

CONSIDER USING A SELF-HELP LAW COACH

As discussed throughout this book, a law coach is a lawyer who does not represent you in your case but is willing to provide you legal advice as you handle the case on your own. The coach will charge you a fee only for the time spent consulting with you, and should help you educate yourself so you can do as much as possible on your own. Hiring a coach can be a sensible and affordable compromise between going it entirely alone and hiring and paying a lawyer to be involved in every aspect of your mediation.

There are many ways to use a lawyer or law coach in mediation. We've explained the various tasks a lawyer can help you with in earlier chapers. For example, a lawyer can:

- Tell you whether the law provides a remedy for your dispute.
- Help you identify the legal issues in your dispute and estimate what a judge or jury might award if you took your case to court.
- Advise you, during a mediation session or between sessions, about the legal consequences of various settlement options.
- Review the mediated agreement before you sign it to make sure it does not compromise any of your legal rights in ways you did not intend.
- Help you prepare your case for arbitration, if you choose to arbitrate after an unsuccessful mediation.

If you need more information about some legal aspect of your case, your best bet will usually be to look it up yourself.

1. What to Look for in a Lawyer

In trying to find the right lawyer or law coach to support your mediation effort, there are many factors to consider. Of course, you'll want to find a lawyer you feel comfortable with. If the lawyer will handle your entire case, you will be spending lots of time together. Even if you're hiring a law coach, your comfort level is still important—you want to be able to communicate with, understand, and trust your lawyer.

This section covers a few other considerations, including expertise, attitude towards mediation, and fees.

a. Is Special Expertise Required?

Some lawyers have experience handling a variety of legal issues, such as wills, divorces, business contracts, and injury claims. If your case involves a relatively small amount of money or property, a generalist like this may be just what you need.

But these days, the law can be so complex and change so fast that more complicated issues are usually handled by people who specialize in particular areas of the law. Specialists often charge a little more, but they are probably worth it, for two reasons: First, they won't need to do as much time-consuming research, and second, you are likely to get a more specific answer from a specialist than a generalist could provide.

For example, if you believe you have been the victim of sexual harassment by your boss, you really should use a lawyer who specializes in representing employees in employment law cases and has some experience with sexual harassment cases. Similarly, if your case concerns a dispute with your partner in a small business, you should use a lawyer who specializes in issues of small business ownership.

b. Does the Lawyer Support Mediation?

To some extent, the type of lawyer you choose will depend on whether you want the lawyer to counsel you throughout the mediation or want only an initial consultation. The lawyer's personality and attitude towards self-help law doesn't matter much when it comes to giving legal advice, but it can make a world of difference if you want the lawyer to coach you on a continuous basis.

If you do need a law coach, you should make it very clear from the first interview that you want to work with a lawyer who understands and supports mediation. This means a lawyer who accepts that mediation sometimes involves compromise and that what you settle for in mediation can be influenced by, but should not be determined only by, what the lawyer believes a judge or jury might give. For example, you might tell the lawyer you are interviewing that you will want him to help you prepare for your mediation, but you do not anticipate the need for him to attend the actual sessions. And you might also ask that he be available to review the anticipated written settlement agreement before you sign it.

There is always the risk that a lawyer who wants your business will claim to support mediation, when in fact her attitude is fairly negative. To probe a little deeper for hidden bias, ask the following questions:

- Has the lawyer ever worked with clients going through mediation? If so, what did the lawyer think of the process? Was it successful for the client? The way lawyers talk about their prior experiences in mediation often reveals whether they really support and respect the process, or think it's a waste of time.

- Has the lawyer had any mediation training? There are two types of mediation training available to lawyers these days. One is training to be an actual mediator; the other is training in how to represent clients effectively in the course of a mediation. Both show an interest in mediation but the second type suggests a more serious professional desire to help clients through the mediation process. This is particularly true if the training to be a mediator was very limited and the lawyer didn't have to pay for it.

c. Fees

When you hire a lawyer to help you with mediation, make sure you understand how fees will be computed. Don't expect any special price break because you are mediating; most lawyers will charge you their normal hourly rate. The key is to define, in advance, when and how the lawyer will help you. For example, if the lawyer says it will take three hours to advise you on the legal aspects of your case before the mediation and another three hours to review and discuss any proposed written settlement, you'll know that your bill will be six times the lawyer's hourly fee (unless, of course, you call the lawyer during the mediation and ask for additional advice).

2. Finding the Right Lawyer

Don't expect to locate a good lawyer just by looking in the phone book, consulting a law directory, or reading an advertisement. There's not enough information in these sources to help you make an informed choice. Lawyer referral services operated by bar associations also won't give you much to go on. Generally, these services make little attempt to evaluate a lawyer's skill and experience. They simply supply the names of lawyers who have listed with the service, often accepting the lawyers' own descriptions of their skills and specialties.

The best way to find a good lawyer is to talk to people you know who may have used the kind of lawyer you are seeking. This includes your personal network of friends, relatives, coworkers, and members of your church, synagogue, book group, or bowling league. If someone you know and respect can recommend a lawyer who helped with a legal problem that's similar to yours, you are probably on the right track. Of course, a friend's or colleague's satisfaction with the work of a particular lawyer is no guarantee that you will also be satisfied, but it's a lot more to go on than a flashy advertisement on the back cover of the local phone book.

Other good resources are people in your community involved in the type of activity that resulted in your dispute. For example, if you want a lawyer who specializes in small business ownership disputes, call the director of the local small business council and ask for names of three or four lawyers who do that kind of work. If you do not have a business council or similar group in your town, then pick some successful small local businesses and ask the owners or managers who they use for legal advice

You may also want to talk to professional people in your community who have frequent contact with lawyers and can make informed judgments about the quality of their work. For example, by speaking to your banker, accountant, insurance agent, or real estate agent, you can probably develop a short list of lawyers known for their work in these areas.

Once you have the names of several lawyers, it's time to do a little research. A good source of information about lawyers is the Martindale-Hubbell Law Directory, available at most law libraries, some local public libraries, and online at www.martindale.com. This resource contains biographical sketches of most practicing lawyers, including information about their experience, specialties, education, the professional organizations to which they belong, and the cases they have handled. Many firms also list their major clients in the directory—good indication of the types of problems these lawyers have tackled. But don't be overly impressed by the length of a particular lawyer's entry—lawyers purchase the space.

With the names of several good prospects, you can begin meeting and interviewing some lawyers. If you tell lawyers in advance that you are shopping around, most will be willing to speak to you for a half hour or so at no charge so you can size them up and make an informed decision. Of course, this is far more appropriate if yours is a large complicated mediation for which you will need considerable legal help than if it's a much smaller dispute for which you want only an hour's legal help. In this situation, most local lawyers will do fine, and you should expect to pay for their time.

B. Legal Research

References to federal and state laws that affect mediation are scattered throughout this book. Some of these laws require or allow judges to refer disputes to mediation; others establish rules and procedures for government-run mediation programs. You can find these statutes yourself and read more about them. You can also research the specific laws involved in your dispute—for example, laws about noise limits in your neighborhood, how contracts should be interpreted, or protecting the environment.

Doing a little legal research to prepare for your mediation should not be difficult once you understand a few basics. Which legal research method you should use depends on what you need to find out. Usually, people preparing for mediation want to research the law in order to:

- understand a particular area of the law

- find and read a statute, regulation, ordinance, court decision, or piece of pending legislation (usually called a bill), or

- find the answer to a specific legal question.

This section explains how to use legal research to accomplish each of these tasks.

Need more detailed information on legal research? Check out these resources:

- *Legal Research: How to Find & Understand the Law*, by Stephen Elias & Susan Levinkind (Nolo), is an easy to use book that provides step-by-step instructions on how to find legal information, both in the law library and online. It includes numerous examples and exercises.

- *Gilbert's Law Summaries: Legal Research, Writing and Analysis*, by Peter Honigsberg (Harcourt Brace), is a no-nonsense guide to commonly used law library resources.

- *The Virtual Chase*, at www.virtualchase.com, offers guides to researching various legal topics, as well as general research tips and legal resources.

1. Learning About a Particular Area of the Law

You may need to do legal research to understand the law that applies to your dispute. For example, you may want to know:

- "Do my partner and I have to follow any legal rules when selling or dividing up our business?"

- "Am I entitled to a share of my former spouse's pension on divorce?"

- "Do I have the right to take time off work to care for a sick family member?"

Questions like these can be answered without regard to your specific circumstances; they involve a general understanding of the law. To find this type of information about a legal topic, you should turn to legal background materials.

Legal background materials are books, articles, and encyclopedia entries in which experts summarize and explain the basic principles of a legal subject area, such as landlord-tenant law, criminal law, or employment law. These materials come in many forms; they can be found in law libraries and public libraries, and many are also available on the Internet.

HOW TO FIND A LAW LIBRARY

Most counties have law libraries in the government buildings or courthouses at the county seat. These libraries are open to the public. County libraries are a good place to go if you're looking for legal encyclopedias, treatises, state laws, and court cases.

Law schools also maintain libraries for their students and staff. Although public access to some law school libraries is restricted, many are open to the general public—especially if the law school is part of a university that receives state funding.

Finally, don't limit yourself to law libraries. Most major public libraries in urban areas contain both local and state laws, self-help law books, and directories of organizations. Public libraries are also good sources of city, county, and state information. And if you're working with a lawyer, ask to use the lawyer's own library. Most law firms have large collections of books for their lawyers to use; even solo practitioners probably have a few shelves of books.

Here are a number of legal background resources that you may find useful:

- **Self-Help Law Books.** Self-help law books, such as those published by Nolo, are written in plain English for a nonlawyer audience. They are an excellent starting point for cracking any legal area that is new to you. Law libraries, public libraries, and bookstores (including Nolo's online bookstore at www.nolo.com) often carry self-help law books. Nolo publishes titles on employment law, neighbor law, small business issues, criminal law, divorce, child custody, and much more.

- **Organizations and Advocacy Groups.** Many nonprofit and professional organizations or advocacy groups—such as tenants' rights groups, the American Association of Retired People (AARP), and local business groups—publish articles or booklets on particular legal topics. Think about which groups might have the information you need and then look for them in the Yellow Pages or on the Web. Most public libraries have reference books that list organizations and associations by topic—these books are an easy way to find leads.

- **Legal Encyclopedias.** You can often find a good introduction to your topic in a legal encyclopedia. The legal encyclopedias most commonly found in law libraries are *American Jurisprudence* and *Corpus Juris*. Many states have legal encyclopedias that are state-specific—for example, *Texas Jurisprudence*.

- **The Nutshell Series.** Another good introduction to legal topics is the Nutshell series, as in *Torts in a Nutshell* and *Intellectual Property in a Nutshell*, published by West Group. These books are available in most law libraries and some bookstores.

- **Treatises.** If you have the time and patience to delve deeply into a subject, you can find comprehensive books—generally known as treatises—on virtually every legal topic. For example, if you want to know about some aspect of trademark law, you could use *McCarthy on Trademarks*, a multivolume treatise on all aspects of trademark law.

- **West's Legal Desk Reference.** This book, by Statsky, Hussey, Diamond, and Nakamura, lists background materials both by state and by legal topic. In addition, *West's Legal Desk Reference* provides keywords and phrases that will help you use the other resources you may need during your research.

- **Internet Resources.** Nolo's Legal Encyclopedia, available free at www.nolo.com, explains many common legal issues in plain English. The other major legal websites (listed below) also provide helpful information and links to specific areas of the law. Finally, U.S. and local government agency sites provide basic legal information for consumers, such as state marriage license requirements or publications on different legal topics. For example, if you visit the website of the Equal Employment Opportunity Commission, at www.eeoc.gov, you will find factsheets, information on antidiscrimination laws, materials on the agency's mediation program, and much more. To find government agencies online, see "Finding Court and Government Agency Websites", in Section 2, below.

 The best legal websites. In addition to our own website at www.nolo.com, Nolo's favorite legal websites are:

- FindLaw, www.findlaw.com

- The National Federation of Paralegal Associations, www.paralegals.org (click "Legal Resources")

- Reflaw: The Virtual Law Library Reference Desk at Washburn University School of Law Library, www.washlaw.edu/reflaw/reflaw.html

- The Library of Congress Guide to Law Online, www.loc.gov/law/guide

- The Legal Information Institute at Cornell Law School, www.law.cornell.edu

- Legal Research from Jurist, http://jurist.law.pitt.edu/legalresearch.htm.

2. Finding a Specific Law

There are many reasons why you might need to find a specific statute, regulation, ordinance, or court decision. For example, you might want to find out whether your state has any laws requiring mediation. Or, you may want to look up your state's laws on a particular topic—boundary disputes, enforcement of contracts, or child support, for example. No matter what you're looking for, finding a specific law is relatively straightforward. The steps to take depend on what type of law you seek.

a. City or County Laws

You can usually get copies of city or county laws (often called "ordinances") from the office of the city or county clerk. The main branch of your public library is also likely to have a collected set of these laws. Once you get there, ask the reference librarian for help.

Many local ordinances are also available on the Web. Your city, county, or state website may have these laws, or a particular department—like the health or planning department—may post its regulations on its home page. Municipal Codes, maintained by the Seattle Public Library, has links to codes from many U.S. cities: you can find it at www.spl.org/selectedsites/municode.html.

b. State or Federal Statutes and Regulations

Rules established by state and federal governments are called statutes and regulations. Federal statutes are passed by the United States Congress, while state statutes are passed by state legislatures. Regulations are issued by state or federal administrative agencies (such as the U.S. Department of Transportation or the State Department of Health) to explain, implement, and enforce statutes.

You can find statutes and regulations in the library or on the Internet. You can also use legal background materials to figure out which statute or regulation you should read.

Finding statutes and regulations at the library

State and federal statutes and regulations can be found at a law library or the main branch of a public library. Depending on the state, statutes are compiled in books called codes, revised statutes, annotated statutes, or compiled laws. For example, the federal statutes are contained in a series called *United States Code*, and the Vermont statutes are found in a series called *Vermont Statutes Annotated*. (The term "annotated" means that the statutes are accompanied by information about their history and court decisions that have interpreted them.) Once you've located the books you need, search for the specific statute by its citation or by looking up key words in the index.

After you find a law in the statute books, it's important to look at the update pamphlet in the front or back of the book (called the "pocket part") to make sure your statute hasn't been amended or deleted. Pocket parts are published only once a year, so brand-new statutes may not be included in the pocket part. Law libraries subscribe to services and periodicals that update these books on a more frequent basis than the pocket parts. Ask the law librarian to help you find the most recent version of the statute.

Most federal regulations are published in the *Code of Federal Regulations (C.F.R.)*, a well-indexed set of books organized by subject. If you don't have a citation for the regulation you want, check the index. To make sure the regulation is current, look at the monthly pamphlet that accompanies the books, called *C.F.R.-L.S.A. (List of C.F.R. Sections Affected)*.

State regulations may be harder to find. If you know which agency publishes the regulation you want, you can usually call and get a copy. Many states also keep a portion of their regulations in a series of books called the Administrative Code. Check the table of contents. If the regulation is not in an Administrative Code, look for loose-leaf manuals published by the individual agency. If you find a regulation in the Administrative Code or loose-leaf manual, you should still call the agency to make sure the regulation hasn't recently changed.

HOW TO READ A CITATION FOR A STATUTE OR REGULATION

A citation is an abbreviated reference that tells you where to find a legal resource. Citations for statutes usually include the name of the set of books where the statute appears, the volume or title number, and the section where you can find the statute. For example:

- 42 U.S.C. § 2000e is the citation of Title VII of the Civil Rights Act, which protects workers from discrimination. You can find the text of the law in title 42 of the United States Code, section 2000e.
- Ariz. Rev. Stat. Ann. § 33-1321 is the citation to Arizona's law on tenant security deposits. You can find the text of the law in title 33 of the Arizona Revised Statutes Annotated, section 1321.

Citations for regulations usually include the name of the code where the regulations can be found, and the volume and section number. For example:

- You can find the regulations interpreting the Fair Credit Reporting Act at 16 C.F.R. § 600.1—volume 16 of the Code of Federal Regulations, section 600.1.
- You can find California's regulations on pregnancy discrimination at 2 C.C.R. § 7291.2—title 2 of the California Code of Regulations, section 7291.2.

Finding statutes and regulations online

You can find federal statutes, the entire *Code of Federal Regulations,* and state statutes by visiting Nolo's Legal Research Center at www.nolo.com/lawcenter/statute/index.cfm. For state regulations, check the agency's website on your state's home page. All state websites have a link to government resources, including a list of state agencies. If the regulations aren't posted online, the information on the agency's website may answer your question—or give you a phone number or email address to contact for help. Another source of state regulations is FindLaw, at www.findlaw.com. Check under "U.S. State Resources." The major websites listed earlier in Section 1 also provide access to state and federal statutes.

Using background materials to find statutes and regulations

When looking for a particular statute or regulation (state or federal), you may want to consult background materials, which often include relevant laws. For example, *Collier on Bankruptcy,* the leading bankruptcy treatise, contains a complete set of the federal bankruptcy laws. Even if the background resource does not include the text of the statutes or regulations, it will provide citations to the relevant laws and the books in which they are found.

Finding the latest legislation

If you are looking for a brand-new statute, you may have to search online for recently enacted legislation, because there is often a delay between the date a statute is passed and the date it shows up in the overall compilation of laws. Almost every state provides links to its legislature where you can find pending and recently enacted legislation. These sites contain not only the most current version of a bill, but also its history. For help locating your state's website, see below. To find out about pending federal legislation or to read the latest version of a bill, go to the United States Congress website at http://thomas.loc.gov.

FINDING COURT AND GOVERNMENT AGENCY WEBSITES

Many courts and government agencies provide statutes and case law, plus other useful items like forms, answers to frequently asked questions, and downloadable pamphlets on various legal topics. To find your state's website, open your browser and type in www.state.<your state's postal code>.us or www.<your state's postal code>.gov. Your state's postal code is the two-letter abbreviation you use for mailing addresses. For example, NY is the postal code for New York, so to find New York's state website, type in www.state.ny.us or www.ny.gov.

Nolo's Legal Research Center (www.nolo.com/lawcenter/statute/index.cfm) provides links to courts across the country and access to small claims court information for most states. You can also find local, state, and federal court websites on the National Center for State Courts' website at www.ncsconline.org. The federal judiciary's website at www.uscourts.gov lists federal court websites.

---

c. State Case Law

State case law consists of the rules established by courts in court decisions (or "court opinions"). Court decisions do one of two things. First, courts interpret statutes, regulations, and ordinances so that we know how they apply to real-life situations. Second, courts make rules that are not found in statutes, regulations, or ordinances. These rules are called the "common law."

Finding state cases in the library

State cases are found in a series of books called reporters. For example, California cases are contained in the California Reporter. You can also find state cases in books known as "regional reporters." These volumes contain cases from several states in a geographical region. For example, the Atlantic Reporter contains cases from several eastern states, including Delaware and Maryland.

Finding cases when you have a citation

A citation indicates the name of the reporter, the volume number, and the page where the case appears. For example, 21 Cal.App.3d 446 tells you that the case is in California Appellate Reports, 3rd Series, Volume 21, on page 446.

Finding cases when you know the name

If you don't have a citation but you know the name of one or both of the parties in the case—for instance, in the case named *Jones v. Smith*, Jones and Smith are the names of the parties—you can use a "case digest" to find the citation. There are digests for individual states as well as federal and general digests. Look for the parties' names in the digest's Table of Cases. If you don't know the name of the case or the citation, then it will be very difficult to find the case in the law library.

Finding state cases on the Web

If the case is recent (within the last ten years), there's a good chance that it's available free on the Internet. A good place to start is FindLaw at www.findlaw.com. Also, most state court websites now publish recent cases.

If the case is older, you can still find it on the Internet, but you may have to pay a private company for access to its database. (Your local law library may also have online legal resources available for searching.) VersusLaw, at www.versusLaw.com, maintains an excellent library of older state court cases. You can do unlimited research on VersusLaw for $9.95 per month. You can also get state cases online through Lexis and Westlaw, commercial online legal research services. (For more information, see "Using Westlaw and Lexis to Do Legal Research on the Web", below.)

d. Federal Case Law

Federal case law consists of the rules established by federal courts. Like state cases, you can find federal case law both in the library and on the Web.

Finding federal cases in the library

Cases decided by the U.S. Supreme Court are published in three different series of reporters. All three contain the same cases. The names of these series are:

- *United States Reports*

- *Supreme Court Reporter*, and

- *Supreme Court Reports: Lawyers' Edition*.

Well-stocked law libraries also have cases from other federal courts, including the Federal Circuit Courts of Appeal (federal appellate courts), U.S. District Courts (federal trial courts), and specialized courts such as bankruptcy or tax court.

To find a case in the Supreme Court reporters or any of the volumes containing other federal cases, follow the guidelines for finding state cases by citation or case name, above.

Finding U.S. Supreme Court cases on the Web

Nolo's Legal Research Center, available at www.nolo.com/lawcenter/ statute/index.cfm, provides U.S. Supreme Court cases decided within the last hundred years.

Finding other federal cases on the Web

FindLaw, at www.findlaw.com, contains cases decided by the Federal Circuit Courts of Appeal going back to 1995, some bankruptcy opinions, and recent tax court cases. The Cornell Law School Legal Information Institute provides access to all federal appellate court cases, some District Court cases, and some bankruptcy opinions (www.law.cornell .edu/federal/opinions.html). VersusLaw (explained above) also has some U.S. District Court cases and some bankruptcy opinions. If you can't find the case you're looking for on one of these websites, your best bet is to use Westlaw or Lexis.

USING LEXIS AND WESTLAW TO DO LEGAL RESEARCH ON THE WEB

Lexis and Westlaw are the chief electronic legal databases that contain the full text of many of the legal resources found in law libraries, including almost all reported cases from state and federal courts, all federal statutes, the statutes of most states, federal regulations, law review articles, commonly used treatises, and practice manuals.

Although Westlaw and Lexis databases are available over the Internet, subscriptions are pricey. However, both offer some free and some fee-based services to nonsubscribers that are helpful and reasonably priced (between $9 and $12 per document). To find out more about these services, visit Westlaw at www.westlaw.com or Lexis at www.lexis.com.

3. Finding Answers to Specific Legal Questions

It's one thing to track down information on a recent case or statute or to read up on general information about a legal topic. It's quite another to confidently answer a question about how the law might apply to your own situation, such as:

- "I live in North Dakota and my former spouse and I own a business together. What share of the business am I entitled to in the divorce?"

- "My neighbor's tree is blocking my view. Do I have the right to trim it or cut it down?"

- "I run a business. Another company has opened nearby, and its logo is similar to mine. Can I force them to change their look?"

These are the types of questions that people have traditionally asked lawyers. To answer such questions, you often need to look at all of the legal resources we have mentioned thus far. You must also make sure that the law you find is current. If you want to undertake this type of legal research on your own, we recommend that you use a comprehensive legal research guide that walks you through the process step by step. (See the list of resources in Section 1, above.) Here, we can provide just a brief overview of what you'll need to do.

When seeking the answer to a specific legal question, your ultimate goal is to predict, as near as possible, how a judge would rule if presented with the issues and facts of your case. The closer your facts are to the facts in previous cases or the more directly a statute applies to your situation, the more likely you'll be able to predict what a judge would decide. Sometimes, your question is so basic that the answer is easy to find. But more often, a statute won't address each facet of your situation and the facts of other cases won't match up 100%. Because of this, legal research cannot always provide a definitive answer. (That's why lawyers often hem and haw when asked a legal question.)

a. Basic or Common Legal Questions

If your legal question is basic and general (such as "Will I have to mediate if I file a lawsuit in small claims court?" or "What kinds of expenses are child support payments supposed to cover?"), then you should begin your research by consulting one or more of the background resources discussed above. The answers to these types of questions are usually based on general legal information rather than on the nuances of your particular circumstances.

If your question is common and straightforward (such as "Can the state garnish my wages if I fall behind on child support payments?" or "What is the fee for filing a civil lawsuit?") then it should be quite easy to find an answer, since these kinds of questions rely on factual information that many people need to know. Finding this kind of information doesn't involve any special legal research methods. Think of the government branches or agencies that are likely to have the answers. For example, the state court for your county probably has filing fees posted on its website, or you can call the court clerk. And every state has an agency that handles child support payments. Look on your state's home page to find the agency website or a public information number. You can find phone numbers for city, county, state, and U.S. government agencies in the Government Pages section at the front of your local telephone book.

In some cases, the quickest way to find an answer is by contacting an organization or advocacy group that specializes in the subject of your question. Do you want to know the current estate tax rate? An organization that advocates for seniors, such as the American Association of Retired People (AARP), may know the answer. If you're looking for information on evictions, a local advocacy group such as a tenants' rights union should be able to help. You can find almost any organization or advocacy group on the Internet. Most Yellow Pages also include listings of community resources.

b. Complex Legal Questions

If you can't get an answer to your legal question from a background resource—usually because your question involves unique facts related to your situation—you'll need to do more detailed research. Build on the information you found in the background materials.

HOW MUCH IS A BROKEN ARM WORTH?

If you have been injured in a car crash or other accident and will be mediating with an insurance company over how much they will pay you for the accident, a little research can help you learn what a judge or jury might give you for the same type of injury. You can use this information as a benchmark to evaluate whatever offers may be made to you in mediation.

In many states, you can find a weekly or monthly publication called a "jury verdict reporter" in the law library. Ask the law librarian if one is published in your state. In the index to these reporters, you can look up whatever type of injury you have, such as abdominal injuries, ankle injuries, arm injuries, and so on, then find recent awards for those types of cases. If your state does not have a jury verdict reporter, look for an easy-to-use book called *What's It Worth? A Guide to Current Personal Injury Awards and Settlements.* This book, published annually by Michie Company, lists injury-related awards for the whole country.

For more on evaluating personal injuries, see the chapter entitled "How Much is Your Claim for Injuries Worth?," in *How to Win Your Personal Injury Claim,* by Joseph Matthews (Nolo).

To proceed further, first search for statutes, regulations, or ordinances that address your question. If you find relevant statutes, look for cases that have interpreted them. To do this at a law library, you can:

- look at the summaries of cases that follow the statute in an annotated code book

- use *Shepard's Citations for Statutes* (a book that provides a complete list of cases that mention a particular statute, regulation, or constitutional provision), and

- search for cases in "case digests" (books that list cases by subject).

If you can't find a relevant statute or other legislative enactment, you need to look for case law only. To do this at a law library, you can:

- read any relevant cases mentioned in the background materials

- search in case digests by subject area or key words.

- if you find a relevant case, read the cases that it mentions, and

- if you find a relevant case, use *Shepard's Citations for Cases* to find more cases that apply. (*Shepard's* provides a complete list of cases that mention your case.)

c. Making Sure the Law Is Up to Date

Because the law changes rapidly, you must make sure that the principles stated in your cases and statutes are still valid. A case may no longer be helpful to you if a more recent case has questioned its reasoning, ruled a different way, or expressly stated that your case is no longer good law. Likewise, you should check to make sure your statute has not been changed or eliminated.

Updating your research in the library

If you are using the law library, there are a few things you should do to make sure your research is up to date.

- **Background Resources.** If you use background materials, be sure to check the pocket part; it contains changes and new developments in the law.

- **Statutes.** Books containing statutes and regulations also contain pocket parts. Be sure to check these as well. Also check law library periodicals that contain more recent statutory updates.

- **Cases.** You can check the validity of every case you find by using *Shepard's Citations for Cases*. *Shepard's* will list every case that mentions your case, and tell you the reasons why it was mentioned. For example, it might show that a later case overruled your case, which means your case is no longer valid. Using *Shepard's Citations* is not simple—ask the law librarian for help.

Updating your research on the Web

On the Internet, the updating process is easier, but might cost some money.

- **Statutes.** If you're checking a state statute, visit your state's website for current legislative developments. If you need federal information, track Congress's legislative developments at http://thomas.loc.gov. You can also get the most recent version of a statute (for a fee) through Westlaw or Lexis.

- **Cases.** You can check the validity of cases by using www.westlaw.com or *Shepard's* at www.lexis.com. Each service charges $4.25 for each case you check.

d. Information on Mediation and Dispute Resolution

If you need to do additional research about the laws relating to mediation, an excellent legal research tool is a two-volume treatise called *Mediation: Law, Policy, and Practice*, by Nancy H. Rogers and Craig A. McEwen (Clark, Boardman Callaghan). In addition to discussing many of the substantive legal issues that can arise in mediation, the book includes tables listing mediation laws by subject matter in all 50 states and the federal government, as well as lengthy excerpts from many of these laws. Although it's written for use by lawyers, the organization and writing is generally clear enough so that much of it should be useful to nonlawyers, too. It should be available at many of the larger law libraries.

Here are some other resources on mediation:

- www.mediate.com. This website offers lots of free information on mediation, including articles, book reviews, mediator referrals, and much more.

- www.acrnet.org. The website of the Association for Conflict Resolution has a library of free articles on mediation.

- *Dispute Resolution Journal*, published by the American Arbitration Association. This journal is widely available in law libraries and is especially strong on issues involving mediation of employment and business disputes.

- *Dispute Resolution Magazine*, published by the American Bar Association Section of Dispute Resolution. This is a magazine for lawyers that includes well-written articles on a variety of issues, such as divorce and family mediation, new state laws affecting mediation, and the lawyer's role in preparing clients for mediation. ■

Sample Mediation Rules

This set of mediation rules is used by a private dispute resolution company with which Peter has been associated, Empire Mediation & Arbitration, Inc., based in Rochester, New York. These rules are typical and should be similar those used by mediators or mediation services handling a general variety of cases.

1. **Mediation defined/role of the mediator:** Mediation is a voluntary process in which the parties to the dispute meet together confidentially with a neutral third party called a "mediator." The mediator does not take sides and has no authority to make a decision, but works with the parties to help them evaluate their goals and options in order to find a solution to the dispute satisfactory to all sides.

2. **Initiating the process:** Any party to a dispute may begin mediation by sending to Empire Mediation & Arbitration, Inc. ("Empire") a completed Submission Form.

3. **Agreement to mediate:** Empire will contact all parties to a dispute to determine their willingness to participate in mediation. If the parties agree to participate, each will sign an "Agreement to Mediate" before the commencement of the first mediation session.

4. **Appointment of mediator:** From its panel of mediators, Empire will propose to the parties the names of one or more mediators qualified and available to mediate their case. The panelist will be chosen by agreement of all the parties.

5. **Scheduling/notice of mediation:** Empire will schedule the mediation at a time and place convenient to all parties, and notify the parties in writing of the date, time and location of the session. The mediation may be rescheduled upon a party's request but a rescheduling fee will be assessed against the requesting party.

6. **Representation at session:** Each party must be represented at the mediation by a person with authority to settle the dispute. Individuals may be represented by legal counsel, and counsel are encouraged to have their clients participate. Insurance companies may be represented by claims staff or defense counsel. Other business corporations may be represented by executive staff or counsel. It is not necessary for witnesses to attend the mediation, but if they do, their testimony will be heard at the mediator's discretion.

7. **Rules of evidence:** The rules of evidence common to judicial and arbitral proceedings do not apply in mediation. Any statement, document or other record offered by the parties will be admissible unless the mediator, in his or her sole discretion, finds it to be irrelevant or otherwise inappropriate in the session.

8. **Session procedure — opening statements:** The mediator will commence the session with an Opening Statement in which he or she will explain the purposes and procedures of the session. The parties will then make their opening statements, explaining their positions on the issues in dispute, including the presentation of any documents, photographs and oral or written summaries of witness testimony that would be helpful to the mediator in understanding the case.

9. **Session procedure—private caucuses:** During the mediation, the mediator may meet in private caucus with each of the parties and counsel, to explore positions and settlement options. Any information disclosed to the mediator in the caucus will be kept confidential unless the party expressly tells the mediator it may be disclosed to the other parties.

10. **Confidentiality:** The mediation session constitutes a settlement negotiation and statements made during the mediation by the parties are inadmissible, to the extent allowed by law, in subsequent judicial or arbitral proceedings relating to the dispute. The parties will maintain the confidentiality of the mediation and not introduce as evidence in any future arbitral or judicial proceeding statements made by the mediator or by any other party or subpoena a mediator to testify or produce records in any such proceeding. Evidence otherwise discoverable or admissible is not made inadmissible or non-discoverable because of its use in mediation.

11. **No record:** No stenographic or other record of the mediation will be made.

12. **Conclusion of the mediation:** The mediation will conclude when the parties have reached a settlement agreement, or upon the oral or written request of the parties or at the discretion of the mediator.

13. **Settlement documents:** If a settlement agreement is reached during the mediation, the parties will make their own arrangements for the drafting and later execution of settlement documents.

14. **Exclusion of liability:** Mediators conducting sessions for Empire act as independent contractors; they are not employees of the company. Neither mediators nor the company act as legal counsel for any of the parties in the dispute. Parties have the right to legal counsel and are encouraged to obtain legal advice in connection with a dispute.

Parties not represented by counsel at a mediation may condition a settlement agreement upon review by their attorney. Neither mediators nor the company are necessary parties in judicial proceedings relating to mediation, and neither the mediator nor the company will be liable to any party for an act or omission in connection with a mediation conducted under these rules.

Standards of Conduct for Mediators

These standards were developed by three professional groups: the American Arbitration Association, the American Bar Association, and the Society of Professionals in Dispute Resolution, and appear here by permission of those organizations.

The three organizations intend these Standards to apply to all types of mediation, but recognize that in some cases the application of these Standards may be affected by laws or contractual agreements.

I. Self-Determination:

A Mediator Shall Recognize that Mediation is Based on the Principle of Self-Determination by the Parties.

Self-determination is the fundamental principle of mediation. It requires that the mediation process rely upon the ability of the parties to reach a voluntary, uncoerced agreement. Any party may withdraw from mediation at any time.

COMMENTS: The mediator may provide information about the process, raise issues, and help parties explore options. The primary role of the mediator is to facilitate a voluntary resolution of a dispute. Parties shall be given the opportunity to consider all proposed options.

A mediator cannot personally ensure that each party has made a fully informed choice to reach a particular agreement, but it is a good practice for the mediator to make the parties aware of the importance of consulting other professionals, where appropriate, to help them make informed decisions.

II. Impartiality:

A Mediator Shall Conduct the Mediation in an Impartial Manner.

The concept of mediator impartiality is central to the mediation process. A mediator shall mediate only those matters in which she or he can remain impartial and evenhanded. If at any time the mediator is unable to conduct the process in an impartial manner, the mediator is obligated to withdraw.

COMMENTS: A mediator shall avoid conduct that gives the appearance of partiality toward one of the parties. The quality of the mediation process is enhanced when the parties have confidence in the impartiality of the mediator.

When mediators are appointed by a court or institution, the appointing agency shall make reasonable efforts to ensure that mediators serve impartially.

A mediator should guard against partiality or prejudice based on the parties' personal characteristics, background or performance at the mediation.

III. Conflicts of Interest:

A Mediator Shall Disclose all Actual and Potential Conflicts of Interest Reasonably Known to the Mediator. After Disclosure, the Mediator Shall Decline to Mediate Unless all Parties Choose to Retain the Mediator. The Need to Protect Against Conflicts of Interest Also Governs Conduct that Occurs During and After the Mediation.

A conflict of interest is a dealing or relationship that might create an impression of possible bias. The basic approach to questions of conflict of interest is consistent with the concept of self-determination. The mediator has a responsibility to disclose all actual and potential conflicts that are reasonably known to the mediator and could reasonably be seen as raising a question about impartiality. If all parties agree to mediate after being informed of conflicts, the mediator may proceed with the mediation. If, however, the conflict of interest casts serious doubt on the integrity of the process, the mediator shall decline to proceed.

A mediator must avoid the appearance of conflict of interest both during and after the mediation. Without the consent of all parties, a mediator shall not subsequently establish a professional relationship with one of the parties in a related matter, or in an unrelated matter under circumstances which would raise legitimate questions about the integrity of the mediation process.

COMMENTS: A mediator shall avoid conflicts of interest in recommending the services of other professionals. A mediator may make reference to professional referral services or associations which maintain rosters of qualified professionals.

Potential conflicts of interest may arise between administrators of mediation programs and mediators and there may be strong pressures on the mediator to settle a particular case or cases. The mediator's commitment must be to the parties and the process. Pressures from outside of the mediation process should never influence the mediator to coerce parties to settle.

IV. Competence:

A Mediator Shall Mediate Only When the Mediator Has the Necessary Qualifications to Satisfy the Reasonable Expectations of the Parties.

Any person may be selected as a mediator, provided that the parties are satisfied with the mediator's qualifications. Training and experience in mediation, however, are often necessary for effective mediation. A person who offers herself or himself as available to serve as a mediator gives parties and the public the expectation that she or he has the competency to mediate effectively. In court-connected or other forms of mandated mediation, it is essential that mediators assigned to the parties have the requisite training and experience.

COMMENTS: Mediators should have information available for the parties regarding their relevant training, education and experience.

The requirements for appearing on the list of mediators must be made public and available to interested persons.

When mediators are appointed by a court or institution, the appointing agency shall make reasonable efforts to ensure that each mediator is qualified for the particular mediation.

V. Confidentiality:

A Mediator Shall Maintain the Reasonable Expectations of the Parties with Regard to Confidentiality.

The reasonable expectations of the parties with regard to confidentiality shall be met by the mediator. The parties' expectations of confidentiality depend on the circumstances of the mediation and any agreements they may make. A mediator shall not disclose any matter that a party expects to be confidential unless given permission by all parties or unless required by law or other public policy.

COMMENTS: The parties may make their own rules with respect to confidentiality, or the accepted practice of an individual mediator or institution may dictate a particular set of expectations. Since the parties' expectations regarding confidentiality are important, the mediator should discuss these expectations with the parties.

If the mediator holds private sessions with a party, the nature of these sessions with regard to confidentiality should be discussed prior to undertaking such sessions.

In order to protect the integrity of the mediation, a mediator should avoid communicating information about how the parties acted in the mediation process, the merits of the case, or settlement offers. The mediator may report, if required, whether parties appeared at a scheduled mediation.

Where the parties have agreed that all or a portion of the information disclosed during a mediation is confidential, the parties' agreement should be respected by the mediator.

Confidentiality should not be construed to limit or prohibit the effective monitoring, research, or evaluation of mediation programs by responsible persons. Under appropriate circumstances, researchers may be permitted to obtain access to statistical data and, with the permission of the parties, to individual case files, observations of live mediations, and interviews with participants.

VI. Quality of the Process:

A Mediator Shall Conduct the Mediation Fairly, Diligently, and in a Manner Consistent with the Principle of Self-Determination by the Parties.

A mediator shall work to ensure a quality process and to encourage mutual respect among the parties. A quality process requires a commitment by the mediator to diligence and procedural fairness. There should be adequate opportunity for each party in the mediation to participate in the discussions. The parties decide when they will reach an agreement or terminate a mediation.

COMMENTS: A mediator may agree to mediate only when he or she is prepared to commit the attention essential to an effective mediation.

Mediators should only accept cases when they can satisfy the reasonable expectations of the parties concerning the timing of the process. A mediator should not allow a mediation to be unduly delayed by the parties or their representatives.

The presence or absence of persons at a mediation depends on the agreement of the parties and mediator. The parties and mediator may agree that others may be excluded from particular sessions or from the entire mediation process.

The primary purpose of a mediator is to facilitate the parties' voluntary agreement. This role differs substantially from other professional-client relationships. Mixing the role of a mediator and the role of a professional advising a client is problematic, and mediators must strive to distinguish between the roles. A mediator should, therefore, refrain from providing professional advice. Where appropriate, a mediator should recommend that parties seek outside professional advice, or consider resolving their dispute through arbitration, counseling, neutral evaluation, or other processes. A mediator who undertakes, at the request of the parties, an additional dispute resolution role in the same matter assumes increased responsibilities and obligations that may be governed by the standards of other professions.

A mediator shall withdraw from a mediation when incapable of serving or when unable to remain impartial.

A mediator shall withdraw from the mediation or postpone a session if the mediation is being used to further illegal conduct, or if a party is unable to participate due to drug, alcohol, or other physical or mental incapacity.

Mediators should not permit their behavior in the mediation process to be guided by a desire for a high settlement rate.

VII.   Advertising and Solicitation:

A Mediator Shall Be Truthful in Advertising and Solicitation for Mediation.

Advertising or any other communication with the public concerning services offered or regarding the education, training, and expertise of the mediator shall be truthful. Mediators shall refrain from promises and guarantees of results.

COMMENTS: It is imperative that communication with the public educate and instill confidence in the process.

In an advertisement or other communication to the public. a mediator may make reference to meeting state, national, or private organization qualifications only if the entity referred to has a procedure for qualifying mediators and the mediator has been duly granted the requisite status.

VIII.   Fees:

A Mediator Shall Fully Disclose and Explain the Basis of Compensation, Fees, and Charges to the Parties.

The parties should be provided sufficient information about fees at the outset of a mediation to determine if they wish to retain the services of a mediator. If a mediator charges fees, the fees shall be reasonable considering among other things, the mediation service, the type and complexity of the matter, the expertise of the mediator, the time required, and the rates customary in the community. The better practice in reaching an understanding about fees is to set down the arrangements in a written agreement.

COMMENTS: A mediator who withdraws from a mediation should return any unearned fee to the parties.

A mediator should not enter into a fee agreement which is contingent upon the result of the mediation or amount of the settlement.

Co-mediators who share a fee should hold to standards of reasonableness in determining the allocation of fees.

A mediator should not accept a fee for referral of a matter to another mediator or to any other person.

IX.   Obligations to the Mediation Process:
Mediators Have a Duty to Improve the Practice of Mediation.

COMMENTS: Mediators are regarded as knowledgeable in the process of mediation. They have an obligation to use their knowledge to help educate the public about mediation; to make mediation accessible to those who would like to use it; to correct abuses; and to improve their professional skills and abilities. ∎

National and Regional Mediation Organizations and Services

You can contact the organizations listed below for more information about mediation in general, such as career and training opportunities, state and federal legislation, and references to specific mediators or mediation services in your area.

The mediation services listed include private dispute resolution companies as well as nonprofit associations that provide mediation, arbitration, and other dispute resolution services for actual cases.

Mediation Organizations

American Bar Association
Section on Dispute Resolution
740 15th St., NW
Washington, DC 20005
202-662-1000 (phone)
www.abanet.org/home.html
Monitors and provides information on dispute
resolution and the courts, and pending and
enacted dispute resolution legislation.

Association for Conflict Resolution
1015 18th St. NW
Washington, DC 20036
202-464-9700 (phone)
www.acrnet.org
A membership organization for conflict
resolution professionals. Check out their
website for information on mediation, and
referrals to member mediators in your area.

Association of Family and Conciliation Courts
6515 Grand Teton Plaza, Suite 210
Madison, WI 53719
608-664-3750 (phone)
www.afccnet.org
Monitors and provides information on
court-sponsored divorce and family
mediation and arbitration programs.

Conflict Resolution Center International
204 37th Street
Pittsburgh, PA 15201
412-687-6210 (phone)
www.conflictres.org
Provides information to individuals and
communities working to resolve neighborhood disputes, and racial, ethnic, and
religious conflicts.

CPR Institute for Dispute Resolution
366 Madison Avenue
New York, NY 10017
212-949-6490 (phone)
www.cpradr.org
Encourages large businesses and law firms to
use mediation and other dispute resolution
techniques (through its "ADR Pledge") as a
first resort to settle disputes.

Mediate.com
P.O. Box 51090
Eugene, OR 97405
541-345-1629 (phone)
www.mediate.com
A website devoted to mediation, with lots of
free articles and other resources, as well as
referrals.

National Association for Community Mediation
1527 New Hampshire Avenue, NW
Washington, DC 20036
202-667-9700 (phone)
www.nafmc.org
Supports the growth of nonprofit, community
mediation centers, and provides contact
information for hundreds of centers nationally.

National Center for State Courts
300 Newport Avenue
Williamsburg, VA 23185
800-616-6164 (phone)
www.ncsconline.org
Compiles and analyzes statistics on court-
connected ADR programs around the country.

Mediation Services

American Arbitration Association
335 Madison Avenue, Floor 10
New York, NY 10017
212-716-5800 (phone)
www.adr.org

Arbitration Forums, Inc.
3350 Buschwood Park Drive
Building 3, Suite 295
Tampa, FL 33618
888-272-3453 (phone)
www.arbfile.org

Asian Pacific American Dispute
1145 Wilshire Boulevard, 2nd Floor
Los Angeles, CA 90017
213-977-7500 (phone)
www.apalc.org

CDR Associates
100 Arapahoe Avenue, Suite 12
Boulder, CO 80302
800-MEDIATE (phone)
www.mediate.org

Center for Dispute Settlement
300 State Street, Suite 301
Rochester, NY 14614
585-546-5110 (phone)
www.cdsadr.org

Empire Mediation & Arbitration, Inc.
625 Panorama Trail # 2
Rochester, NY 14625
585-381-6830

Federal Mediation and Conciliation Service
2100 K Street, NW
Washington, DC 20427
202-606-8100 (phone)
Fax: 202-606-4251
www.fmcs.gov

Institute for Christian Conciliation
1537 Avenue D, Suite 352
Billings, MT 59102
406-256-1583 (phone)
www.Hispeace.org

Judicial Arbitration and Mediation Services
(JAMS)
1920 Main St, Suite 300
Irvine, CA 92614
949-224-1810
www.jamsadr.com

The Keystone Center
1020 16th Street, NW, Second Floor
Washington, DC 20036
202-452-1590
www.keystone.org

Lesbian and Gay Community Services
208 West 13th Street
New York, NY 10011
212-620-7310
www.gaycenter.org

Resolute Systems, Inc.
1550 North Prospect Avenue
Milwaukee, WI 53202
800-776-6060 (phone)
www.resolutesystems.com

Resolve, Inc
1310 Broadway
Somerville, MA 02144
888-623-0744
www.resolve.org

Settlement Consultants International Inc.
P.O. Box 181496
Dallas, TX 75218
214-661-3771
www.solutionswithconsensus.com

U.S. Arbitration and Mediation, Inc.
720 Olive Street, Suite 2020
Saint Louis, MO 63101
314-231-4642 (phone)
www.usam.com ■

Statewide Mediation Offices

Many states now have, or are in the process of forming, special offices to coordinate mediation services within the state. Some offices are sponsored or partly funded by state governments; others are independent nonprofit organizations that assume this role themselves. These offices specialize in mediating disputes involving public policy issues, and many can also provide information on mediators and mediation services located within their states.

ALABAMA
Alabama Center for Dispute Resolution
P.O. Box 671
Montgomery, AL 36101
334-269-1515
www.alabamaadr.org

ARIZONA
Arizona Supreme Court ADR Program
1501 W. Washington Street
Phoenix, AZ 85007
602-542-9255

ARKANSAS
Arkansas ADR Commission
625 Marshall Street
Little Rock, AR 72201
501-682-9400

CALIFORNIA
Common Ground Law & Public Policy Programs
University of California, Davis Research Park
Davis, CA 95616
530-754-7060
http://universityextension.ucdavis.edu/
commonground/index.asp

COLORADO
Office of Dispute Resolution
Colorado Judicial Department
1301 Pennsylvania Street, Suite 110
Denver, CO 80203
303-837-3672
www.courts.state.co.us/chs/court/mediation/
odrindex.htm

FLORIDA
Florida Conflict Resolution Consortium
2031 East Paul Dirac Dr.
Tallahassee, FL 32310
850-644-6320
http://consensus.fsu.edu

Florida Dispute Resolution Center
Supreme Court Building
Tallahassee, FL 32399
850-921-2910
www.flcourts.org/osca/divisions/adr/
brochure.html

GEORGIA
Georgia Commission on Dispute Resolution
244 Washington Street, SW
Atlanta, GA 30334
404-463-3788
www.ganet.org/gadr

HAWAII
Center for Alternative Dispute Resolution
417 S. King Street, Room 207
Honolulu, HI 96813
808-539-4980

MARYLAND
Mediation and Conflict Resolution Office
900 Commerce Road
Annapolis, MD 21401
410-841-2260
www.courts.state.md.us/macro

MASSACHUSETTS

Office of Dispute Resolution
One Ashburton Place, Room 501
Boston, MA 02108
617-727-2224 (phone)
www.state.ma.us/modr

MICHIGAN

Office of Dispute Resolution
State Court Administrative Office
P.O. Box 30048
Lansing, MI 48909
517-373-4839
www.courts.michigan.gov/scao/dispute/
odr.htm

MINNESOTA

Minnesota Alternative Dispute Resolution
www.courts.state.mn.us/adr/index.html

MONTANA

Montana Consensus Council
1301 Lockey, 3rd Floor
Department of Administration
State Capitol
Helena, MT 59620
406-444-2075
http://mcc.state.mt.us/css/default.asp

NEBRASKA

Office of Dispute Resolution
P.O. Box 98910
Lincoln, NE 68509
402-471-3148
http://court.not.org.odr

NEW JERSEY

New Jersey Office of Complementary Dispute
Resolution
www.judiciary.state.nj.us/services/cdr.htm

NEW YORK

New York State Forum on Conflict &
Consensus, Inc.
255 River Street, 4th Floor
Troy, NY 12180
518-687-2240
www.nysdra.org

NORTH DAKOTA

North Dakota Consensus Council, Inc.
1003 E. Interstate Avenue, Suite 7
Bismarck, ND 58503
701-224-0588
www.agree.org

OHIO

Ohio Commission on Dispute
Resolution and Conflict Management
77 South High Street
Columbus, OH 43215
614-752-9595
http://disputeresolution.ohio.gov

OREGON

Oregon Dispute Resolution Commission
1201 Court Street NE, Suite 305
Salem, OR 97310
503-378-2877
www.odrc.state.or.us/index.html

TENNESSEE
Tennessee Administrative Office of the Courts
511 Union Street, Suite 600
Nashville, TN 37219
800-448-7970
www.tsc.state.tn.us/index.htm

TEXAS
Center for Public Policy Dispute Resolution
School of Law, Univ. of Texas at Austin
727 East Dean Keeton Street
Austin, TX 78705
512-471-3507
www.utexas.edu/law/academics/centers/
cppdr/index.html

VERMONT
The Governor's Commission on
Dispute Resolution
109 State Street, 4th Floor
Montpelier, VT 05609
802-828-3217

VIRGINIA
Dispute Resolution Services
Supreme Court of Virginia
100 North Ninth Street
Richmond, VA 23219
804-786-6455
www.courts.state.va.us/drs/mediators.htm

WASHINGTON
Washington State ADR
1206 Quince Street SE
P.O. Box 41170
Olympia, WA 98504
360-753-3365
www.courts.wa.gov

WISCONSIN
Wisconsin Supreme Court–Court-Annexed ADR
P.O. Box 1688
Madison, WI 53701
www.courts.state.wi.us/circuit/
Alternative_Dispute_Resolution_Clearinghouse.htm

Index

P

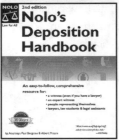

Y our comments make a big difference in the development and revision of Nolo books and software. Please take a few minutes and register your Nolo product—and your comments—with us. Not only will your input make a difference, you'll receive special offers available only to registered owners of Nolo products on our newest books and software. Register now by:

PHONE
1-800-728-3555

FAX
1-800-645-0895

EMAIL
cs@nolo.com

or **MAIL** us
this registration card

give us
Your 2 cents

fold here

Registration Card

NAME _____ DATE _____

ADDRESS _____

_____

CITY _____ STATE _____ ZIP _____

PHONE _____ EMAIL _____

WHERE DID YOU HEAR ABOUT THIS PRODUCT? _____

WHERE DID YOU PURCHASE THIS PRODUCT? _____

DID YOU CONSULT A LAWYER? (PLEASE CIRCLE ONE)   YES   NO   NOT APPLICABLE

DID YOU FIND THIS BOOK HELPFUL?   (VERY)   5   4   3   2   1   (NOT AT ALL)

COMMENTS _____

_____

_____

WAS IT EASY TO USE?   (VERY EASY)   5   4   3   2   1   (VERY DIFFICULT)

We occasionally make our mailing list available to carefully selected companies whose products may be of interest to you.
☐ If you do not wish to receive mailings from these companies, please check this box.
☐ You can quote me in future Nolo promotional materials.
  Daytime phone number _____.

MEDL 1.0